SEX,
GENDER,
and CHRISTIANITY

SEX, GENDER, *and* CHRISTIANITY

Edited by
PRISCILLA POPE-LEVISON
and JOHN R. LEVISON

CASCADE *Books* · Eugene, Oregon

7/29/13
WW
$34.50

SEX, GENDER, AND CHRISTIANITY

Cascade Books
An Imprint of Wipf and Stock Publishers
199 W. 8th Ave., Suite 3
Eugene, OR 97401

www.wipfandstock.com

ISBN 13: 978-1-62032-015-0

Cataloguing-in-Publication data:

Sex, gender, and Christiantity / edited by Priscilla Pope-Levison and John R. Levison, with a foreword by Patricia O'Connell Killen.

xxii + 250 pp. ; 23 cm. Includes bibliographical references and index.

ISBN 13: 978-1-62032-015-0

1. Sex—Religious aspects—Christianity. 2. Sex role—Religious aspects—Christianity. I. Title.

BT708 S465 2012

Manufactured in the U.S.A.

To our colleagues in the School of Theology
at Seattle Pacific University

Contents

Contents

Contributors

David G. Allen, Professor and Chair, Gender, Women & Sexuality Studies, University of Washington, Seattle, Washington

Karen Trimble Alliaume, Associate Professor of Theology and Co-Director of Women's Studies, Lewis University, Romeoville, Illinois

Brian Bantum, Assistant Professor of Theology, Seattle Pacific University, Seattle, Washington

Mikee C. Delony, Assistant Professor of English, Abilene Christian University, Abilene, Texas

James G. Dixon III, Professor and Chair of English & Theatre, Grove City College, Grove City, Pennsylvania

Antonios Finitsis, Associate Professor of Hebrew Bible, Pacific Lutheran University, Tacoma, Washington

Theresa J. FitzPatrick, Term Professor of English, Concordia University, St. Paul, St. Paul, Minnesota

Allyson Jule, Professor of Education and Co-Director of the Gender Studies Institute, Trinity Western University, Langley, British Columbia, Canada

Patricia O'Connell Killen, Academic Vice President and Professor of Religious Studies, Gonzaga University, Spokane, Washington

John R. (Jack) Levison, Professor of New Testament, Seattle Pacific University, Seattle, Washington

Contributors

Priscilla Pope-Levison, Professor of Theology and Assistant Director of Women's Studies, Seattle Pacific University and Affiliate Faculty, Gender, Women & Sexuality Studies, University of Washington, Seattle, Washington

Caryn D. Riswold, Associate Professor of Religion & Gender and Women's Studies, Illinois College, Jacksonville, Illinois.

Tina Schermer Sellers, Professor of Marriage & Family Therapy, Seattle Pacific University, Seattle, Washington

Acknowledgments

THE LAUGHTER FROM OUR deck on June 19, 2010, kicked off what would be a robust Lilly Fellows Summer Seminar on Gender and Christianity. Along with daily discussions of sex, gender, and Christianity, we enjoyed animated happy hours, a tour of Theo's Chocolate (a very Seattle-esque, fair trade chocolate), a weekend getaway at Seattle Pacific University's historic Camp Casey on the breathtaking shores of Whidbey Island, a day trip to majestic Mt. Rainier, a reception at Steelhead Diner, a favorite haunt of ours at Pike Place Market, a spectacular dinner at Tony Finitsis's house, and a final sunset celebration at Richmond Beach Saltwater Park. This book is the byproduct of the *esprit-du-corps* that developed during that momentous summer month.

Several individuals at Seattle Pacific University contributed to the success of this seminar. Doug Strong, Dean of the School of Theology, hosted a reception for seminar participants. Margaret Diddams, Director of the Center for Scholarship and Faculty Development, planned and led a day trip to Mt. Rainier. University Communications, especially Kathy Henning, Jennifer Gilnett, and Rich Kim, created an eye-catching poster, which we sent to all Lilly Fellows member colleges and universities. Conference Services arranged for housing in a single building with sparkling kitchens and brand new pots and pans from Ikea; we were told that seminar participants would listen for laughter and gather in whichever apartment was the source of this giddiness. Bryce Nelson and Robin Maas of the Seattle Pacific University Library offered us a light-filled seminar room with kitchen facilities, and Steve Perisho arranged for all seminar participants to have library privileges. David Rither in Instructional Technology Services helped to film the video, *Impossible Promises and Broken Hearts*. Lastly, former president Phil Eaton footed the bill for a closing reception.

Our assistants for the seminar were Christa Mazzone Palmberg and Catherine "Cat" Gipe. Christa did much of the startup work of advertising, corresponding with potential applicants, and organization. Cat took over from her during the seminar and did all sorts of wonderful things, especially unparalleled hospitality—from welcome packets to adventures in Seattle's clubs and historic haunts. Cat also lent insight as a college student, with websites, college experiences, and personal reflections. She was a resource all her own, and we, as the leaders of the seminar, were gratified to note the extent to which participants expressed their delight in Cat.

The seminar happened in the first place because of the Lilly Fellows Program, which is housed at Valparaiso University. More than just financial support, the Lilly Fellows Program Staff—Joe Creech, Program Director, and Kathy Sutherland, Program Coordinator—were accessible and amiable colleagues. We are saddened to recall as well John Paul, whose initial enthusiasm for the seminar gave impetus and shape to our application; John Paul died before the seminar members met on our deck on that memorable June 19.

Foreword

IDEAS ABOUT SEX AND gender in Christianity evoke intense, explosive reactions. Why? Because, on the one hand, religion orients humans to boundary experiences such as sex, pain, and death, which bring the contingent character of human existence squarely into focus. Religion helps to manage contingency by situating such experiences within a meaningful narrative and symbolic system. On the other hand, this same powerful symbol system and meaningful narrative also orients and guides humans in ordinary, daily interactions. Human communities appeal to religion to warrant social structures and conventions—to establish and maintain social order.

Sex and gender relationships are a pivot of religion's ability to reinforce both boundary crossing (sex, pain, and death) and boundary maintenance (social order). Therefore, in times of large-scale demographic, economic, political, and cultural change—which are also times of religious reconfiguration—tensions surrounding ideas about sex and gender in Christianity increase. During such periods, certain individuals transgress conventional sexual mores and norms for gender relationships by claiming to be divinely inspired or to have discovered new meanings in sacred texts. Such individuals believe these acts of transgression, which often upend the social order, bring the divine and the human closer. At the same time, other individuals, typically in reaction to these transgressions, reaffirm conventional sexual mores and norms for gender relationships. They understand this reaffirmation to be a clear marker of a more trustworthy, divinely established social order.

History is rife with transgressors of conventional sexual mores and gender relationships in Christianity. Consider Mother Ann Lee and the United Society of Believers (the Shakers) with their teaching of universal celibacy as the antidote to the original sin of sexual intercourse; the early Latter Day Saints' practice of polygamy; or the 2003 election of V. Eugene Robinson, an openly gay priest, as Episcopal bishop of New Hampshire.

History is rife as well with defenders of conventional sexual mores and gender relationships in Christianity. Consider Phyllis Schafly's and the National Council of Catholic Women's opposition to the Equal Rights Amendment. Recall James Dobson's Focus on the Family. Notice pastor Mark Driscoll's preaching on gender relationships through Mars Hill Church in Seattle.

What becomes clear about the transgressors and defenders of conventional gender relationships in Christianity, when looked at more closely, is that, while they appear to be diametrically opposed, in fact they reach differing conclusions by participating in shared practices. Both interpret sacred texts and their own experience; both warrant their ideas about gender with divine approbation; and both try to contain primal human energies such as human sexuality within stable categories—whether in transgression or maintenance of social order. The conflict over gender relationships, then, is a conflict over fidelity to God because, at a deep level, it is a conflict over the ordering of primal human energy in relationship to the source of life.

The contributors to this volume understand the significance of sex and gender in Christianity, not only in the past, but now. They are keenly aware of how, in the midst of a period of intense social change as we are, positions on gender relationships within Christianity get presented in simplistic terms that fail to do the topic justice and that cause harm to Christians and their communities. The authors are not content with superficial discussion. They know that much is at stake for the Christian community, for society, and for individual lives in how young adults come to make sense of gender relationships in relation to their faith—or fail to do so. The contributors know that perspectives on these topics, which students bring with them to college, profoundly affect their personal relationships, their behavior in the classroom, their sense of vocation, and their ways of relating to whatever theological heritage will be theirs over the long haul. The authors are unwilling to ignore sex and gender in Christianity as topics in their teaching even though they know, firsthand, how contentious these issues are on many church-related campuses today.

The contributors defuse the tension and open up space for genuine conversation on these topics in two ways. First, as the editors note, they choose to go at the topic "slant," employing indirection to draw students into thoughtful consideration of gender in Christianity. Secondly, the contributors address sex and gender from multidisciplinary perspectives and across different historical periods. In doing so they confront readers with the complexities involved in any consideration of sex and gender, including their profoundly contextualized character. And the essays, cumulatively, undercut claims to obvious meaning and timeless, unchanging understandings of sex and gender relationships in Christianity by exposing and embracing the complexity of issues across disciplines and historical eras.

Finally, another element adds to the power of this volume: the authors' compassion for their students. The contributors succeed in constructing hospitable space in their writing. Without stifling their own passion for their topics, blurring the force of their questions, or softening the precision of their analyses, each author constructs an intellectual space within which a reader can be herself, a space for reflection. That is no small accomplishment. It will be crucial to the volume working so well in teaching.

Patricia O'Connell Killen

INTRODUCTION

Beyond Polarization

PRISCILLA POPE-LEVISON *and* JOHN R. LEVISON

Two Students at an Impasse

THE FIRST DAY OF the Lilly Fellows Summer Seminar on Gender and Christianity began with two Seattle Pacific University students, Nick and Cat, seated at the head of the table. Nick is a member of Mars Hill Church, a large and influential church in Seattle pastored by Mark Driscoll, a champion of the complementarian position, according to which men retain final authority in the church and in marriage.[1] Cat is a feminist who believes that women should have equal access to every position in the church and equal authority in marriage. Cat and Nick represent, if not two ends of the spectrum, at least disparate and distant places on the spectrum. Although they knew each other—Cat, in fact, recommended that we ask Nick to participate—their respective views of gender roles led to an impasse and, eventually, to a neglected friendship.

The situation of estrangement in which Nick and Cat found themselves is representative of many students—administrators and faculty too—on college and university campuses. Students, as we expressed it in our application for a Lilly Fellows Summer Seminar, "reflect a bewildering range of perspectives on the relationship between sex, gender, and

1. For more on the complementarian position in this volume, see Pope-Levison, "Separate Spheres and Complementarianism in American Christianity."

Christianity. These perceptions, unwittingly or consciously, influence their choice of vocation, their personal associations, even the ways in which they participate in class." It was our contention, as potential directors, that "professors with a textured understanding of the wide expanse of these perspectives will be uniquely equipped to mentor students in every dimension of their educational experience." Therefore, we proposed a seminar that would *"create a cadre of significantly well-informed faculty who take the initiative to catalyze discussion and action on their campuses directed toward a rapprochement among students, staff, and faculty who often hold seemingly incompatible views of gender and Christianity."*

While leading this seminar, we discovered that it is not always beneficial or efficient to deal with issues related to gender and Christianity, as well as sex, in a head-on, confrontational manner. This approach can polarize. As the result of what we learned during the month the seminar participants spent together, we decided to approach the issues a bit more obliquely—to tell the truth but tell it slant, as the poet Emily Dickinson put it. Therefore, to address sex, gender, and Christianity on a slant, from less alarming and more indirect angles, we present in this volume a collection of first-rate articles that represent a variety of disciplines, from the social sciences to the humanities and theology. All of them deal, in varying degrees, with these three issues, yet none of them contains a frontal assault on any given position. The result, we hope, will be the ability to create an atmosphere of intelligent inquiry in which people will be able to discuss sex, gender, and Christianity in a shared space—a safe space, if you will, that allows for earnest and honest conversation. To provide focus to these issues, we have organized the articles in this book around three primary poles: church, sexuality, and society.

Gender, Authority, and the Church

The authority of women in the church is hotly debated throughout the contemporary church, from prominent evangelicals to Roman Catholics and Orthodox Christians. Prompting even-handed discussions on the topic is extremely difficult. This issue is best approached from indirect angles.

Rather than asking whether women can be ministers or priests, a more durable and indirect solution can be to unmask deleterious ideologies that have persisted through the centuries. John R. (Jack) Levison does this with respect to the figure of Eve, the progenitrix of Judaism,

Christianity, and Islam—and a figure well known by those outside of these faiths. Levison's analysis of this beleaguered figure shows that, at least in her opinion, Eve is far less culpable than the tradition has made her out to be. Levison identifies and interprets a key literary source, the Greek *Life of Adam and Eve*, in which a woman (Eve) interprets her *own* religious experience in a way that contravenes the dominant ideology of denigration.

Mikee Delony's interpretation of Chaucer's *Canterbury Tales* offers a similar assessment of the wife of Bath. Delony discovers in the world of this contentious woman an unexpected space for considering women's authority to interpret Scripture. Students might expect to discuss this issue in relation to scripture, such as the New Testament letters of 1 Corinthians (ch. 14) and 1 Timothy (ch. 2). They will hardly expect Chaucer's bawdy tale of the wife of Bath to provide a point of conversation on women, authority, and the interpretation of scripture.

Priscilla Pope-Levison addresses women's authority in the church through the lens of history—not disembodied history but the history of nineteenth- and twentieth-century women who felt God's call to preach. Pope-Levison offers several models from the past that are still operative today, including opposition to women's preaching from the complementarian position and unabashed support from evangelical women called to preach. This article, then, presents both poles of the debate—all of this fodder for a classroom conversation that does not put students immediately on the defensive.

Caryn Riswold brings us up to date when she begins her article with a Twitter interchange between a middle-aged woman who characterizes Christianity as hopelessly patriarchal and a young man who believes that feminism distorts Christianity. In her compelling article, Riswold challenges this polarity and carves out a common ground where a traditionalist and a rejectionist can talk. She does this by appealing to a breadth of theologians, from the apostle Paul to Martin Luther to contemporary feminist theologian Mary Streufert. This is a promising model for students such as Cat and Nick, who may, if a professor calls their attention to articles such as these, discover a dose of détente.

Gender, Race, and Society

Safe spaces are hard to find—or to create—but Theresa FitzPatrick turns to her own students to show us how the writings of Sylvia Plath from the 1960s offer a safe space for considering the polarity between men and women in the realms of sexuality, vocation, and gender. In a rare combination of pedagogy, literary criticism, and actual student online responses, FitzPatrick's essay provides a real-life example of how a professor can nudge her students beyond polarization and toward conversation.

David Allen, the first male director of a women studies program at a major university, guides us through the rich literature of masculinity studies. Sometimes dispassionate, sometimes autobiographical, but always insightful, Allen focuses upon how men have been taught to feel, to believe, and to behave. His article creates a safe space where men—and women—can discuss the construction of masculinities.

Brian Bantum expands the discussion of gender by identifying its intersection with race. In largely uncharted territory, Bantum creates a new paradigm beyond polarization, in which race and gender offer different yet related theological challenges. This essay can stimulate conversations about gender, race, humanity as *imago Dei*, and the consequences of these for Christian discipleship.

Vociferous and many are the voices that blame feminism for the crumbling of our society. (On this, see Pope-Levison's treatment of the Danvers Statement.) What to do? How can students—and their professors—navigate the confusing rapids of these conversations? Allyson Jule addresses these questions by turning to an unexpected corner of popular culture. In a witty and winsome analysis of the television and movie series *Sex and the City*, Jule opens the curtain to the new girl order in contemporary culture. Rather than putting people on the defensive, Jule offers students the opportunity to assess the culture that surrounds and influences them.

Gender, Sexuality, and Marriage

An interest in and concern for sexuality pervades college and university campuses, yet what issue is harder to discuss in a college classroom than sexuality? Statistics cited in the online video accompanying this volume—https://sites.google.com/site/impossiblepromisespresentation/—indicate that the majority of students either have lied or been lied to about their sexual activities. It might be unrealistic, therefore, to assume that students in a college classroom will discuss sexuality with honesty and openness. However, what if professors address the issue obliquely? Karen Trimble Alliaume does exactly this by opening her essay with the entertaining world of romance novels. By flying under the radar of student frisson when it comes to sexuality, Trimble Alliaume opens the door to conversation, once again, in a shared and safe space. Students can talk about the so-called purity culture in Protestantism and Catholicism—its strengths and weaknesses—with reference to romance novels, without necessarily revealing their own sexual activities or proclivities.

The issue of the respective roles of husbands and wives is seething in all corners of the church. For instance, the contemporary backlash against feminism has led many men and women to embrace complementarian roles, in which the wife defers to the husband's authority. Trying to talk about this in a college or seminary classroom can often turn into a Nick-and-Cat impasse, with intelligent students unwilling, or perhaps unable, to engage students who hold to opposing positions. What if a professor approached the issue of marriage non-confrontationally, via Shakespeare? Jim Dixon's article on companionate marriage provides just such an approach. Dixon traces the development of companionate marriage in Shakespeare's plays and in this way provides students with various models of marriage they can discuss without rancor or indicting their classroom nemeses.

Tina Sellers's article on spirituality and sexuality offers a similar opportunity. Sellers's sensitive exploration of ancient Jewish literature on sexuality offers students the opportunity to discuss these critical issues through the experiences of a time-honored culture. Further, Sellers, as a marriage and family therapist with particular expertise in sexuality, sets up an atmosphere of inquiry that may go a long way to promoting honest conversation, free of shame and defensiveness.

In addition to an insightful and useful collection of articles, readers have available to them an online video and brochure that will be an excellent tool for opening up a conversation about sex, gender, and Christianity on college campuses. Tony Finitsis, producer of this video, offers suggestions and advice for using it in the classroom to help open up myriad questions and issues students face around these issues. Because its tone is peaceable and its message frank, this video has the potential to crack open well-guarded façades.

Two Students in Conversation

There are signs of hope that the impasse over sex, gender, and Christianity can be overcome. Nick and Cat, as the result of preparing for the first day of our seminar, actually found themselves able to talk about what divides them, what keeps them apart. With that hope in mind, we make the modest proposal that resolution and reformation will result if we develop the ability to deal with sex, gender, and Christianity obliquely, if we tell the truth but tell it slant. This is precisely what the essays in this book do, as they provide safe and intellectually sound spaces for discussing essential questions about the relationship between sex, gender, and Christianity.

PART ONE

Gender, Authority,
and the Church

1

Ideology and Experience in the Greek *Life of Adam and Eve*[1]

John R. (Jack) Levison

I. The Prevalent Ideology

A. *Eve's Enduring Legacy*

THE OPENING SCENE OF the television series *Desperate Housewives* begins with Jetsonesque music from the sixties and a medieval portrait of Eve that moves as Eve plucks the apple from the tree and hands it to Adam. In the final moment of this opening scene, the apple falls into the hand

---

1. I originally presented the gist of this article in 2006 as "Women's Religious Experience in the Greek *Life of Adam and Eve*" at the national Society of Biblical Literature meeting in Washington, DC. In 2007, I presented a version of this article at a seminar in the Classical, Near Eastern, and Religious Studies Department at the University of British Columbia, under the auspices of the President's Advisory Committee on Lectures and with the co-sponsorship of Vancouver School of Theology. Subsequently, I was invited to write this article, which I did for *Experientia*, vol. 2, *From Text to Experience*, edited by Colleen Shantz and Rodney A. Werline (Early Judaism and Its Literature; SBL Symposium Series 40; Atlanta: Society of Biblical Literature, forthcoming). Its content is so appropriate for the Lilly Fellows Gender and Christianity Seminar that we decided to include it in this volume as well. This article is particularly important because of the position that Genesis 1–3, and especially the figure of Eve, plays in discussions of gender roles among proponents of complementarianism. See, for example, Köstenberger, *God, Marriage, and Family*, 21–28, 44.

of one of the desperate housewives, who are mesmerizing a generation of those who inhabit TV Land. The more recent trailer begins with a split-second image of a serpent and apple. The first time I saw the connection between *Desperate Housewives* and Eve was in a U-Bahn station in Munich, on a billboard where five women—the desperate housewives—are lying in a huge box of apples. When I returned to Seattle, my students explained the whole "affair" to me.

The metamorphosis of Eve into Adam's desperate housewife, of course, antedates the invention of televisions and subways. Two millennia ago, imaginations nearly went wild in their efforts to excoriate and isolate her, so much so that when Joan Wallach Scott contends that the establishment of gender requires "culturally available symbols that evoke multiple (and often contradictory) representations," where does she turn?—to "Eve and Mary as symbols of woman, in the Western Christian tradition."[2] The resonance of these figures runs deep. Scott discerns in Mary and Eve "myths of light and dark, purification and pollution, innocence and corruption."[3]

The representation of vulnerability to deception and a tendency toward seduction coalesced around Eve in Jewish and Christian antiquity.[4] For example, Ben Sira, who taught toward the beginning of the second century BCE, offered the young men in his academy this instruction: "From a woman [or 'wife'] is the beginning of sin, and on account of her we all die" (Sirach 25:24).[5] Early in the first century CE, the Alexandrian philosopher Philo Judaeus accepted as axiomatic that woman, when created, would become for Adam the beginning of a sinful life (*On the Creation* 151–52).[6] In his allegory of the soul, pleasure is represented by the serpent, the mind by Adam, and sense perception by woman. "Pleasure," he writes, "does not venture to bring her wiles and deceptions to bear on the man, but on the woman, and by her means on him" (*On the Creation* 165–66). Elsewhere he explains why the serpent spoke to the woman; quite simply, "woman is more accustomed to being deceived than man" (*Questions and Answers on Genesis* 1.33). The infamous passage in 1 Timothy 2 draws a similar association between Eve and womankind: "I

2. Scott, "Gender," 1067.

3. Ibid.

4. For a sampling of interpretations, see Kvam, Schearing, and Ziegler, *Eve & Adam*, 41–155.

5. I argued that this reference is to the evil wife rather than an evil Eve in "Is Eve to Blame?"

6. Quotations of Philo Judaeus are from the Loeb Classical Library.

permit no woman to teach or to have authority over a man; she is to keep silent. For Adam was formed first, then Eve; and Adam was not deceived, but the woman was deceived and became a transgressor" (1 Tim 2:12–14). Of course, no ancient author can match Tertullian's extended rant, in which he condemns all women for being Eve, the devil's gateway (*On the Apparel of Women* 1.1).

B. *The Greek Life of Adam and Eve*

Though Tertullian's may be the most infamous excoriation, a more detailed demonization of Eve can be located in the less well-known *Apocalypse of Moses*, or the Greek *Life of Adam and Eve* (*GLAE*), a pseudepigraphon composed sometime during the first three centuries CE. Tischendorf initially published this text in the middle of the nineteenth century.[7] This pseudepigraphon, which is, in part, an inventive interpretation of Genesis 2–5, can be divided into four neat sections: patrimony, pain, parenesis, and pardoning.

Patrimony (1:1—5:3; retelling Gen 4:1—5:5). Long after the births of Cain and Abel, in a dream—a nightmare, really—Eve learns of the murder of Abel by Cain. Patrimony, however, does not belong to Cain; therefore, God commands Adam not to reveal to Cain the mystery that Adam alone knows. God then promises that Seth will be born to replace Abel. Adam— he is given credit, not Eve—makes or produces thirty sons and thirty daughters. After this flurry of births, an unknown condition—they do not yet know how to identify illness—befalls Adam, who gathers his children around him in traditional testamentary fashion.

Pain (6:1—14:2). Adam proposes that Seth and Eve should travel to paradise, beg God to send an angel into paradise to retrieve the oil of mercy, and return with the oil to alleviate Adam's inscrutable suffering. This otherwise smooth story (6:1–2; 9:1–3; 13:1—14:2) is interrupted twice, first by Adam's autobiographical recollection of the first sin (6:3—8:2), then by a wild animal that attacks Seth and accuses Eve of initiating, by her greed, the dominion over the wild animals (10:1—12:2). The scene ends

---

7. Tischendorf, *Apocalypses Apocryphae*, 1–23. There is intense debate about whether the composition was written originally in Hebrew by a Jewish author (Dochhorn, *Apokalypse des Mose*, 105–72) or in Greek by a Christian author (e.g., Stone, *History of the Literature*, 58–61; Tromp, *Life of Adam and Eve*, 65–78; and Jonge, "Christian Origin," 347–63, esp. 363).

when the archangel Michael denies Seth's request, so he and his mother return incapable of relieving Adam's duress.

Parenesis (14:3—30:1; retelling Gen 3:1–24). After Seth and Eve return from paradise, Adam again indicts Eve, providing an occasion for her to reveal her own perspective on the primeval sin in what might be called the Testament of Eve. Eve recounts, in a flourish of biblical and unbiblical elements: the envy of the devil; the entrance of the serpent, the devil's tool, into paradise; Eve's inability to resist the devil's trickery; Eve's taking of the fruit; Eve's ability to persuade Adam to eat; God's awesome entry into paradise on a chariot; the curses; and the expulsion of the first pair from paradise, despite angelic pleas for mercy. Eve does more than recount the story; the intention of her testament is parenetic. Eve ends her testament: "Now therefore, my children, I have disclosed to you the way in which we were deceived. And you yourselves—guard yourselves so as not to disregard what is good" (*GLAE* 30:1).

Pardoning (31:1—43:4). Following the Testament of Eve, Adam attempts to assuage Eve's anxiety by promising their shared destinies. Eve then confesses her sin repeatedly and is subsequently instructed by an angel to watch Adam's ascent. While she is watching, God's chariot arrives in paradise, replete with an entourage consisting of angels, the sun, and the moon. Seth explains to Eve what she sees, including the inability of the sun and moon to shine in the presence of God. The story continues with the burial of Adam's body and the sealing of his tomb until the burial of Eve should take place. Eve is subsequently buried, and the archangel Michael delivers final instructions about this burial to Seth.

C. Eve, the Prevalent Ideology, and the Greek Life of Adam and Eve

In the first thirteen chapters, there is much to be said about Eve—nearly all of it negative. Adam begins his autobiographical account of the first sin with the words, "When God made us, both me and your mother, through whom I am also dying" (7:1).[8] Eve, in turn, blames herself for Adam's pain and sickness, to the extent that she begs to take half of his disease from him: "My lord, Adam, get up, give to me half of your disease, and I will endure it because on account of me this has happened to you, on account

---

8. All translations of *GLAE* are my own, based upon the critical edition of Tromp, *The Life of Adam and Eve in Greek*. I have preserved awkward Hebraisms and some of the wooden qualities of the original Greek. Occasionally I add words, which are marked by brackets. Other sigla adopted from Tromp, such as double brackets, indicate textual variants.

of me you are meeting with troubles" (9:2). When Adam sends her subsequently with their son, Seth, to retrieve healing oil from paradise, she encounters a wild beast, who blames her—and particularly her greed—for the animal rebellion:

> Oh, Eve, your greed is not about us, nor your weeping, but about you, since the dominion of the wild animals came to be from you. How was your mouth opened to eat from the tree about which God commanded you not to eat from it? For this reason also our natures were altered. Now, therefore, you will not be able to endure [it] if I begin to cross-examine you. (11:1–2)

The animal stands back only when Seth commands it because Seth is the image of God—Eve, presumably, is not. In the first thirteen chapters of *GLAE*, then, Adam blames Eve for his death, Eve blames herself for Adam's pain and disease, and the wild animal blames Eve for the sharpening of its teeth, that is, for animal rebellion. These thirteen chapters express to a daunting extent, and with an extensive amount of detail, the prevalent ideology about Eve.

The exclamation point is put to these scenes when Adam indicts Eve in these words: "Oh, Eve, what did you bring about among us? You have brought upon us enormous anger, which is death's exercise of dominion over all of our race?" (14:2). Such incendiary language is usually reserved for Adam, and occasionally for Eve, in Jewish apocalypses that attempted to make sense of the devastation of Jerusalem in 70 CE.[9] *4 Ezra* contains this indictment: "And you laid upon him one commandment of yours; but he transgressed it, and immediately you appointed death for him and for his descendants" (3:7). *2 Baruch* laments, "For when he transgressed, untimely death came into being, mourning was mentioned, affliction was prepared, illness was created" (56:6).[10] In chapter fourteen of *GLAE*,

---

9. The apocalyptic authors of *4 Ezra* (3:4–11, 20–27; 4:26–32; 6:45–59; 7:11–14, 62–74, 116–31) and *2 Baruch* (4:1–7; 14:17–19; 17:1—18:2; 19:8; 23:4–5; 48:42–47; 54:13–19; 56:6–10), during the decades following the destruction of Jerusalem in 70 CE, accentuate the effects of the sin of Adam—and Eve in *2 Baruch*—by viewing him as the inaugurator of the present evil age.

10. They also question Adam's (and Eve's for *2 Baruch*) place in the problem of ongoing moral depravity. The author of *4 Ezra* appears to blame Adam: "O Adam, what have you done?" Yet there is a measure of ambivalence when he continues, "For what good is it to us, if an eternal age has been promised to us, but we have done deeds that bring death?" (7:117–20). Ultimately, the angel lays responsibility at the individual's feet: "This is the meaning of the contest which every person who is born on earth shall wage" (7:127–28). Although the question in *2 Baruch* is the same— "O Adam, what did you do to all who were born after you? (48:42)—the answer is

however, this is *Eve's* doing, not Adam's. This is Eve's sin, not Adam's. This is her greed, not his.

The finale of *GLAE* begins in much the same way that the first part ended. After a brief interchange between Eve and Adam, Eve "got up and went outside. And having fallen upon the earth, she said repeatedly,

> I sinned, God,
> I sinned, father of all,
> I sinned against you,
> I sinned against your chosen angels,
> I sinned against the cherubim,
> I sinned against your immovable throne,
> I sinned, Lord,
> I sinned much,
> I sinned in your eyes,
> And because of me has all sin come about in the creation.
> (*GLAE* 32:1–2)

Throughout the final chapters, Eve incessantly weeps, perplexed and chagrinned by Adam's death and pending fate—with the hope of burial by his side. When she cannot understand something, such as why the two dark heavenly apparitions cannot shine, she turns to Seth for answers (34:1—36:3). The deference Eve pays to Seth, who understands what she does not, takes the reader back to Eve and Seth's encounter with the wild animal. In that instance, Eve could not forestall the animal's attack; only Seth, the image of God, could (10:1—12:2).

The Greek *Life of Adam and Eve*, then, comprises a, perhaps even *the*, quintessential expression of a prevalent negative ideology of Eve. Yet such vilification characterizes only the first thirteen and the final twelve chapters of *GLAE*. Eve is a very different figure in the middle section, chapters 14–30, in which we are able to discern a subversive ideology that poses a challenge to the prevalent negative ideology, which swirls around Eve in the remainder of this text.

---

crisper than in *4 Ezra*. While Adam brought physical death to the present evil age, individuals have the capacity to determine their destinies in the age to come: "For, although Adam sinned first and has brought death upon all who were not in his own time, yet each of them who has been born from him has prepared for himself [or herself] the coming torment" (54:15). In other words, "Adam is, therefore, not the cause, except only for himself, but each of us has become our own Adam" (54:16). For English translations of pseudepigraphical texts, see Charlesworth, *Old Testament Pseudepigrapha*.

II. The Subversive Ideology of Eve's Testament

Against the backdrop of the prevalent ideology, according to which Eve introduced sickness, death, and animal chaos into the world, we will be able to appreciate the many ways in which the middle portion of the Greek *Life of Adam and Eve* forcefully projects an alternative, even subversive ideology. This middle portion can aptly be designated the Testament of Eve, for Eve gathers her children to tell them about how she and Adam sinned. Such scenarios and stories are the essential characteristics of ancient Jewish testaments.

A. *The Testamentary Genre and a Female Narrator*

Our extant Jewish sources contain no testaments set into the mouth of a woman; in no instance does a Jewish woman gather her children in preparation for death and offer final words to them. The pseudepigraphical *Testaments of the Twelve Patriarchs*, for example, contains no comparable testaments of the matriarchs.[11]

The exception occurs in chapters 15–30 of the Greek *Life of Adam and Eve*. This is a literary and cultural anomaly; this anomaly alone, in my opinion, suggests subversion. Here Eve is, in a real sense, the author of her own story. She, the first *woman*, is the ideal figure who informs their children while Adam writhes in the throes of pain (15:1; 30:1). She, not Adam, is the one who says, "I have disclosed to you the way in which we were deceived" (30:1). Yet Eve's testament is subversive in more salutary ways than this.[12]

11. According to a conversation with Sarah Johnston, extant Greek and Roman sources do not contain testaments set into the mouth of a woman, with the possible exception of Euripides's *Alcestis*, in which Alcestis, as she is dying, speaks briefly to her children about how they should live the rest of their lives. Alcestis, however, is a distant cousin to Eve; her words are brief, her authority far more limited, her story constrained by her role as dutiful wife and mother. Even if we admit the resemblance between Alcestis and Eve, we are compelled to admit that only in this rare instance does a Greek or Roman woman gather her children in preparation for death and offer final words to them.

12. For indications of why this should be read as an independent unit within *GLAE* (e.g., a different view of the location of paradise from the remainder of *GLAE*), see my essay "The Exoneration of Eve." Further, there are two textual insertions in *GLAE*, 13:3–5 and 29:7–13, that may indicate the conjoining of originally independent parts of *GLAE*. In short, chs. 15–30 (with ch. 14 added as a transition) may have formed a separate unit.

PART ONE: Gender, Authority, and the Church

B. Two Testaments, Two Perspectives

Within the first thirteen chapters of *GLAE*, Adam delivers his own auto-biographical narrative of the first sin and its horrific consequences. The narrative is far shorter than Eve's, measuring but two chapters, but it is long enough to present the prevalent ideology about Eve, and, therefore, to suggest how radically the perspective of Eve's testament diverges from his testament. It provides, in other words, an ample illustration of the prevalent ideology, with which the subversive ideology can be contrasted. It will be beneficial, before proceeding, to set these testaments side by side.

Topics	Adam's Version	Eve's Version
Typical introduction to a testament	5:1 And Adam produced thirty sons and thirty daughters. And Adam lived nine hundred and thirty years, 2 and, having fallen into disease [and] crying out with a loud voice, he says, "Let all my sons come to me so that I may see them before I die." 3 And all gathered (for the world was settled in three regions)	14:3 And Adam says to Eve, "Call all our children and the children of our children, and reveal to them the manner of our sinful neglect."
Seth's response	6:1 And Seth, answering, says to him, "You don't remember, do you, father, paradise from which [fruits] you used to eat—and you grieved? 2 If this is so, reveal [it] to me, and I myself will go and bring to you fruit from paradise. For I will place excrement upon my head, and I will weep and pray, and my Lord will hear me and will send his angel, and I will bring to you so that the pain will leave you." 3 Adam says to him, "No, my son Seth, but disease and pains, I have." Seth says to him, "And how did they come to you?"	

Topics	Adam's Version	Eve's Version
	⁷:¹ And Adam said to him,	¹⁵:¹ Then Eve says to them: Listen, all my children and the children of my children, and I will reveal to you how the enemy deceived us.
Division of labor in paradise	"When God made us, both me and your mother, through whom I am also dying, he gave to us every plant in paradise, but about one he commanded us not to eat from it, through which also we are dying. ² And the hour for the angels who were guarding your mother to ascend and to worship the Lord drew near.	² And it just so happened that we were tending paradise, each of us the portion allotted to him, whatever region [was] from God, and I myself tended in my allotment—south and west. ³ And the devil went into the allotment of Adam, where the wild animals were (since God had divided the wild animals; all the males he had given to your father, and all the females he had given to me.)
Serpent deceived		¹⁶:¹ And the devil spoke to the serpent, saying, "Get up. Come to me." ² And, having gotten up, he went to him. And the devil says to him, "I hear that you are shrewder than all the wild animals. Listen to me, and I will become friends with you. ³ Why are you eating from the weeds of Adam and not from paradise? Get up and come, and let us make him to be thrown out of paradise, as also we were thrown out through him." ⁴ The serpent says to him, "I am afraid that perhaps the Lord will be angry with me." ⁵ The devil says to him, "Stop being afraid. Become a tool for me, and I myself will speak through your mouth one word aimed at deceiving them."

PART ONE: Gender, Authority, and the Church

Topics	Adam's Version	Eve's Version
Eve deceived		[17:1] And immediately he became suspended next to the walls of paradise. And when the angels ascended to worship God, then Satan was transformed into [the] appearance of an angel and praised God with hymns— just like the angels. [2] And as I peeped out of the wall, I saw him—similar to an angel. And he says to me, "Are you Eve?" And I said to him, "I am." And he says to me, "What are you doing in paradise?" [3] And I said to him, "God placed us [here] to tend and to eat from it." [4] The devil answered through the mouth of the serpent, "You are doing well. But you are eating from every plant, aren't you?" [5] And I said, "Yes, from all of them we are eating, except one only, which is well inside paradise, about which God commanded us, 'Do not eat from it, since with death you will die.'" [18:1] Then the serpent says to me, "God lives—because I grieve for you [two], for I do not want you to be ignorant. Come therefore and eat and consider the value of the tree." [2] But I said to him, "I am afraid that perhaps God will be angry with me, just as he said to us." [3] And he says to me, "Stop being afraid. For when you eat, your eyes will be opened, and you will be as gods, knowing what is good and what is evil. [4] And because God knew this, that you will be just like him, he bore a grudge against you and said, 'Do not eat from it.' [5] But you, turn your attention to the plant, and you will see intense glory." But I was afraid to take from the fruit, and he says to me, "Come, I will give [it] to you. Follow me."

Topics	Adam's Version	Eve's Version
Trick about the oath		¹⁹:¹ And I opened, and he entered inside into paradise. And he passed through ahead of me. And after walking a bit, he turned and says to me, "Because I have changed my mind, I will not give to you to eat, unless you swear to me that you [will] give [it] also to your husband." ² But I myself said to him, "I don't know with what kind of oath I will swear to you. Nevertheless, what I know I say to you: By the throne of the Authoritative One and the cherubim and the tree of life, I will give also to my husband."
	And the enemy gave to her	³ When he had extracted from me the oath, then he came and placed upon the fruit which he gave to me the venom of his wickedness [[this is of desire. For desire is of all sin.]] And after having bent the branch to the ground, I took from the fruit,
	and she ate from the tree, knowing that I was not very near her—nor the holy angels.	and I ate.
Eve weeps about her oath		²⁰:¹ And at that very hour my eyes were opened, and I knew that I was naked of the righteousness with which I had been clothed. ² And I wept, saying, "What did you bring about, that I have been estranged from my glory?" ³ And I began to weep about the oath. And that one got down from the plant and became invisible. ⁴ And I was searching in my region for leaves so that I could hide my shame, and I did not find [any]. For the leaves had fallen off all the plants of my region, except for the fig alone. ⁵ And having taken the leaves from it, I made for myself loin-cloths.

Topics	Adam's Version	Eve's Version
Eve gives Adam the fruit		[21:1] And I cried out at that very hour, saying, "Adam, Adam, where are you? Get up, come to me, and I will show you an enormous mystery." [2] But when your father came, I spoke to him words of lawlessness, which brought us down from intense glory. [3] For when he came, I opened my mouth, and the devil was speaking, and I began to give harsh counsel to him, saying, "Come, my lord Adam, listen to me and eat from the fruit of the tree (about) which God said to us not to eat from it, and you will be as God." [4] And answering, your father said, "I am afraid that perhaps God will be angry with me." But I said to him, "Stop being afraid, for when you eat, you will be knowledgeable (about) good and evil." [5] And then after having quickly persuaded him, he ate, and his eyes were opened, and he became aware of his nakedness. [6] And he says to me, "Oh, evil woman, what did you bring about among us? You have estranged me from the glory of God."
	[3] Then she gave also to me to eat,	

Topics	Adam's Version	Eve's Version
God's entry to paradise	[8:1] And God was angry with us. And coming into paradise,	[22:1] And at that very hour we heard the archangel Michael sounding the trumpet and calling the angels and saying, [2] "These things says the Lord, 'Come with me into paradise and hear the sentence with which I am going to sentence Adam.'" And when we heard the archangel sounding the trumpet, we said, "Look, God is coming into paradise to sentence us. And we were afraid, and we hid. [3] And God came into paradise mounted upon a cherubim-throne, and the angels were praising him with hymns. And when God entered, the plants of Adam's allotment sprouted—and all of mine. [4] And the throne of God was established firmly where the tree of life was.
	the Authoritative One called me with a frightful voice, saying, "Adam, where are you?"And why do you hide yourself from my face? A building cannot be hidden from the one who built it, can it?	[23:1] And God called Adam, saying, "Adam, where have you gone into hiding, thinking that I will not find you? A building will not be hidden from the one who built it, will it?"

Topics	Adam's Version	Eve's Version
		[2] Then answering, your father said, "Not, my Lord, are we hiding from you because we think that we (cannot) be found by you, but I am afraid because I am naked, and I stood in awe of your power, Authoritative One." [3] God says to him, "Who made known to you that you are naked, unless you disregarded my command—to keep it?" [4] Then Adam remembered the word which I had spoken to him, "Free of danger from God I will make you." [5] And having turned to me, he said, "Why did you do this?" And I said, "The serpent deceived me."
Curse of Adam	[2] And he says, "Since you disregarded my covenant and my command you disobeyed, I have inflicted upon your body seventy blows. The first disease of a blow: violence to the eyes. The second [is a disease of] a blow to hearing–and in this way, one after the other, all the blows to your body will follow closely behind."	[24:1] And God says to Adam, "Since you disobeyed my command and listened to your wife, cursed is the earth on your account. [2] You will work it, and it will not give its produce. Thorny and prickly plants it will sprout for you, and with (the) sweat of your face you will eat bread. And you will be in various diseases, [having been] oppressed by bitterness, [and] you will not taste sweetness—[3] [having been] oppressed by burning heat and constrained by cold. And wild animals, which you used to rule, will rise up in revolt against you with anarchy because my command you did not keep."

Topics	Adam's Version	Eve's Version
Curse of Eve		[25:1] And having turned toward me, the Lord says, "Since you yourself listened to the serpent and disobeyed my command, you will be in various diseases, and in unendurable pains [2] you will give birth to children [[in many ways.]] And in one hour you will come to give birth and you will lose your life from your intense bodily anguish and childbirth pains. [3] And you will confess and say, 'Lord, Lord, save me, and I will not return to the sin of the flesh.' [4] On account of this, on the basis of your words I will sentence you—on account of the enmity which the enemy placed in you. And having turned again to your husband, (and) he himself will rule you."

Topics	Adam's Version	Eve's Version
Curse of serpent		26:1 And after he had said these things to me, he said to the serpent with intense anger, saying to him, "Since you did this and became an ungrateful tool, so that you could deceive the careless of heart, cursed are you from all domestic animals. 2 You will be deprived of your food, which you used to eat, and dust you will eat all the days of your life. Upon your breast and upon your belly you will go, lacking both your hands and feet. 3 There will be left to you neither ear nor wing nor one body part of these with which you enticed with your wickedness and caused them to be thrown out of paradise. 4 And I will place enmity between you and between their seed. And he himself will (closely) watch your head, and you the heel of that one, until the day of judgment."

Topics	Adam's Version	Eve's Version
Expulsion from paradise Adam's plea & confession		27:1 Having said these things, he commands his angels to throw us out of paradise. 2 And while they were driving us out and wailing out loud, your father Adam begged the angels, saying, "Allow me a little (time) so that I may beg God to have compassion and show me mercy, for I only sinned." 3 And they themselves stopped driving him out. And Adam cried out with weeping, saying, "Forgive me, Lord, what I have done." 4 Then God says to his angels, "Why did you stop throwing Adam out of paradise? The sinful act is not mine, is it, or did I hand down a sentence wickedly?" 5 Then the angels, having fallen upon the earth, worshipped the Lord, saying, "You are just, Lord, and you hand down fair sentences."

Topics	Adam's Version	Eve's Version
Refusal of mercy		[28:1] And having turned toward Adam, he said, "I will not allow you from now on to be in paradise." [2] And answering, Adam said, "Lord, give to me from the plant of life so that I may eat before I am thrown out." [3] Then the Lord spoke to Adam, "You will not take now from it. For it was determined that the cherubim and the fiery sword which revolves should guard it on your account so that you may not taste from it and be immortal forever. [4] And you have the enmity which the enemy placed in you. But when you go out of paradise, if you guard yourself from all wickedness—as if longing to die—again, when the resurrection happens, I will raise you, and (it) will be given to you from the tree of life, and you will be immortal forever."

Topics	Adam's Version	Eve's Version
Expulsion complete		[29:1] And having said these things, the Lord commanded his angels to throw us out of paradise. [2] And your father wept in the presence of the angels in paradise, and the angels say to him, "What do you want us to do for you, Adam?" [3] And answering, your father said to the angels, "Look, you are throwing me out. I beg you: Allow me to take away fragrances out of paradise so that, after I go out, I may present an offering to God, so that God will hear me." [4] And having approached, the angels said to the Lord, "Jael, eternal king, command that incenses of fragrance from paradise be given to Adam." [5] And God commanded that it be allowed to Adam that he should take fragrances and seeds for his sustenance. [6] And having left him, the angels brought four kinds: saffron, spikenard, aromatic cane, and cinnamon—and other seeds for his sustenance. And having taken these, he went out of paradise. And we came to be upon the earth.
Parenetic conclusion		[30:1] Now therefore, my children, I have disclosed to you the way in which we were deceived. And you yourselves—guard yourselves so as not to disregard what is good.

Considerable differences of opinion about Eve distinguish the two testaments. First, there is no doubt about where responsibility lies for the primeval sin and its consequences. Adam refers to Eve as "your mother, through whom I am also dying" (7:1). In contrast, although Eve in her testament admits to being deceived, it is Adam who offers the most unequivocal admission of guilt. As the angels drive him from paradise, he begs for a brief reprieve to elicit God's mercy; he says, "[F]or I only sinned" (27:2). When the angels relent, he weeps and cries, "Forgive me, Lord, what I have done" (27:3). The weight of sin that Adam lays on Eve's shoulders in *his* testament rests principally upon Adam's shoulders in *her* testament.

Second, the explanation for Eve's vulnerability differs in the two testaments. According to Adam, the angels who were charged with guarding Eve had ascended to worship (7:2). The enemy gave the fruit to Eve, "knowing that I was not very near her—nor the holy angels" (7:2). (Though it is only a matter of innuendo, Adam may be suggesting that Eve was alone because he was at worship with the angels.) Eve offers a different explanation of how the serpent so easily approached her. Note the repetition that Eve adopts to underscore the partitioning of paradise and sexes, as she recalls,

> And it just so happened, that we were tending paradise, each of us the portion allotted to him, whatever region [was] from God, and I myself tended in my allotment—south and west. And the devil went into the allotment of Adam, where the wild animals were (since God had divided the wild animals; all the males he had given to your father, and all the females he had given to me). (15:2–3)

Eve's testament clearly communicates that Eve was not originally one who was guarded, but one who guarded. There is no angelic escort, and certainly no male one. This is a decidedly autonomous woman.

Equally significant is the third difference between the testaments: the divine division of paradise into a female and a male portion. What is clear here is that the laxity of a *man* with respect to his *male* animals allows Satan entrée into paradise. To quote this again in order to appreciate the implications of this division: "And the devil went into the allotment of *Adam*, where the wild animals were (since God had divided the wild animals; *all the males he had given to your father*, and all the females he had given to me)." The detail of the division of paradise is strong enough perhaps to offer firm pressure against the prevalent ideology, according to which Eve was responsible for the entrance of Satan, sin, and death.

Adam and Eve's testaments in the Greek *Life of Adam and Eve* offer two very different perspectives on the symbol that was Eve. In Adam's testament, which is caught in the web of the prevalent ideology, Eve is the one through whom human beings die because she, left unguarded, succumbed immediately to the enemy. In Eve's testament, which expresses a subversive ideology, Adam alone admits to being culpable—and he is right, from Eve's perspective, because he did not adequately guard his male portion of paradise.

III. From Text to Experience

The observation that the Testament of Eve evinces a subversive ideology does not of itself require us to acknowledge that it is a window into religious experience in antiquity. Further, the besetting difficulty of the Testament of Eve is that its narrator is fictionalized. Few women, outside the world of Harry Potter or *GLAE*, could claim to have conversed with satanically inspired snakes, eaten fruit that wrested death from immortality, or had the capacity to undo the submission of wild animals through her greed. Is it possible to make the leap from this fictionalized Eve, even one who champions a subversive ideology, to real women in antiquity?

In order to answer this question, we should perhaps lift a page from a longstanding debate between women's and gender studies. In pioneering work on women's history, on the one hand, scholars in *women's* studies in religion have tended to employ ancient literature as documents, as resources for the lives of real women, for social history. On the other hand, scholars who prefer *gender* studies in religion have tended to employ ancient literature as literary texts, as resources for cultural and intellectual history. In short, women's studies deals with lived history, gender studies with ideologies.[13]

The solution to this tension between women's studies and gender studies, between social history and cultural history, may prove illuminating for the discovery of religious experience in antiquity. Elizabeth Clark, by appealing to the pioneering insights of Joan Wallach Scott, explains that the impasse between social history and intellectual history, between the lives of women and discourses about women, is not insurmountable because discourse is not merely rhetoric or narrative; *discourse rather takes shape in the context of concrete social, economic, and political organizations.* The ability to understand gender in terms of discourse (in our case an autobiographical narrative, or testament, in the mouth of a woman) arises from the realization that gender is "a means of representing

---

13. Clark ("Engendering the Study of Religion," 237) distinguishes between "women's history (with its focus on social, political, and economic forces) and gender history (with an edge on the production of knowledge)," though she also recognizes that they "need to be kept in tandem."

ideas about social order and social organization."[14] Therefore, "to study
the meaning of the rhetoric pertaining to women—in addition to raising
up women as agents and victims—enlarges our historical perspective."[15]
Amy Hollywood, in her response to Clark, assesses the value of texts succinctly in these terms: "Knowledge of prevalent ideologies is itself a kind
of historical knowledge."[16]

If a bifurcation between historical events and rhetorical discourse
fails to hold the day, if women's actual experience can be related to discourses about or by women, then identifying the *ideologies* that permeate
the Testament of Eve may be a means of discerning *experience* as well.
This is not a simple transition, and I will make it with caution and care.
Still, if it is possible to discern experience—including religious experience—through the lens of literary discourse, then the Testament of Eve
may be a principal, perhaps even indispensable discourse that leads to the
world of experience in antiquity. While this experience may be reflected
in details as mundane as Eve's calling Adam "lord" or as remarkable as
her responsibility to guard the primeval garden, it may also be expressed
in subtle, less apparent ways, to which we may now turn our attention.

IV. The Testament of Eve and Religious Experience

A. The Tweaking of the Testamentary Genre

The complex role women played in antiquity is discernible in Eve's capacity to construct a testament, delivered when all of her children are gathered together. She, it seems, is the agent of her own story. She, not Adam,
concludes the story with the words, "*I* have disclosed to you . . ." (30:1).
Nonetheless, it is not her story exclusively. This is a shared story—". . .
how *we* were deceived." Her children, further, are not gathered for her
death but in anticipation of Adam's. Eve's agency, in short, is constrained
by the pervasive presence of Adam, her husband, though not to the extent that her voice is effaced and her agency expunged.

Another constraint on Eve's story is the presence of a more ancient
story. She cannot, consequently, exonerate herself, as that would undermine the older story of Genesis 1–4, of which *GLAE* is a revision. Still,

14. Ibid., 236.
15. Ibid., 241.
16. Hollywood, "Response to Elizabeth Clark," 249.

she proves herself to be an agent with a level of autonomy in the way she revises that first story. She does not merely repeat the story or claim responsibility for the first sin. Her retelling is more subtle in two respects. First, its testamentary quality renders it more universally applicable. This is not just a story about her and her husband; this is a story that reflects the experience of all people. Second, the way in which Eve offers inside views of her experience prompts readers to sympathize with her: though a sinner, and the first sinner, her actions are understandable, her transgression forgivable. These two dimensions of Eve's story, and the insight they bring to religious experience, comprise the substance of what is left to say about the Testament of Eve.

B. Parenesis and the Experience of Deception

The universal significance of this testament is discernible in its parenetic character. In other words, Eve's retelling of the primeval story in this testamentary form is an indication that it is intended to offer instruction—parenesis—in the struggle for righteousness that is integral to religious experience. The rhetorical discourse of a testament, simply put, offers insight into how religious experience was perceived in antiquity.

The *Testaments of the Twelve Patriarchs* provide stellar examples of the transformation of ancient biblical stories into universal lessons. In these testaments, Israel's male ancestors function as narrators who retell their stories from the book of Genesis. One of the apparent purposes of these retellings is to shape the religious experience of the testaments' readers. Several testamentary figures are preoccupied with urging their children— and by extension the readers—to avoid sexual sin. For example, the story of Reuben, who in a sliver of Genesis sleeps with Jacob's concubine, Bilhah (Gen 35:22), explodes in the *Testaments of the Twelve Patriarchs* into a tirade against sexual promiscuity. This tirade is not about personal animus or private sin; it is rife with generalizations about women and men: men should not devote their attention to the beauty of women (*T. Rub.* 4:1); because women are evil, they must scheme about how to entice men with their looks (5:1), like a prostitute (5:4); men should therefore protect their senses from women (6:1); men should even order their wives and daughters not to adorn themselves so as to seduce men's sound minds (5:5). On and on it goes, with stereotypes and generalizations that extend far beyond Genesis 35 into the world of extramarital sexual activity. The *Testament of*

Reuben is less about Reuben than about the treachery of women and the ways in which men can avoid their morally fatal grip.[17]

The point of this brief excursus into the *Testaments of the Twelve Patriarchs* is to underscore that testaments transmuted the specificity of a biblical text into universal parenesis in an effort to shape religious experience. The rhetorical discourse of a testament, in other words, provides a window into the experience of its readers—or what the author considered their experience, or potential experience, to comprise. The rhetorical shape of the Testament of Eve points in the same direction. In this testament, Eve transforms details of the biblical story in a way that renders them applicable to the experience of all readers of the text. In several ways, then, Eve offers insight into the religious experience of all people.

First and foremost, the recurring pattern of deception communicates to Eve's children—and by implication all readers of the testament—precisely how to avoid disregarding what is good, how to steer clear of finding themselves vulnerable to deceit. The deception of the serpent, Eve, and Adam proceed precisely along five identical steps, in each of the three instances: (1) the deceiver approaches and arouses desire (16:1; 18:1; 21:1); (2) the deceiver invites the soon-to-be deceived to follow (16:3; 18:1; 21:3); (3) the soon-to-be deceived hesitates—"I fear lest the LORD/God be angry with me" (16:4; 18:2; 21:4); (4) the deceiver responds with the words, "fear not," accompanied by a part truth intended to allay fear (16:5; 18:3–4; 21:4); (5) the deceived acquiesces (17:1; 19:3; 21:5). This pattern repeats with variations. The deception of the serpent is the paradigm that sets out the basic elements in the process of deception. The deception of Adam, marked by brevity, indicates how easily the unguarded victim falls prey to deception. The deception of Eve exposes the complexity and inner turmoil of the process. The repetition of this pattern is an indication that this testament is aimed, at least in part, at bolstering the integrity of the religious experience of its readers: three different characters—representing animals, men, and women—manage to find themselves deceived and in the throes of transgression.

This pattern is characterized as well by verisimilitude. Notwithstanding the presence of a talking serpent, the pattern is realistic, and its parenesis down to earth: desire enters human experience; hesitation holds desire off—but only temporarily; a part truth or rationalization allays that fear, preparing the way to succumb to deception, so that the apparent

17. See further *Testament of Simeon* 5. In another testament, Judah urges his children to avoid promiscuity, drunkenness, and greed (*Testament of Judah* 15–19).

good is now within reach. Such a lucid pattern of sin belongs to more than the primeval pair and the talking serpent; this is a common pattern of sin, a pervasive prototype of authentic and flawed religious experience.

Despite the recurrence and verisimilitude of this pattern, should readers of this testament fail to grasp the likelihood that this tragic experience will overtake them, Eve makes one final appeal, in which she emphasizes that this is not just a story but an experience to which her hearers too are liable: "Now therefore, my children, I have disclosed to you the way in which we were deceived. *And you yourselves—guard yourselves so as not to disregard what is good*" (emphasis mine). There is a clear lesson to be learned here, a lesson to be applied in pursuit of what is good. This is not only Eve's personal story—or Adam's—but a testament told to steel her children, and by extension all readers, to guard themselves so as not to disregard what is good.

C. The Power of Inside Views

Though constrained by the biblical story, as well as the prevalent ideology about women, according to which Eve succumbed to sin because weak-willed, salacious, and seductive women precipitate sin, Eve is still able to revise the story in such a way that she is not entirely, or ultimately, culpable for the first sin. Rather than adopting the tactic of omission—leaving out the sordid details of Genesis—Eve preserves the negative elements of the original story but expresses them in a way that serves to exonerate her. She accomplishes this with subtle narrative details and by offering inside views of her experience. In other words, in her own testament, Eve, while guilty of actions similar to those in Genesis 3, evokes sympathy because the reader can empathize with her inner experience of being deceived.

This is an effective narrative technique. Wayne Booth, for example, notices the importance of inside views in this respect when he writes, "*If an author wants intense sympathy for characters who do not have strong virtues to recommend them, then the psychic vividness of prolonged and deep inside views will help them.*"[18] He also points to Shakespeare's "elaborate rhetoric" by which he controls reader sympathies even with a criminal: "Macbeth's suffering conscience," notes Booth, "dramatized at length, speaks a stronger message than is carried by his undramatized

---

18. Emphasis is Booth's; see Booth, *Rhetoric of Fiction*, 377–78. See as well Scholes and Kellogg, *Nature of Narrative*, 170–71.

crimes."[19] Along a similar vein, Booth writes of Emma in Jane Austen's novel by the same name: "Sympathy for Emma can be heightened by withholding inside views of others as well as by granting them of her . . ."[20] By the same token, sympathy for Eve is heightened by withholding inside views of Adam and the serpent—the others who are deceived—and by granting inside views of her own experience. The narrative in *GLAE* contains precisely these sorts of inside views of Eve that are possessed of the potential to evoke a resonance between her experience of being deceived by an evil, inhuman being—her negative religious experience, we might venture—and the experience of the readers (or hearers) of this testament.

This, then, is the heart of the matter: the portrait of Eve in this independent testament offers a compelling narrative in which inside views of Eve embody a subversive ideology, according to which Eve is not nearly as culpable as the prevalent ancient ideology would suggest. Already in the first of five steps on the path toward deception—the approach of the deceiver—Eve explains her perception, in 17:1–2, in such a way that she may be accused only of an inadvertent sin, for she emphasizes through repetition that Satan looked very much like an angel: "And immediately he became suspended next to the walls of paradise. And when the angels ascended to worship God, then Satan was transformed into [the] appearance of an angel and praised God with hymns—just like the angels" (17:1). What other conclusion could Eve have drawn? Here, in paradise, was an angelic figure who spoke with her. Her error, set in this light, is entirely understandable.

Equally significant are the dialogue and inner view that this encounter precipitates in the third step of the process of deception. Like the serpent before her and Adam after her, Eve too verbally confesses her fear. This verbalization leads in *GLAE* to the dialogue that occurs in Genesis 3 between the serpent and the woman. Yet at the conclusion of that dialogue—and this is what is noteworthy—Eve continues to feel fear. In 18:5, she recalls, "But I was afraid to take from the fruit."

The force of Eve's resistance, which is an extra step in the process of deception, is apparent when Eve's unwillingness to be deceived is compared with Adam's instance of recollection, which pales in comparison with the intensity of Eve's resistance. Eve in *GLAE* 21:4–5 remembers, "And answering, your father said, 'I am afraid that perhaps God will be angry with me.' But I said to him, 'Stop being afraid, for when you eat, you will

19. Booth, *Rhetoric of Fiction*, 115.
20. Ibid., 249.

be knowledgeable (about) good and evil.' And then after having quickly persuaded him, he ate, and his eyes were opened, and he became aware of his nakedness." By her own account, Eve was able "quickly" to persuade Adam, to dissolve his fear—a fear that can hardly even be characterized as resolve. If proponents of the prevalent ideology saw in Eve a figure who was particularly prone to deception, this portrait in the Testament of Eve offers an alternative point of view. The serpent succumbed to deception readily. Adam succumbed to deception quickly. Only Eve expressed her fear, entered into a lengthy conversation, and *felt* continued fear; only Eve resisted deception.

This subversive ideology gains further momentum in the subsequent scene (chs. 19–20), in which Eve as narrator depicts her acquiescence by expanding upon the laconic words of Genesis 3:6: "[A]nd she also gave some to her husband with her." Eve communicates to her children that she did not intend to give an evil fruit to her husband; rather, Satan tricked her by extracting from her an oath that she would give this fruit—this presumably good fruit—to her husband as well. That is, Eve agreed to share the fruit with Adam while she still thought it was possessed of God's glory. Only *after* she ate did Eve realize the predicament in which she had placed herself. She was bound by an oath to give the pernicious fruit to Adam. In good faith, Eve had promised to share the glorious fruit with Adam; after eating it, she discovered that she was compelled to offer him the harmful fruit. Her mistake was not intentional; on the contrary, she was deceived, duped into giving the fruit she now knew to be evil to her husband. And her response? Her response was to weep. Eve recalls, "And I began to weep about the oath" (*GLAE* 20:3).

In summary, throughout the detailed process of deception, Eve divulges something unique and self-exonerating, typically by offering inside views of her experience. These views have the potential to evoke reader sympathy for her predicament and her eventual plight. When the deceiver approaches, he looks to Eve and acts very much as an angel should. Her naïveté, in other words, is understandable and perhaps even forgivable. Despite the apparent angelic likeness of Satan, she still offers resistance, so much so that Satan does not quickly deceive her. Even her culpability with respect to the deception of Adam diminishes. She was bound by an oath she took when she thought the fruit a good thing; when she found out the truth, she wept.

If the discourse of the Testament of Eve and the ideology it champions are a reflection of social history, then we have learned much about

29

conceptions of religious experience in antiquity. Eve, in contrast to Adam and the serpent, is a good person duped by a deceiver. Despite her resistance, she succumbs, bound further by the goodness of her intention not to withhold the fruit from her husband. Everything has gone wrong, though the readers, represented by Eve's children, are able to empathize with this tragic figure, since the pattern of deception is so subtle yet so realistic, it reflects an actual experience that may overtake them at any time. This, of course, is the gist of Eve's conclusion: "Now therefore, my children, I have disclosed to you the way in which we were deceived. *And you yourselves—guard yourselves so as not to disregard what is good.*"

V. Conclusion

Several dimensions of the Testament of Eve identify it is as a window into ideologies, prevalent and subversive, and religious experience in antiquity. First, the Testament of Eve is rife with *sympathy* toward Eve. The other characters are developed without inside views, inner tensions, and various elements that evoke a reader's sympathy. In contrast, a reader learns about Eve's feelings, her resistance, and her regret. The reader can empathize with her inability to recognize Satan disguised as an angelic being. The reader can sense in her tears a fidelity to Adam, to whom she does not want to give the fruit, though she is bound by an oath. This sympathy is a subtle subversion of the prevalent ideology, in which the first woman, because she was a woman, became the source of sin and the cause of Adam's downfall.

Second, the *initiative* of Eve is evident in the fundamental observation that this is not a story told *about* Eve. Although it is not exclusively her story, and though it is told to children gathered prior to her husband's death, this is a story told *by* Eve. From the perspective of Jewish antiquity, it must be said that the placement of a testament in her mouth would have served to raise her status. Further, Eve offers clear, even perspicacious insight into religious experience, into the protracted process of deception, into unwitting betrayal.

Third, Eve is *autonomous* in her testament. She is shown at first to be the guardian of her portion of paradise rather than, as in the prevalent ideology, one who needs angelic—and presumably Adamic—protection. She is also, unlike the serpent and Adam, resistant to deception; her fall is protracted, her demise a struggle.

Fourth, Eve is able in her testament to communicate sympathy, initiative, and autonomy despite the dependence of her story upon Genesis 3. These are adaptations, additions, and nuanced developments of the biblical text. Despite her incorporation of much of Genesis 3 in this testament, Eve is able nonetheless to imbue her character with virtue tinged by naïveté.

Fifth, this testament offers a clear alternative to the prevalent ideology. This is not simply about an autonomous narrative character who evokes reader sympathy through inside views, who conveys an elaborate assessment of deception, who takes the initiative to guard paradise alongside Adam, though in a different portion. We can say still more. Because we know the prevalent ideology about Eve in particular and womankind in general, we can recognize in this testament a narrative that subtly undermines the prevalent ideology. Other texts thought possibly to be authored by women—the *Testament of Job* and *Joseph and Aseneth*—have to do with women for whom there was no longstanding tradition of denigration. The scenario is otherwise with the figure of Eve, who came to symbolize vulnerability to deception, the capacity to seduce, and, frankly, all things wicked that could be associated with women. This is not simply a sympathetic take on an autonomous woman, but a subtle, even subversive recasting of the alleged progenitrix of evil.

Sixth, the Testament of Eve is a window into religious experience in antiquity. By recounting a finely honed, down-to-earth pattern of deception, which repeats three times with wide variation, Eve offers a lesson in flawed religious experience—a lesson intended to prevent her children from succumbing, even inadvertently, to sin. This testament is also a window into women's experience in antiquity. Eve's retelling of the primeval sin goes a long way to undermine Adam's version. Yet it does so under constraint. Eve must offer evocative inside views and a variety of details, such as the serpent's entering through Adam's portion of the garden, to destabilize the prevalent ideology obliquely rather than directly. Such a subtle but forceful literary effort may correspond to the clever and circuitous means women were compelled to adopt to maintain their status in a world dominated by men.

Bibliography

Booth, Wayne C., *The Rhetoric of Fiction*. 2nd ed. Chicago: University of Chicago, 1983.

Charlesworth, James. H., editor. *Old Testament Pseudepigrapha*. 2 vols. Garden City, NY: Doubleday, 1983, 1985.

Clark, Elizabeth. "Engendering the Study of Religion." In *The Future of the Study of Religion: Proceedings of Congress 2000*, edited by Slavica Jakelic and Lori Pearson, 217–42. Numen Book Series; Studies in the History of Religions 103. Leiden: Brill, 2004.

Dochhorn, Jan, *Die Apokalypse des Mose: Text, Übersetzung, Kommentar. Texts and Studies in Ancient Judaism* 106. Tübingen: Mohr/Siebeck, 2005.

Hollywood, Amy. "Agency and Evidence in Feminist Studies of Religion: A Response to Elizabeth Clark." In *The Future of the Study of Religion: Proceedings of Congress 2000*, edited by Slavica Jakelic and Lori Pearson, 243–49. Numen Book Series; Studies in the History of Religions 103. Leiden: Brill, 2004.

Jonge, Marinus de."The Christian Origin of the *Greek Life of Adam and Eve*." In *Literature on Adam and Eve: Collected Essays*, edited by Gary Anderson, Michael Stone, and Johannes Tromp, 347–63. *Studia in Veteris Testamenti Pseudepigrapha* 15. Leiden: Brill, 2000.

Köstenberger, Andreas J. *God, Marriage, and Family: Rebuilding the Biblical Foundation*. 2nd ed. Wheaton, IL: Crossway, 2010.

Kvam, Kristen E., Linda S. Schearing, and Valarie H. Ziegler, editors. *Eve & Adam: Jewish, Christian, and Muslim Readings on Genesis and Gender*. Bloomington: Indiana University Press, 1999.

Levison, John R. (Jack). "Is Eve to Blame? A Contextual Analysis of Sirach 25:24." *Catholic Biblical Quarterly* 47 (1985) 617–23.

———. "The Exoneration of Eve in the Apocalypse of Moses 15–30." *Journal for the Study of Judaism and Related Literature* 20 (1989) 135–50.

Scholes, Robert, and Robert Kellogg. *The Nature of Narrative*. New York: Oxford University Press, 1966.

Scott, Joan Wallach. "Gender: A Useful Category of Historical Analysis." *American Historical Review* 91/5 (1986) 1053–75.

Stone, Michael E. *A History of the Literature of Adam and Eve. Early Judaism and its Literature* 3. Atlanta: Scholars Press, 1992.

Tischendorf, Constantin von. *Apocalypses Apocryphae Mosis, Esdrae, Pauli, Johannis, item Mariae dormitio*. Hildesheim, 1966.

Tromp, Johannes. *The Life of Adam and Eve and Related Literature*. Sheffield: Sheffield Academic, 1997.

———. *The Life of Adam and Eve in Greek: A Critical Edition*. Pseudepigrapha Veteris Testamenti Graece 6. Leiden: Brill, 2005.

2

Weaving the Sermon[1]
The Wife of Bath's Preaching Body
in the *Canterbury Tales*

MIKEE DELONY

I am convinced that when the strands of women's experience, thinking, and embodiment are interwoven they comprise a large portion of the distinctiveness of women's preaching from a feminist perspective.

—CHRISTINE M. SMITH

THE WIFE OF BATH[2] figures prominently as a character on pilgrimage to Canterbury Cathedral in Geoffrey Chaucer's late fourteenth-century long

1. I borrow these words, "Weaving the Sermon," from the title of Christine M. Smith's book, *Weaving the Sermon: Preaching in a Feminist Perspective*.

2. Most often referred to by scholars as the "Wife of Bath" or, simply, the "Wife," Chaucer provides a lesser-known given name for his character when her husband calls her "Alisoun" in the *Prologue* to the *Wife of Bath's Tale* (804). Geoffrey Chaucer wrote *The Canterbury Tales* between 1380 and 1400. As a vehicle for the tales he plans to tell, he creates a frame narrative of a religious pilgrimage from London to Canterbury Cathedral. In the opening section, the *General Prologue*, Chaucer's narrator presents generally satirical portraits of most of the travelers who represent many of England's populace, from the aristocratic knight to the humble plowman. The pilgrims and their host, Tabbard Inn owner Harry Bailey, devise a tale-telling contest to help pass the time as they travel to Canterbury. Many of the pilgrims are members of the Catholic

poem, the *Canterbury Tales*. Soon after her textual creation, she steps nimbly off the manuscript page and into cultural history as an outspoken female preacher who weaves together a subversive reading of authoritative texts, including scripture, with her own female experience in an oppressive, patriarchal milieu. Indeed, she is a literary creation, literally inscribed into parchment more than six hundred years ago, yet those who have read and analyzed the Wife of Bath through the centuries treat her as a living, breathing, female body.[3] Her outspoken, feisty behavior has been celebrated as "a figure of extraordinary authority," who acts as "an expert witness on marriage," notable as "the only pilgrim in the *Canterbury Tales* to compete with Chaucer for the authority of authorship. . . . Mistaken for an author, Chaucer's Wife [of Bath] . . . consequently appears to be a female speaker whose subjectivity is compellingly accessible."[4] A middle-aged, partially deaf widow who makes a habit of traveling on pilgrimages, the Wife of Bath is wealthy, unruly, talkative, lonely, and, I argue, a vehicle through which Chaucer critiques his culture's objectification and subjugation of women as well as the medieval church's explicitly misogynous discourse. Additionally, by providing the storytelling Wife with a trade, Chaucer emphasizes her proficiency in that most feminine of occupations—weaving—as she weaves together separate threads into both textiles and texts.

"And I was yong and ful of ragerye, Stibourne and strong, and joly as pye"[5]: The Wife of Bath's Portrait

Readers first encounter the Wife of Bath in the *General Prologue* to the *Canterbury Tales* through the eyes of Chaucer's narrator, who *seems* to

---

clergy, and others represent rising middle-class professions such as merchant, lawyer, and doctor. The Wife of Bath is the only woman not of a religious order and the only woman traveling alone. Although she is named a Wife, she is actually a widow five times over and claims to be on the lookout for husband number six.

3. See Harvey, *Ventriloquized*, 15. Harvey notes that in their groundbreaking study of the woman writer, *The Madwoman in the Attic*, Sandra Gilbert and Susan Gubar include the Wife of Bath in their list of resisting woman writers.

4. Desmond, *Ovid's Art*, 117, 118.

5. *Prologue* to the *Wife of Bath's Tale* (hereafter ProWBT) 455–56. All quotations from the *Canterbury Tales* are from Geoffrey Chaucer, *Riverside Chaucer*. All further references to the Wife of Bath's *Prologue* are noted parenthetically by line number in the text. All translations from Middle English, located in the footnotes, are my own.

tell his audience a great deal about her; however, he actually reveals only snippets of information, carefully crafted descriptions of a few individual body parts and clothing choices, concise, selectively worded snatches of biography, and brief snapshots of social behavior:

> A good WIF was ther OF biside BATHE,
> But she was somdel deef, and that was scathe.
> Of clooth-makyng she hadde swich an haunt
> She passed hem of Ypres and of Gaunt.
> In al the parisshe wif ne was ther noon
> That to the offrynge bifore hire sholde goon;
> And if ther dide, certeyn so wrooth was she
> That she was out of alle charitee.
> Hir coverchiefs ful fyne weren of ground;
> I dorste swere they weyeden ten pound
> That on a Sonday weren upon hir heed.
> Hir hosen weren of fyn scarlet reed,
> Ful streite yteyd, and shoes ful moyste and newe.
> Boold was hir face, and fair, and reed of hewe.
> She was a worthy womman al hir lyve:
> Housbondes at chirche dore she hadde fyve,
> Withouten oother compaignye in youthe—
> But thereof nedeth nat to speke as nowthe.
> And thries hadde she been at Jerusalem;
> She hadde passed many a straunge strem;
> At Rome she hadde been, and at Boloigne,
> In Galice at Seint-Jame, and at Coloigne.
> She koude muchel of wandrynge by the weye.
> Gat-tothed was she, soothly for to seye.
> Upon an amblere esily she sat,
> Ywympled wel, and on hir heed an hat
> As brood as is a bokeler or a targe;
> A foot-mantel aboute hir hipes large,
> And on hir feet a paire of spores sharpe.
> In felaweshipe wel koude she laughe and carpe.
> Of remedies of love she knew per chaunce,
> For she koude of that art the olde daunce.[6]
> (*General Prologue*, 445–76)

6. *General Prologue* 445–76. "A good woman was from near Bath, but sadly she was somewhat deaf. Her cloth-making or weaving skill surpassed those in Ypres and Gaunt, and no woman in her parish was able to precede her to the offering table. If someone preceded her, her anger would cause her to lose her kindness toward others. Her Sunday head coverings were woven of the finest linen, and, I swear, must have weighed ten pounds. Her red hose were woven of the finest wool, straight and tied

Chaucer's narrator describes her fair skin, ruddy complexion, and the gap between her front teeth, which signified sexual lasciviousness in the Middle Ages. He praises her prowess as a weaver and describes her fine, if somewhat ostentatious, clothing—red wool stockings and fine linen headdresses for church and serviceable riding attire for pilgrimages. The narrator's description of the Wife's characteristics and professions as wife, traveler, and cloth-maker seems filled with admiration, yet Chaucer's clever use of language suggests a complicated, layered portrait, which only grudgingly yields its riches to the astute and careful reader. His audience witnesses her wealth and pride in her insistence on being the first to give to the Sunday offering (the person with the largest gift goes first), her jockeying for social position, and her improper fondness for culturally questionable behavior, including laughter, gossip, love potions, and lovemaking.

Chaucer's portrait of the Wife is as ambiguous and contradictory as is her liminal status as a widow—neither virgin nor wife—and her propensity to ignore social custom, propriety, and morality. Instead she chooses to please herself, exacerbating cultural angst about the danger of loose (in both senses of the word) women, characteristics exemplified by her presence on this pilgrimage, traveling unaccompanied as the "only woman . . . not affiliated with a religious order."[7] In this way, Chaucer chooses "to put words of the most profound wisdom into the mouth of a character who embodied some of the most virulent antifeminism of his time,"[8] ironically and purposefully choosing this unreliable woman of questionable character to preach a powerful sermon in which she—or he—critiques both the patriarchal church and the culture's oppressive social structures.

---

tightly, and her leather shoes were made of moist and new leather. Her face was both bold and fair, and she had a ruddy complexion. She was a worthy woman all her life. She legally married five husbands, in addition to other male companions in her youth, but there's no need to speak of that now. An avid pilgrim, she has traveled to Jerusalem three times, crossing many foreign rivers in her travels. She has traveled to sacred sites in Rome and Bologne, to Saint James' shrine, and to Cologne. She often wandered by the way. She had a gap between her front teeth, and sat easily upon her horse. In addition to her widow's wimple, she wore on her head a hat as large as a small shield. She wore a large covering over her skirts to protect them from the mud, and also wore a pair of sharp spurs on her feet. She could laugh and joke with her companions, and knew well the remedies of love as well as art of lovemaking."

7. Gotfried, "Conflict and Relationship," 204.

8. Minnis, *Fallible Authors*, 5.

"Of clooth-makyng she hadde swich a haunt, She passed hem of Ypres and of Gaunt":[9] The Wife of Bath as Weaver of Texts and Textiles

Chaucer's narrator's characterization of the Wife's weaving ability as surpassing that of Flemish weavers, considered the finest in Europe,[10] taps into the audience's collective understanding of the feminine power of weaving, a craft that, as Smith explains, has "for ages . . . symbolized in a powerful way the connections women have to the earth, to the cycles of life *an*d death, and to female power and creativity.[11] Whether weaving cloth, baskets, rugs, or stories, women weave to provide hope, income, beauty, artistic expression, and self-sufficiency, no matter the era, culture, or generation. Chaucer's occupational choice for his most colorful and outspoken female character echoes identification for his immediate audience as well as for contemporary readers, who recognize that weaving cloth provides not only a fine wardrobe and excellent business reputation, but also acts as a metaphor for speaking, storytelling, and, in the Wife's case, preaching sermons.

The metaphor of weaving connects the Wife as well to the long history of classical women weavers. When Penelope, Odysseus's wife in the *Odyssey*, is beset by dozens of greedy suitors who hope to marry her and take control of Odysseus's property, she uses the pretext of weaving her father-in-law's shroud—work she unweaves every night—to delay a confrontation with these persistent men. In the Greek myth of Philomena and Procne, Philomena's brother-in-law rapes and then silences her by cutting out her tongue. In response, Philomena weaves a tapestry that silently yet powerfully reveals her horrifying story. In the ancient Greek drama *Lysistrata*, women take over the government to end a long war and use a weaving metaphor to explain their peace plan. Furthermore, the Wife's hometown of Bath links her to the virgin Greek goddess Athena—goddess of war, wisdom, and handicrafts—and provides classical authority, important to medieval authors, for the Wife's oral tapestry that resounds with wisdom as it challenges the masculine control of sacred knowledge and understanding.[12] Moreover, as we shall see in the next section, in addition to weaving textiles, the Wife weaves a sermon in which she uses her

9. *General Prologue* 447–48.

10. See Stabel, "Guilds in Late Medieval," 187–212.

11. Smith, *Weaving the Sermon*, 1, 15.

12. O'Brien, "Troubling Waters," 382.

own life story both to illustrate and to resist the prevalent misogynistic theological, and cultural teachings about women in the Middle Ages.

"My joly body schal a tale telle"[13]: The Wife of Bath's Preaching Female Body

In the narrative frame preceding her own *Prologue* (the *Epilogue* to the preceding *Man of Law's Tale*), the Wife of Bath literally pushes herself forward in the tale-telling queue in order to tell the next tale, her voice preceding her body into the scene. She interrupts the host, who is in the midst of choosing the Parson to speak next, and asserts that *she* will be the next storyteller:

> And therfore, Hoost, I warne thee bforn,
> My joly body schal a tale telle.[14]

Barrie Ruth Straus reminds us that Chaucer's "remarkable insertion of a female voice [is] something rarely heard not only in the *Canterbury Tales* and medieval literature but in the literary canon."[15] The Wife of Bath clarifies from the first ringing words of her *Prologue* that she intends to provide her own sermon, based not on male-authored, male-glossed texts,[16] but upon her own feminine text and feminine gloss in the form of her *Prologue's* approach and authority provided by experience—the physical, social, and emotional *experience* centered in the physical text of her female body:

> Experience, though noon auctoritee
> Were in this world, is right ynogh for me
> To speke of wo that is in mariage."[17]

13. *Epilogue* to the *Man of Law's Tale*, 1185

14. *Epilogue* to the *Man of Law's Tale*, 1184–85. "And therefore, Host, I announce that I'm first in line; / My jolly body shall tell a tale."

15. Strauss, "Subversive Discourse," 529. See also Dinshaw, *Chaucer's Sexual Poetics*; Carruthers, "Wife of Bath"; Russell, *Chaucer and the Trivium*, 204; Pearsall, *Canterbury Tales*, xii; Desmond, *Ovid's Art*, 126; Goodspeed-Chadwick, "Sexual Politics"; Moore, "(Re)Creations"; Hanning, "From Eva and Ave," 582; and Minnis, *Fallible Authors*, 25.

16. The word *gloss* refers to the medieval scribal practice of including interpretations of the scripture and commentaries on the scripture on the same manuscript page as the scripture.

17. ProWBT 1–3. "Experience rather than authority in this world is good enough for me to speak of the woe that is in marriage."

Certainly, she reads and glosses patristic texts, but her primary text is always her own body—virginal and violated, adored and abused, venerated and vilified, pleasured and punished, speaking and silenced. Her body is her only secure commodity, her only authentic text, and she insists on controlling it—giving, withholding, selling—when and where she chooses:

> And therfore every man this tale I telle,
> Wynne whoso may, for al is for to selle;[18]

The articulation of the Wife of Bath as text includes reader recognition of her corporeal body as a bruised and damaged text, with inscriptions of patriarchy purposefully etched into her skin, a violent process beginning with forced sexual intercourse at age twelve by an aging husband in a marriage most likely arranged by her father. In her *Prologue* she describes being "bete on every bon,"[19] and this repetitive domestic violence leaves her body bruised, broken, and partially deaf. In this way, the Wife of Bath both *reads* and *writes* her literal, physical body as her text.

Reclaiming women from the margins of historical, cultural, religious, and literary narratives necessarily includes the recovery of the female body from the universalizing claims of the masculine as normative. As Susan Bordo writes, the body "is a medium of culture,"[20] a "surface on which the central rules, hierarchies, and even metaphysical commitments of culture are inscribed and thus reinforced through the concrete language of the body."[21] Throughout much of Western history, the female body has been designated as an inferior, material entity, particularly in comparison to the idealized, enclosed, spiritualized male body. Ian Maclean succinctly summarizes influential classical theories of the biologically sexed body:

> the best endowed with powers of procreation, and the hottest. Such a creature is the male, who implants his semen in the female to the end of procreating males. If, however, there is some lack of generative heat, or if climatic conditions are adverse, then creation is not perfected and a female results.[22]

18. ProWBT 413–14. "And therefore I tell this tale to every man, I earn however I may because everything [including my body] is for sale."
19. ProWBT 511. "beaten on every bone."
20. Bordo, "The Body," 90.
21. Bordo, *Unbearable Weight*, 165.
22. Maclean, *Renaissance Notion*, 8.

Similarly, Aristotle stated, "we should look upon the female state as being as it were a deformity, though one, which occurs in the ordinary course of nature."[23] Medievalist Elizabeth Robertson explains that in the study of medieval gender construction, a "woman's essential materiality arises primarily from Hippocratic, Aristotelian, and Galenic medical views of women as they were synthesized with theological commentaries on Genesis" in ways that continued and reinforced classical patriarchal misogyny.[24] Later, the medieval church linked Aristotle's ideas of female physical inferiority with "the doctrine of original sin" and assumed that the misogynist laws, customs, and beliefs that controlled and restricted women's bodies existed "to compensate for woman's fundamental character defect inherited from Eve,"[25] the source of the fall in Genesis and the introduction of sin and evil into the previously Edenic world. Thus, in the Middle Ages, the combination of classical and Christian misogynistic teaching continually exacerbated fears of unruly females and reinforced the belief about female bodies as unstable containers of sexual and cultural sins. For example, Minnis notes that "in Chaucer's day . . . [h]alf of the human race was deemed fallible because its members lived in the wrong kind of material body, the inferior female rather than the superior male form."[26]

Chaucer's textual construction of the Wife of Bath as metaphorically conflated with her corporeal female body would not appear unusual to a medieval audience. Monica Potkay Brzezinski and Regula Meyer Evitt explain that medieval culture "considered a text, like a human being, to comprise a body and a soul."[27] Additionally, medieval church fathers feminized their manuscript texts by speaking of them as if they were literal female bodies. For example, in Jerome's treatise on preparing pagan classical texts for Christian consumption, he describes the manuscript text as a captive, pagan, female body that he must clean and prepare for intimacy:

23. Hallissy, *Clean Maids,* 9.

24. Robertson, "Medieval Medical," 142. Medieval and scholastic writers still based their assumptions about the human body, and particularly the female body, on the classical writings of Hippocrates, Aristotle, and Galen, all of whom deemed the male body as the human model and the female body an abnormality, a deformed male, and even monstrous. See also Green, *Trotula,* and Miller, *Medieval Monstrosity.*

25. Hallissy, *Clean Wives,* 9.

26. Minnis, *Fallible Authors,* 2.

27. Potkay and Evitt, *Minding the Body,* 25.

It is surprising that I, too, admiring the fairness of her form and the grace of her eloquence, desire to make that secular wisdom, which is my captive and handmaid, a matron of the true Israel? Or that shaving off and cutting away all in her that is dead whether this be idolatry, pleasure, error or lust, I take her to myself clean and pure and begot by her servants for the Lord of the Sabaoth?[28]

If one regards the material text as a seductive object, a female body which must be unveiled before the eyes of the trained scholar, exposing her naked truth to her reader's gaze, then reading becomes "a kind of sexual mastery, an act of bodily control (stripping, penetrating, even sometimes cleansing) which is represented along the lines of a male prerogative."[29]

In the six hundred years since Chaucer first created this notable female character, Alisoun of Bath has become her own person. Even more, she *is* a body. She is a living, breathing, aging, sweating, speaking body that spills out of Chaucer's medieval text and overrides the phallic pens and word processors of critics who try to silence her and move her back within the boundaries of male-authored, male-constructed texts.

"Experience, though noon auctoritee Were in the world, is right ynogh for me To speke of wo that is in mariage"[30]: The Wife of Bath's Female Challenge to Authority

When the Wife of Bath begins the *Prologue* to her *Tale* with the above lines, she challenges centuries of venerated written authorities—medieval *auctors*[31]—the very basis for medieval scholastic theory and religious dogma, thus calling in to question the cumulative wisdom from centuries

---

28. Copeland, "Why Women," 257.

29. Ibid., 258.

30. ProWBT 1–3. "Experience rather than authority in this world is good enough for me to speak of the woe of marriage."

31. The Middle English word *auctor* refers to the authority of writers, both classical and religious, dating back to the classical period. In particular, the Wife challenges generations of clerical writings about scriptural interpretation, which often carried as much authorial weight as Scripture itself. Even among secular authorities, as Minnis explains, the "*auctor* was held to be not only a writer but also an 'authority' in the sense of a person whose words were judged worthy of imitation and belief" (*Fallible Authors*, xiv).

of philosophical and theological thought.[32] Neither her sex, nor her possible illiteracy, nor her hearing disability, nor even the risk of being labeled a heretic discourages the Wife from co-opting the male ability to read, gloss, and preach her interpretation of sacred texts. Using language similar to that of more recent arguments against women's ordination, Susan Sage Heinzelman reminds us that, in the case of the Wife, in addition to the impropriety of a woman's public speaking, "a woman preacher [is] a highly troubling figure in a society in which women were prevented from officiating in any religious service, much less preaching."[33] Moreover, Minnis explains that the Wife of Bath

> displays in sensational form so many of the fallibilities then (in the fourteenth-century) deemed endemic to her sex, dares to quote the Bible, bandy about authoritative documents just like a schoolman, enthusiastically defend female sexual desire, and tell a moral tale which suggests that true nobility comes from God alone and is unaffected by class or gender. And all this in an age in which Wycliffite nonconformity was developing the proposition that virtuous women had more right to preach than vicious men, and (in certain situations) could administer the sacraments.[34]

For this reason, in similar fashion to female ministers, who, according to Roxanne Mountford, must learn to "accommodate themselves to the physicality of preaching" in a pulpit spatially constructed for a male body and to modify rhetoric long practiced by male clergy,[35] the Wife must also work within a masculine discourse because she has no other language available. Like women ministers who create a woman's sermon

---

32. In order to fully appreciate the Wife's performance as a speaking body who preaches in her *Prologue*, we must review the powerful, masculine tradition of literary and biblical interpretation that she defies when she presumes to present her own experience-based female exposition on female desire for mastery in marriage. The sacred *auctors* of the Middle Ages comprised a vast compendium of ancient texts as well as classical and medieval commentary on Scripture, science, medicine, literature, and other valuable texts. According to Copeland, "[m]edieval hermeneutical practice defines its ideological relationship with antiquity in terms of continuity or of an organic and inevitable lineage"; moreover, "this assumption of lineal continuity is directly expressed in linguistic ties of medieval academic discourse with antiquity" (*Rhetoric*, 257).

33. Heinzelman, "Termes Queinte," 177.

34. Minnis, *Fallible Authors*, xiv–xv.

35. Mountford, *Gendered Pulpit*, 3.

by weaving together women's experiences, the Wife reweaves strands of masculine pronouncements into a feminine discourse centered on personal narrative and the female body.

Throughout her *Prologue*, the Wife references scribal "glossing" of both texts and bodies. The medieval practice of glossing is similar to today's practice of adding historical and theological information to study bibles or biblical commentaries. Extant medieval manuscripts reveal that scholarly interpretations and opinions often left little room on the page for the scriptural text. Moreover, indiscriminate scribal glossing was a serious problem in the Middle Ages because the clerical copyists often inserted their own opinions into both the scriptural text and the commentary, thus blurring the boundary between Holy Scripture and religious tradition. Copeland explains that by the fourteenth century "commentary substitute[d] itself for the text . . . inserting itself into the *auctoritas* of that text, hence appropriating that authority, and to varying degrees performing in lieu of the text."[36]

Prologues were among the most common of these extratextual glosses and an important component of medieval textual construction. In their narrative prologues, medieval authors writing in Latin or the vernacular revealed "sophisticated and often still-influential traditions of thinking, not only about hermeneutics and rhetoric but about pedagogy and literacy, language, linguistics and textuality, historiography, fiction, genre, translation, and much else."[37] The Wife of Bath's *Prologue* serves as a somewhat unconventional example of such authoritative pretextual musing by exhibiting simultaneously a wide-ranging knowledge along with her own feminine gloss upon ancient medical, scriptural, literary, and philosophical texts, interwoven with sermon texts regularly employed by the clergy, local gossip, medieval romances, and *fabliaux*.[38]

In addition to scriptural exegesis and scribal glossing, the Wife refutes clerical charges against wives by describing the ways she manipulates her five husbands in order to survive in an androcentric culture. She prefaces the story of her marriages with more than one hundred fifty lines of misogynist rhetoric and concludes her narrative with another hundred lines of a similar rhetoric. In this way, her challenge to

36. Copeland, *Rhetoric, Hermeneutics*, 103.

37. Wogan-Browne et al., *Idea of the Vernacular*, xiii.

38. The *Merriam-Webster Online Dictionary* defines the Old French word *fabliau* as a "short, usually comic, frankly coarse, and often cynical tale in verse" from the Middle Ages.

authorities, based on her own reading and glossing, although seemingly shallow and literal (and thus "feminizing"), instead represents a smartly literate and distinctively female point of view. She knowingly plays the role of the shrewish harridan with an unruly body and uncontrollable speech. Simultaneously, however, she establishes her own space in which to deconstruct misogynist discourse in the dialectic of accommodation and resistance.

More than simply constructing a feminized introduction to her tale, however, the Wife also establishes a new sort of verbal access, presenting a "counter-sermon" that recontextualizes women's bodies, similar to the task the narrator's introduction in the *General Prologue* accomplishes for the literal sense, the fleshly surface of the text. For example, the Wife counters the clerical emphasis on the sexual identity and elimination functions of sexual organs—"thynges smale"[39] as she calls them—and the clerical refusal to acknowledge the pleasurable aspect of sexual activity by noting that no matter what clerks say, her own experience, which they lack, suggests otherwise:

> The experience woot wel it is noght so.
> So that the clerkes be nat with me wrothe,
> I sey this: that they maked ben for bothe;
> That is to seye, for *office* and for *ese*
> Of engendrure, ther we nat God displese.[40]

In addition to avoiding clerical censure, the Wife also implicitly references her access to secret, yet equally valid, female knowledge based on *experience* rather authority. The clerks, by virtue of their male sex and sexual celibacy, cannot know or understand female secrets, even when the Wife *reveals* them in her sermon on the pretext of passing her wisdom on to other wives.[41] Although her pilgrimage audience consists of primarily men and a few nuns, she directs part of her text to wives, teaching them how to work within the oppressive system:

---

39. ProWBT 121. Braun and Kitzinger ("Snatch," 146–58) note that the euphemism "[t]hing has served for both female and male genitalia" since the Middle Ages."

40. ProWBT 123–28 (emphasis added). "But to keep the clerks from being angry with me, I will say that they are made for both, that is to say, for *enjoyment* and for the *function* of procreation, so that we not displease God."

41. For further discussion of the medieval fascination with female secrets, particularly among the celibate male clergy, see Miller, *Medieval Monstrosity*, and Lochrie, *Cover Operations*.

> Ye wise wyves, that kan understonde.
> Thus shulde ye speke and bere hem wrong on honde,
> For half so boldely kan ther no man
> Swere and lyen, as a womman kan.[42]

Minnis notes that her sermon so "blatantly confound[s] . . . expectations that another of Chaucer's fictions, the Friar, is moved to advise her to leave authorities of preaching . . . to the schools of clergy."[43] In his view, her discourses of authority are unfitting in the mouth of a woman, and he interrupts her dialogue to say the following:

> Ye han heer touched, also moot I thee,
> In scole-matere greet difficultee.
> Ye han seyd muche thyng right wel, I seye;
> But, dame, heere as we ryde by the weye,
> Us nedeth nat to speken but of game,
> And lete auctoritees, on Goddes name,
> To prechyng and to scoles of clergye.[44]

Ironically, however, this lecherous representative of the church pays for marriages of village women, or in other words, he provides a generous dowry in order to find husbands for the women he impregnates, marrying off his pregnant young paramours at his own expense.[45] Moreover, the Wife informs her audience that her "scoleiyng"[46] stems from her life experiences, particularly her five marriages, which are literally inscribed on her corporeal body (or text). She defends her multiple marriages and her own objectification of her body as a "marketable commodity," which she admits assists her in negotiating the medieval maze of conflicting models for female behavior. She speaks irreverently

---

42. ProWBT 225–28. "You wise wives must understand that you should speak and accuse your husbands wrongfully because no man can swear and lie half as boldly as a woman can."

43. Minnis, *Fallible Authors*, 23.

44. *Prologue* to the *Friar's Tale* 1271–77. "If I may say so, you have touched here on a subject of great debate in the universities. And you have handled these matters quite well, I say, but woman, as we ride along the way, we do not need to speak of anything so serious. And, in God's name, leave the sermons to preachers and clerical schools."

45. *General Prologue* 211–13.

46. ProWBT 44f. "schooling."

and openly of her own sexuality, asserting that "[i]n wyfhod I wol use myn instrument / As frely as my Makere hath it sent."[47]

In addition to arguing that God provided sexual organs for pleasure, the most likely illiterate Wife preaches from a corporeal text she knows well. Strauss remarks that "[A]gainst the discourse of serious, public masculine learning, of the knowledge that goes with writing and books, the Wife invokes her knowledge of her own experience of the private, female . . . world, a knowledge not considered of the same order as authorized knowledge."[48] She somewhat contemptuously associates masculine knowledge with her fifth husband's book of "wikked wyves," which represents, not true learning, but merry "disport."[49]

For the Wife, authorized "knowledge" is the province of misogynistic clerics whose writings and glossing of scripture malign women falsely, unfairly, and with obvious misinformation since they lack the female "experience." While the Wife speaks from experience, the "clerkes" write fantasies of the virginal feminine perfection found in deceased saintly women, and they malign real women, with whom they have little actual experience:

> The clerk, whan he is oold, and may noght do
> Of Venus werkes worth his olde sho,
> Thanne sit he doun, and writ in his dotage
> That wommen kan nat kepe hir mariage![50]

Chaucer's Wife suggests that the misogynist leanings of clerical writers influence the content of their texts because of their concurrent attraction to and resistance of women. They are trained from adolescence to sublimate their natural sexual desires, either by associating all women with abject filth, a defiled natural body, and sexual sin or by envisioning them as distant, saintly, and ultimately inhuman and non-corporeal spiritual exemplars.

47. ProWBT 149–50. "In wifehood I will use my 'instrument' (my sexual organs) as freely as my Maker intended."

48. Strauss, "Subversive Discourse," 530.

49. ProWBT 670, 685. Jankyn's book of "wikked wyves" (wicked wives) is a fictitious text partially based on an ancient anti-marriage text often quoted by Jerome: Theophrastus' *Golden Book of Marriage*. Additionally the book contains classic stories of scheming, murderous women who actively harm and/or murder their husbands.

50. ProWBT 706–10. "The clerk, when he is old, may not participate in the enjoyment of sex worth his old shoe, Then he sits and writes in his old age that a woman cannot keep their marriage vows."

"For trusteth wel, it is an impossible
That any clerk wol speke good of wyves
But if it be of hooly seintes lyves"[51]:
The Wife's Female Gloss of Scripture

Long before Judith Fetterley envisions the resisting reader in her analysis of the portrayal of women in American literature, the Wife of Bath becomes "a resisting reader rather than assenting reader, and by her refusal to agree with a male depiction of women, begins the process of exorcizing the male mind that has been implanted in us."[52] She begins reminding her audience that clergymen never speak well of women who have not suffered the mutilation and torture of their virginal bodies, the most common subject of female saints' lives, or who are not the most perfect mother of God, the virgin Mary. She continues by transforming the most common litany of women's failings into God-given gifts that enable women to survive in a patriarchal world. Providing her own readings of scripture, she asserts that she possesses as much right as anyone to reread and respeak scripture to suit her own preferences. In one of her *Prologue's* most famous passages, the Wife suggests that if women told the stories, they would be very different from the male-authored tales of women. She evokes a classic fable when she asks,

> Who peyntede the leon, tel me who?
> By God, if wommen hadde writen stories,
> As clerkes han withinne hire oratories,
> They wolde han writen of men moore wikkednesse
> Than al the mark of Adam may redresse.[53]

51. ProWBT 688–90. "But trust this well, it is an impossibility for any clerk to speak well of women unless they are speaking of holy saint's lives."

52. Fetterly, *Resisting Reader*, xxii. Although the Wife is a literary creation of a medieval male writer, which perhaps brings her ultimate success at resistance into question, her insistence on rereading and reglossing traditional authoritative and sacred texts suggests that she—and Chaucer as well—predicts the feminist project of the late twentieth century to resist the assumption that the male point of view or the male reading is the natural if not the universal way of reading. Fetterley continues: "As readers and teachers and scholars [and, I add, as medieval wives], women are taught to think as men, to identify with a male point of view, and to accept as normal and legitimate a male system of values, one of whose central principles is misogyny" (xx).

53. ProWBT 692–96. "Who painted the lion, tell me who? By God, if women had written the stories that the clergy have in their libraries, they would have told more tales of men's wickedness than all humankind could redress."

In this fable, a lion remarks on a painting that depicts a man killing a lion, and asks "who painted the lion," suggesting that the point of view depends on the person in control of the narrative. Likewise the Wife speculates that if women controlled religious and cultural narratives, men rather than women would be blamed for evil.

Basing her own understanding of scripture on her experience as a wife to five different men, the Wife challenges the teaching she claims to have received about the Wedding at Cana:

> That sith that Crist ne wente nevere but onis
> To weddyng in the Cane of Galilee,
> That by the same ensample taughte he me
> That I ne sholde wedded be but ones.[54]

She quite logically questions the prevailing clerical teaching, which argues that because Jesus attended only one wedding a woman should only marry once. This argument highlights her untenable dilemma as a widow who is expected to remain celibate after her husband's death. Yet she is simultaneously encouraged to remarry in order to place her body and property under male oversight and is condemned as sexually insatiable if she does marry. According to Andrew Galloway, sermons on this important text, "Nupiae factae sunt in Chana Galilee," were "preached annually on the second Sunday after Epiphany," and he suggests that Chaucer's medieval audience would have noted immediately a connection between this familiar sermon and the Wife's inclusion of this text in her own "sermon."[55] Thus, the Wife cleverly chooses an ideal scriptural text with many cultural associations to launch her strike against the misogynous glossing of scriptural texts. She aspires to create a new interpretative sermon that will not only support her lifestyle, but also enable her to continue

---

54. ProWBT 11–13. "Since Christ never went but once to a Wedding, that of Cana in Galilee, by that example he [a clerk] taught me that I should only be married once."

55. Galloway, "Marriage Sermons," 6, 8. Galloway bases his discussion on a well-known sermon on the Cana text by the Dominican Jacop da Varazze, archbishop of Genoa, usually identified as "Januenis" in the manuscripts. At least 22 collections of Januenis's sermons are extant, and Galloway suggests that this sermon is similar, if not identical, to the annual lesson preached in local parish churches to members of Chaucer's contemporary audience. Galloway notes the following lines that refer to marriage as her "estaat" (estate or social status): 147–48 (cf. lines 28, 39, 50, 78, 83–84, 149–50), 6.

bistow[ing] the flour of al myn age
In the actes and in fruyt of mariage. [56]

In setting up her catalog of "marital transgressions," the Wife continues to challenge authorial interpretations by reglossing scripture in a seemingly literal manner, arguing, for example, against the accepted allegorical interpretation of Solomon's many wives as representing Jesus and the church. Rather, she implies biblical approval of multiple sexual partners by pointing to Solomon's harem and expresses an ironic desire to be "refresshed half so ofte as he!"[57] She announces that the one scriptural text she "kan . . . wel understonde" is that in which "God bad us for to wexe and multiplye."[58]

Soon after reminding the audience that no man can "[s]weren and lyen as a womman kan,"[59] she begins the lengthy litany of rhetoric traditionally read as the Wife's confession of her own seemingly immoral story;[60] however, her choice to begin each statement with the words "Thou sayst" suggests that she is creating an allegorical defense by embodying and repeating the hatred and venom directed toward women by clerical and cultural authorities. The Wife explains, for example, that her innocent visit to a "gossib or a freend"[61] becomes the basis for her fourth husband's drunken diatribe. She accuses him:

Thou comest hoom as dronken as a mous,
And prechest on thy bench, with yvel preef!"[62]

Some critics define the Middle English phrase *yvel preef* as "bad luck to you"; however, the *Middle English Dictionary* (*MED*) suggests alternative definitions that change the connotation of this phrase from the Wife's threat to the husband's false accusation. According to the *MED*, the

56. ProWBT 113–14. "Bestowing the flower of all her age in the acts and in the fruit of marriage."

57. ProWBT 35–38. The longer passage reads: "We have here the wise King Solomon. I believe he had many wives at once! I wish God would provide for me to be refreshed half as often as he was."

58. ProWBT 27, 28. "God instructed us to increase and multiply."

59. ProWBT 228. "There is no man who can swear and lie as a woman can."

60. Morrison, *Women*, 115 n. 54, provides the following list of lines from the *Wife of Bath's Prologue* in which the Wife insists that husbands preach to their wives: 248, 254, 257, 263, 265, 270, 271, 273, 278, 282, 285, 292, 293, 302, 337, 348, 362, 266, 276.

61. ProWBT 243. "godmother or friend."

62. ProWBT 246–48. "You come home as drunk as a mouse and exclaim on your honor your false proof."

word *yvel*, similar to the modern English word "evil," modifies a noun to denote something false or misrepresented. In this line, the word *yvel* modifies *preef* ("proof"), which refers to the basis of the husband's accusation rather than the Wife's behavior.[63] The Wife's recitation reveals the lose-lose situation of medieval women. On the one hand, if women are rich, they will be accused of "pride";[64] on the other hand, "it is a greet meschief" to marry a "povre womman" because of the "costage" or expense.[65] Further, she observes that although women are desired for their "shap" (258), "fairnesse" (258), ability to "synge or daunce" (259), "gentillesse and daliaunce" (260), or "handes and . . . armes smale" (261), these same characteristics require that women be confined behind the "castel wal" (263) in order to ensure their chastity.[66] Cultural and scholastic assumptions suggest that although a woman may attract a man because of these admirable qualities, she cannot control her desire to covet "every man that she may se, / For as a spanyel she wol on hym lepe" (266–67).[67] The association of promiscuous female sexual desire with the behavior of an indiscriminate bitch recalls Moria Gatens's assertion that one of the hegemonic strategies used to silence the voice of "the other" is to "animalize the subject.[68]

In yet another challenge to authorial interpretation of scripture, Alisoun quotes patristic accusations based on the book of Proverbs, such as "chidyng wyves maken men to flee / Out of hir owene houses,"[69] a statement that contradicts the common medieval sermon appeals for women to use whatever means necessary to convince their husbands of the seriousness of their sins. Of course, a sinning husband would rather

63. ProWBT 108; Mann, *Geoffrey Chaucer*, 219 n. 247. *MED* definitions for *yvel* include: (1) "wicked, depraved, sinful"; (2) "Harmful," "false counsel," "discreditable"; (3) "unlucky," "harmful"; unluckily; (6) "inferior," "defective."

64. ProWBT 252; 248–49: "It is a great mischief to marry a poor woman because of the legal expenses."

65. ProWBT 258–63. "Women are desired for their shape, their beauty, their ability to sing or dance, their high class and flirtatiousness, and their dainty hands and arms, characteristics that require a woman to be literally and figuratively confined behind a castle wall in order to ensure her chastity."

66. PeoWBT 266–67. "Otherwise, she will leap upon every man she encounters like a dog (in heat)."

67. Gatens, "Corporeal Representation," 84.

68. Ibid.

69. ProWBT 279–80. "Chiding women cause men to flee out of their own houses."

call his talkative wife a "shrewe"[70] than hear a litany of his own vices. The Wife complains that men "preyse my beautee" and "poure alwey upon my face,"[71] evoking the idea of a ubiquitous male gaze, yet she says that once married, her husbands ignore her maid and family, seeming to care for little else but her body. Accusing her "olde dotard" husbands of spouting a "barel-ful of lyes,"[72] the Wife expresses frustration with their endless accusations. This suggests another of Gatens's hegemonic strategies for controlling women, "reducing a woman to her sex," which involves displaying her behavior as hysterical and irrational.[73] The Wife returns to a catalogue of female vices, the litany of "Thou seyst," near the end of the *Prologue*. However, this time she repeats the misogynistic sentiment her fifth husband, Jankyn, reads nightly in his book of "wikked wyves." If anything, the rhetoric against women is more virulent in this specialized collection of classical and fictional "[e]mpoysoned" women who regularly murder their husbands.[74]

[F]eele I on my ribbes al by rewe, And evere shal unto myn endyng day"[75]: Patriarchal Marking of the Wife's Textual Body

The Wife's narrative can be read as a boastful story of the miserable lives a careless woman inflicts on her haplessly trapped husbands, men whose most valuable function is to die. She outlives husband after husband, using her inheritances to increase her wealth and improve her social status. However underlying this tale of multiple marriages is the medieval practice of returning young widows to their fathers to be auctioned off again

---

70. ProWBT 284.

71. ProWBT 294–95. "praise my beauty"; "always stare at my face."

72. ProWBT 291, 302. "Aging and decrepit husbands . . . barrel-full of lies."

73. Gatens, "Corporeal Representations," 84.

74. ProWBT 751. "poisonous" or "venemous." The assumption that female menses were necessary to rid a woman of her impure bodily contamination was common in the Middle Ages, even going to far as to suggest that women past menopause grew more and more venomous after the cessation of monthly periods. In this light, Margaret Hallissy suggests that the most threatening combination to medieval society was "the woman who combines the morally venomous power of female sexuality with the asexual power of the mind" (*Venomous Women*, xv).

75. ProWBT 505–7. "Every day I feel the pain in one rib after another, and I shall continue to feel this pain until my dying day."

to a new husband.[76] She explains that her first three husbands were old and kind and the last two were neither old nor kind, and her narrative seems to shift as she talks of husbands four and five. Admitting that she enjoyed the sexual pleasure she received from these younger men, she also acknowledges that she suffered infidelity and physical abuse in these two marriages. Calling her fourth husband a "revelour"[77] with a mistress on the side, the Wife attempts to turn the tables, giving as good as she gets this time. She feigns her own assignations to make him jealous, transitioning from the stereotypical feminine behavior of a cheated-on wife to calmly driving her philandering husband to a frenzy of jealousy and thus feminizing *his* behavior:

> That in his owene grece I made hym frye
> For angre, and for verray jalousye.[78]

In this way, the Wife reverses the *auctors* by showing that a man can also be driven to hysterical behavior and thus perform femaleness.

The Wife's account of her marriage to Jankyn, the Oxford Clerk, may be the *Prologue's* most authentic portrayal of medieval marriage, at least from Chaucer's point of view. After their "daliance"[79] in the fields and after her fourth husband's death, the occasion of the notorious ogling scene where the Wife spends more time at the funeral enjoying her own gaze at Jankyn's legs than mourning her husband's death, her stormy marriage to Jankyn may represent the Wife's rebuttal to the *auctors* who demean women. She realistically depicts the domestic violence that often accompanies medieval marriage, since husbands were expected to beat their wives.[80] However, she also suggests that in this marriage she fights back and refuses to allow the specter of the proverbial "wicked wife," symbolized by the *exempla*[81] in Jankyn's book, to remain in her marriage. Jankyn attempts to control the Wife by using his fists, in the process inscribing her body with painful reminders of his violence. And in a

76. See, for example, Walker, "Widow and Ward," where she notes that a child and the feudal lands were returned to the overlord on the death of the husband. Also see Wright, "De Manneville v. De Manneville."

77. ProWBT 453.

78. ProWBT 487–88. "I made him fry in his own grease of anger and jealousy."

79. ProWBT 565.

80. See, for example, Hanawalt, "Violence."

81. *Merriam-Webster's Online Dictionary:* "An anecdote or short narrative used to point a moral or sustain an argument."

famous scene that prefigures today's understanding of domestic abuse,
Jankyn irrevocably impairs her hearing, beating her for impulsively rip-
ping three pages from his infamous book of wikked wyves, after which
he takes her to bed, where he is so sexually proficient that she forgives his
physical abuse:

> By God, he smoot me ones on the lyst,
> For that I rente out of his book a leef,
> That of the strook myn ere wax al deef.
> . . .
> But in oure bed he was so fressh and gay,
> And therwithal so wel koude he me glose,
> Whan that he wolde han my *bel chose*;
> That thogh he hadde me bete on every bon,
> He koude wynne agayn my love anon. [82]

Significantly, in this passage the Wife uses textual rather than sexual
language when describing her intimate "make-up" sexual relations with
Jankyn. Her statement that he "glose[s]" her body well after he beats her
"on every bon" overtly conflates her female body with a manuscript text.
Simultaneously, she blends Jankyn's profession as a clerk who "glosses"
manuscript texts with his lovemaking to the corporeal text of her body
and emphasizes the violence inherent in both textual and sexual "glossing." Jerry Root links this passage with the Wife's earlier statement about
scribal glossing:

> We can read her 'confession of the flesh' . . . as the scandal of
> the domination of the female body by traditional strategies of
> interpretation. These traditional strategies like her husband
> . . . and like Vinsauf, 'glose' the female body in a gesture that
> at once denies and uses this body. In exegetical practice 'men
> may devyne and glosen, up and doun.' Men move 'up and doun'
> from the text to the 'glose,' substituting the gloss itself for the
> authoritative text. [83]

Reminding us that the purpose of glossing is to uncover a text's underlying meaning, Eve Salisbury suggests that by verbally unveiling her

---

82. ProWBT 634–36; 508–12. "By God, he hit me once on the ear because I tore
a page out of his book [of wicked wives], and Jankyn's blow to my ear made me deaf
. . . But in our bed he was so young and charming, and he could lie to me so well when
he made love to me that, although he had beaten me on every bone, he could win my
love back at once."

83. Root, "Space to Speke," 257.

bruised and battered body, the Wife discloses a heretofore hidden body of evidence,[84] her own textual and sexual body. In this way, although Jankyn is the skilled glosser of her sexual text, the Wife chooses when and where to reveal the underlying meaning of his probing, his beating, and finally his pleasurable, phallic piercing of her sex. At the same time, scribal glossing also gradually asserts its own control over the inscribed text, eventually crowding, enclosing, and overshadowing the text—perhaps her female body—itself. By using the loaded word "gloss" when commenting on Jankyn's sexual skill, the Wife calls her final claim of achieving mastery in marriage into question. On the one hand, she chooses to reveal the glossing experience to her audience, including her "unveiled" beaten body. On the other hand, by allowing her female text to be sexually "glossed" and by forgiving Jankyn's harsh treatment because he is good in bed, the Wife reveals that "talk" about female sovereignty is just that—talk. Unable to resist Jankyn's physical mastery of her body, the Wife can only describe the *possibility* of what women most desire in marriage.

Therefore, with just a few lines of poetry, Chaucer, and by extension his garrulous Wife of Bath, creates a powerful critique of clerical glossing and teachings on marriage. Moreover, the Wife's contemporary audience would have immediately grasped her multilayered words, a richly complex addition to a contemporary conversation about the sexual roles of wives in marriage. Indeed, the *Wife of Bath's Prologue*, and particularly her sermon in the first section, provides considerable evidence that the unruly Wife is actually a savvy rhetor who successfully pits her female experience against centuries of patriarchal learning.

Conclusion: Weaving and Women's Preaching

Feminist theologian Christine Smith links weaving with women's preaching when she writes, "within recent literature of feminist theology, women's published sermons, feminist spirituality, and women's psychology, weaving emerges as an organizing image in women's lives." She then uses William Schulz's words to reiterate the connection between women's weaving and preaching:

> For me the image which begins to get at the type of truth which good preaching embodies is the image of weaving. I am indebted

84. Salisbury, "Chaucer's 'Wife,'" 76.

to feminism for this image, and more specifically to Adrienne Rich who speaks in one of her poems of discovering an old piece of her grandmother's patchwork, never finished, and of taking up the work where the grandmother had left off. . . . A true sermon is a tapestry drawn from tradition, memory, conversations long forgotten, candor, courtesy, pain and passion, fresh insight and fresh metaphor, but all united.[85]

Further, Smith argues that women preachers are distinctive in their weaving of "female experience and the impact of gender enculturation"[86] into their sermons. Like Alisoun of Bath, who wove textiles and words as a mode of female expression and critique of the patriarchal church's interpretation of sacred knowledge, in the same way contemporary clergywomen weave their life stories into sermons that preach women's emancipation and endowment of power.

Bibliography

Bordo, Susan. "The Body and the Reproduction of Femininity." In *Writing on the Body: Female Embodiment and Feminist Theory*, edited by Katie Conboy, Nadia Median, and Sarah Stanbury, 309–26. New York: Columbia University Press, 1997.

———. *Unbearable Weight: Feminism, Western Culture, and the Body*. 2nd ed. Berkeley: University of California Press, 2004.

Braum, Virginia, and Celia Kitzinger. "'Snatch,' 'Hole,' or 'Honey-Pot'?: Semantic Categories and the Problem of Nonspecificity in Female Genital Slang." *The Journal of Sex Research* 38/2 (2001) 146–58.

Carruthers, Mary. "The Wife of Bath and the Painting of Lions." *PMLA* 94/2 (1979) 209–22.

Chaucer, Geoffrey. *The Riverside Chaucer*. Edited by Larry D. Benson. 3rd ed. New York: Houghton Mifflin, 1987.

Copeland, Rita. *Rhetoric, Hermeneutics, and Translation in the Middle Ages: Academic Traditions and Vernacular Texts*. Cambridge: Cambridge University Press, 1991.

———. "Why Women Can't Read." In *Representing Women: Law, Literature, and Feminism*, edited by Susan Sage Heinzelman and Zipporah Batshaw Wiseman, 253–86. Durham: Duke University Press, 1994.

Desmond, Marilyn. *Ovid's Art and the Wife of Bath: The Ethics of Erotic Violence*. Ithaca, NY: Cornell University Press, 2006.

Dinshaw, Carolyn. *Chaucer's Sexual Poetics*. Madison: University of Wisconsin Press, 1989.

Fetterley, Judith. *The Resisting Reader: a Feminist Approach to American Fiction*. Bloomington: University of Indiana Press, 1978.

85. Smith, *Weaving*, 7, 20.
86. Ibid., 9.

Galloway, Andrew. "Marriage Sermons, Polemical Sermons, and *The Wife of Bath's Prologue*: A Generic Excursus." *Studies in the Age of Chaucer* 14 (1992) 3–30.

Gatens, Moria. "Corporeal Representation in/and the Body Politic." In *Writing on the Body: Female Embodiment and Feminist Theory*, edited by Katie Conboy, Nadia Medina, and Sarah Stanbury, 80–89. New York: Columbia University Press, 1997.

Goodspeed-Chadwick, Julie. "Sexual Politics in 'The Wife of Bath's Prologue and Tale'": The Rhetoric of Domestic Violence and Rape." *Readerly/Writerly Texts* 12/1–2 (2005) 155–62.

Gotfried, Barbara. "Conflict and Relationship, Sovereignty and Survival: Parables of Power in the *Wife of Bath's Prologue*." *Chaucer Review* 19/3 (1985) 204.

Green, Monica, editor. *The Trotula: An English Translation of the Medieval Compendium of Women's Medicine*. Translated by Monica Green. Philadelphia: University of Pennsylvania Press, 2002.

Hallissy, Margaret. *Clean Maids, True Wives, Steadfast Widows: Chaucer's Women and Medieval Codes of Conduct*. Westport, CT: Greenwood, 1993.

———. *Venomous Women: Fear of the Female in Literature*. Westport, CT: Greenwood, 1987.

Hanawalt, Barbara. "Violence in the Domestic Milieu of Late Medieval England." In *Violence in Medieval Society*, edited by R. W. Kaeuper, 197–214. Rochester, NY: Boydell, 2000.

Hanning, Robert. "From Eva and Ave to Eglentyne and Allisoun: Chaucer's Insight into the Roles Women Play." *Signs* 2/3 (1977) 580–99.

Harvey, Elizabeth D. *Ventriloquized Voices, Feminist Theory, and English Renaissance Texts*. London: Routledge, 1995.

Heinzelman, Susan Sage. "'Termes Queinte of Lawe' and Quaint Fantasies of Literature." In *Law in the Liberal Arts*, edited by Austin Sarat, 166–92. Ithaca, NY: Cornell University Press, 2005.

Lochrie, Karma. *Covert Operations: The Medieval Uses of Secrecy*. Philadelphia: University of Pennsylvania Press, 1998.

Maclean, Ian. *The Renaissance Notion of Women: A Study in the Fortunes of Scholasticism and Medical Science in European Intellectual Life*. Cambridge: Cambridge University Press, 1982.

Mann, Jill, editor. *Geoffrey Chaucer: The Canterbury Tales*. London: Penguin, 2003.

McSparran, Frances, editor. *Middle English Dictionary*. University of Michigan Digital Library Prod. Service. Online: http://quod.lib.umich.edu/m/med/.

Miller, Sarah Alison. *Medieval Monstrosity and the Female Body*. New York: Routledge, 2010.

Minnis, Alistair J. *Fallible Authors: Chaucer's Pardoner and the Wife of Bath*. Pittsburgh: University of Pennsylvania Press, 2008.

Morrison, Susan Signe. *Women Pilgrims in Late Medieval England: Private Piety as Public Performance*. London: Routledge, 2000.

Mountford, Roxanne. *The Gendered Pulpit: Preaching in American Protestant Spaces*. Carbondale: Southern Illinois University Press, 2005.

O'Brien, Timothy O. "Troubling Waters: The Feminine and the Wife of Bath's Performance." *Modern Language Quarterly* 53 (1992) 377–91.

Pearsall, Derek Albert. *The Canterbury Tales*. London: Allen & Unwin, 1985.

Potkay, Monica Brzezinski, and Regula Meyer Evitt. *Minding the Body: Women and Literature in the Middle Ages, 800–1500*. London: Twayne, 1997.

Robertson, Elizabeth. "Medieval Medical Views of Women and Female Spirituality in the *Ancrene Wisse* and Julian of Norwich's *Showings*." In *Feminist Approaches to the Body in Medieval Literature*, edited by Linda Lomperis and Sarah Stanbury, 142–67. Philadelphia: University of Pennsylvania Press, 1996.

Root, Jerry. "'Space to Speke': The Wife of Bath and the Discourse of Confession." *Chaucer Review* 28/3 (1994) 252–74.

Russell, J. Stephen. *Chaucer and the Trivium: the Mind Song of the* Canterbury Tales. Gainsville: University Press of Florida, 1998.

Salisbury, Eve. "Chaucer's 'Wife,' the Law, and the Middle English Breton Lays." In *Domestic Violence in Medieval Texts*, edited by Eve Salisbury, Georgiana Donovin, and Merrall Llewelyn Price, 73–93. Gainesville: University Press of Florida, 2002.

Smith, Christine M. *Weaving the Sermon: Preaching in a Feminist Perspective*. Louisville: Westminster/John Knox, 1989.

Stabel, Peter. "Guilds in Late Medieval Flanders: Myths and Realities of Guild Life in an Export-Oriented Environment." *Journal of Medieval History* 30/2 (2004) 187–212.

Strauss, Barrie Ruth. "The Subversive Discourse of the Wife of Bath: Phallocentric Discourse and the Imprisonment of Criticism." *English Literary History* 55/3 (1988) 527–54.

Walker, Sue Sheridan. "Widow and Ward: The Feudal Law of Child Custody in Medieval England." *Feminist Studies* 3/3–4 (1976) 104–16.

Wogan-Brown, Jocelyn, Nicholas Watson, Andrew Taylor, and Ruth Evans. "Introduction" in *The Idea of the Vernacular: An Anthology of Middle English Literary Theory* 1280–1520, edited by Jocelyn Wogan-Browne, Nicholas Watson, Andrew Taylor, and Ruth Evans, xiii–xvi. University Park: Pennsylvania State University Press, 1998.

Wright, Danaya C. "De Manneville v. De Manneville: Rethinking the Birth of Custody Law under Patriarchy." *Law and History Review* 17/2 (1999) 247–307.

3

Separate Spheres and Complementarianism in American Christianity

A Century's Perspective

PRISCILLA POPE-LEVISON

A CENTURY AGO, IVA Durham Vennard (1871–1945) resigned as principal of Epworth Evangelistic Institute, a training school in St. Louis for Methodist deaconesses she had founded eight years earlier in 1902.[1] From the outset, prominent Methodist clergymen and laymen in the city labeled Vennard a "dangerous and powerful woman," and they devised plans to oust her as principal.[2] Her detractors objected to the hiring of women faculty to teach courses in theology and the Bible and the training of women in evangelism rather than religious education, because evan-

---

1. The Methodist deaconess movement was one avenue for women at the turn of the twentieth century to reach out beyond their home to ameliorate society's ills. Deaconesses, according to an official church statement, were to undertake these tasks: "minister to the poor, visit the sick, pray with the dying, care for the orphan, seek the wandering, comfort the sorrowing, save the sinning, and relinquishing wholly all other pursuits, devote themselves, in a general way, to such forms of Christian labor as may be suited to their abilities" (Harrison, "Methodist Deaconess," 415). Deaconesses served as nurses, teachers, settlement workers, pastor's assistants, evangelists, and house-to-house visitors.

2. Bowie, *Alabaster and Spikenard*, 136.

gelism veered too close to preaching, which was, in their opinion, solely for the male gender.[3] Further, they charged her with "training women preachers under the guise of deaconess work."[4] Opposition from these men reached a crisis point in the fall of 1909, when Vennard returned from maternity leave—having given birth to her only child, William—to find sweeping changes at Epworth. Indeed, these men staged a coup in her absence, barging in to revise the school charter, remove evangelism courses from the curriculum, and replace female faculty with clergymen who taught Bible and theology. They justified the overhaul by citing the separate spheres ideology,[5] namely that Vennard and her deaconesses had overstepped woman's sphere and moved into man's sphere, where they did not belong. "Methodist preachers do not want deaconesses who study theology," declared the presiding elder of St. Louis Methodism. "We can attend to that ourselves. We want women as helpers who will work with the children, care for the sick, and visit the poor. If our deaconesses are trained in theology they will become critical of the preachers, and that will be the end of the deaconess movement."[6]

Vennard had already heard a clear explication of this separate spheres ideology by the Rev. Dr. A. H. Ames when he issued his annual report as superintendent of a deaconess training school in Washington, DC. Ames delineated separate spheres for the preacher (male) and the deaconess (female). "Preachers and deaconesses represent the two ministries of the Christian Church: the ministry of the Word and the ministry of work; the

---

3. Gender is a "powerful means of orienting world and self"—and church—because it is inextricably tied up with the social construction of what it means to be male and female (Bendroth, *Fundamentalism and Gender*, 6). It is often mistakenly interpreted as synonymous with sex; however, whereas sex is a biological and physical term, gender is a social and cultural term. One learns gender—how to act as male or female—through instruction and observation of family, society, church, school, and other such cultural institutions. The behavior associated with gender—what constitutes a gender role—is constructed according to "organized patterns of behavior we follow that are based on our interpretation of the significance of sex" (Sapiro, *Women in American Society*, 68).

4. Bowie, *Alabaster and Spikenard*, 124.

5. The term "separate spheres" stands as a way to describe, understand, and analyze the traditional distinction between male and female roles in American culture. "The standard rendition depicts the ideology of separate spheres as a dichotomized view of male and female nature and function wherein men, economics, and politics were associated with the public spheres and women, children, religion, and morality with the private sphere" (Taves, "Women and Gender in American Religion(s)," 263).

6. Bowie, *Alabaster and Spikenard*, 145.

expounding and enforcing the message which God has ordained for the quickening and perfecting of souls, and the making that Word real in the removal or mitigation of sorrow, poverty, and pain."[7] Vennard chose to ignore Ames's words, because she envisioned the deaconesses she trained at Epworth to be, first and foremost, evangelists attending to the "ministry of the Word," the very activity Ames consigned to male preachers. She purposefully assigned Epworth deaconesses to preach throughout St. Louis in city missions and hospitals, the jail, juvenile court, and the work house, and in Sunday schools and prayer meetings in urban churches.

However, Vennard's dreams for Epworth did not prevail against the entrenched separate spheres ideology, which prompted her male opponents to impose their will on the institution. She decided to resign shortly after she returned to Epworth from maternity leave, rather than remain as principal of an institution in which she no longer had jurisdiction. In an ironic epitaph to her resignation, the minutes of St. Louis Methodism's Annual Conference declared: "Epworth Deaconess Institute is getting a *firmer grip* on the situation in St. Louis."[8]

Vennard's experience a century ago offers a historical perspective that introduces the first section of this essay, in which the debate over separate spheres will be presented. Currently, the separate spheres position is championed vociferously by a sector of evangelical[9] American Protestants who call themselves "complementarians." Like Vennard's opponents, complementarians view God's binary design as assigning to men and women certain roles that are different yet complementary. In

---

7. Ames, "Lucy Webb Hayes National Training-School." Even Lucy Rider Meyer, founder of the Methodist deaconess movement, adopted a similar stance in her influential article "The Mother in the Church." Meyer applied the separate spheres ideology in her argument that women's "characteristic ministry," unlike the "administrative and teaching ministry of men," was service. Just as mothers served their family, opined Meyer, so deaconesses did the same for church and society. "'The real origin of the [deaconess] work in America was, in the mother-instinct of woman herself, and in that wider conception of woman's 'family duties' that compels her to include in her loving care the great needy world-family as well as the Blessed little domestic circle" (Meyer, "The Mother in the Church," 5).

8. *Minutes of the Forty-Third Session*, 307. Emphasis added.

9. A definition of evangelicalism termed by Mark Noll as "the most serviceable" stems from Bebbington's *Evangelicalism in Modern Britain*: "It stresses four characteristics: biblicism (or reliance on the Bible as ultimate religious authority), conversionism (or an emphasis on the new birth), activism (or energetic, individualistic engagement in personal and social duties), and crucicentrism (or focus on Christ's redeeming work as the heart of true religion)" (Noll, *America's God*, 5).

other words, what Vennard encountered—men preach; women serve—is nothing new. Nevertheless, as this essay will demonstrate in the second section, Vennard and other women evangelists and preachers in the late nineteenth and early twentieth centuries were called by God to preach the gospel, and they persevered despite enormous opposition. The strategies that they developed to circumvent the separate spheres ideology will be presented in the essay's final section. These strategies, which simultaneously utilized and undermined the separate spheres ideology, are remarkable for their ingenuity and instructive as historical precedent for contemporary women and men who struggle with the pervasiveness of complementarianism.

Separate Spheres Then and Now

A century ago, one of the clearest expressions of the separate spheres ideology was tirelessly expressed in articles and lectures by a Roman Catholic lay evangelist, Martha Moore Avery (1851–1929). Women, Avery argued, naturally operated in the social and domestic spheres of human society, men in the civic and economic. Why? Her rationale was simple: God's design. God designed the male and female with certain abilities, preferences, and physical structures, which in turn determined their respective spheres and concomitant roles. For instance, God created woman's physical structure for childbearing, a labor of the domestic sphere. Further, woman's naturally intuitive proclivities were clearly meant for the more interior spheres of social and domestic life, not the exterior spheres of civic and economic life.

> Women's legitimate rights, as the second term of mankind, give her control of the home and of society, and her duties are to keep these environments in good order. . . . Women build in the hearts of the little ones, in the hearts of men, in the world of emotion and intuition. Masculine building, on the other hand, is exterior: men organize governments and build up the intellectual and moral codes that show the designs of Almighty God.
>
> Thus, working together in *complementary spheres*, men and women lay the foundation in the home and build gloriously those nations which honor God.[10]

---

10. Avery, "Spread of Social Disorder," 78. Emphasis added.

Upsetting God's design for these confined, separate gendered spheres created chaos and disorder in the home and nation as exemplified, according to Avery, by the distasteful public debacles generated by the suffragists. Consequently, she championed an anti-suffrage message: "No votes are needed for the women to set their half of the world in order."[11] In other words, only those active in the civic and economic spheres—men—have the need to vote; women's influence in the social and domestic spheres is entirely unrelated to voting matters. Further, she charged suffragists with national destruction due to their "demoralizing influence."

> Suffragists have so long been weaving public opinion with the warp of mental rebellion and the woof of sex discontent that the very foundations of our Republic are being sapped, because of the failure of a vast number of women to do the work God set them to do. Even the mention of her natural qualifications and their corresponding activities is vexatious to those most advanced in denying the true mission of woman. Their insistent iteration is for freedom from all the *limitations of convention.* . . . Moreover, as a consequence of a lack of interior womanliness that is compelling, our country faces the demoralizing influence of vain women, idle women, selfish women, luxurious women with their real rights condemned and their duties unperformed.[12]

A more recent statement, the Danvers Statement, a galvanizing document for complementarians issued in 1987 by the Council for Biblical Manhood and Womanhood, delivers dire warnings for the American nation similar to Avery's. To solidify their position against what they perceive as an encroaching egalitarianism in the home, church, and American society, complementarians indict *feminists*—"the increasing promotion given to feminist egalitarianism"—and *women beyond complementarian roles*—"the widespread ambivalence regarding the values of motherhood, vocational homemaking, and the many ministries historically performed by women."[13] (Evidently no corresponding confusion exists concerning

11. Ibid. Previously, while a socialist, she supported women's suffrage in her pamphlet "Woman: Her Quality, Her Environment, Her Possibility." However when she joined the Catholic Church, she emerged a staunch opponent of women's right to vote. Between 1908 and 1915, the anti-suffrage rhetoric dominated her lectures and articles.

12. Avery, "Spread of Social Disorder," 78.

13. The full text is online at http://www.cbmw.org/Danvers. For more on the Danvers Statement, see Grudem and Piper, *Recovering Biblical Manhood and Womanhood*.

the values of fatherhood, men's vocational work in the home, or ministries men historically perform, because none is mentioned, and males never appear as problematic.) In a concluding catastrophic prediction, similar to Avery's against the suffragists, the Danvers Statement declares, "We are convinced that a denial or neglect of these principles will lead to increasingly destructive consequences in our families, our churches, and the culture at large."

The Danvers Statement and its supporters advocate complementarianism, a new name for the separate spheres ideology. Complementarianism describes simultaneously an equality and a difference between the genders: equality in terms of "a correspondence between man and woman" and difference in terms of roles. Woman's role is to submit to man as his helper; man's role is to lead the woman. "Woman complements man in a way that makes her a helper to him. Her role is not identical to his. Their complementarity allows them to be a partnership in which each needs the other, because each provides something different from what the other provides."[14] For some complementarians, gender roles remain in place even beyond family and church; in other words, women should continue to submit to men as a helper in every context. As the pastor in a large Los Angeles church explains, "I would say that . . . there really shouldn't be a different structure for women in society [than there is] in the church. They would need to submit to men in general . . ." When asked whether a female principal would ever be hired for the school housed at his church, he responded negatively, "because there would be male teachers who would then be required to submit to female leadership, which we believe would be outside the standard of God." Even single women need to be "in the context of submitting [themselves] to men in general."[15]

In the opening chapters of Genesis, complementarians find clear explication of God's design for gender roles. There is equality between the genders—God created male and female in God's image (Gen 1:26–27) and assigned them jointly to take charge of the earth, to steward it together (Gen 1:28–29). Then in Genesis 2, complementarians locate the biblical basis for gender differentiation and concomitant gender roles.[16]

---

14. Clark, *Man and Woman in Christ*, 23–24.

15. Ingersoll, *Evangelical Christian Women*, 19.

16. Curiously, one recent biblical commentator claims there exists a gendered division of labor even in God's stewardship command in Genesis 1, which "assigns to the man the primary responsibility to provide for his wife and children and to the woman the care for and nurture of her family." Unfortunately, he offers no further explanation

For instance, several aspects of Genesis 2 provide complementarians with the clear command for male leadership and female submission, such as the order in which God created the sexes, man first and then woman (Gen 2:7, 21–23); the prior commands God gave just to the man (Gen 2:16–17); the man's naming of the animals (Gen 2:19–20); and the creation of woman to be "a helper" (Gen 2:18). In this way, by setting gender roles in place before the fall in Genesis 3, complementarians contend that they are intrinsic to God's design from the onset of creation.

A complementarian worldview can regulate every aspect of life, from romance to marriage and from career aspirations to parenting. In recent studies of female college students, investigators trace the influence of complementarianism on future plans. The complementarian group was "more likely to aspire to motherhood and full-time homemaker status"; this group also exhibited extremely high agreement with statements such as "The husband is the head of the home" (75.4 percent) and "There will be limitations on what position I can hold in the church because of my gender" (88.6 percent), and with the term "helper-wife" (96.7 percent).[17] According to Donna Freitas in *Sex and the Soul*, women in the complementarian group assume the passive role in romance and dating.

> While evangelical women grow up learning the values of patience and passivity, evangelical men are raised to believe they are *active* when it comes to sex, purity, and romance: they *guard* their women, they *prove* themselves chivalrous by heroic restraint, they *take* a woman's gift [of virginity] as their birthright. Women by contrast, *submit* to their guardian, and they *wait* for their prince to come along and for their purity to *be taken* on their wedding day.[18]

These sentiments reflect the popular Love Waits purity pledge, which has been signed by more than two million people: "Believing that true love waits, I make a commitment to God, myself, my family, my friends, my future mate, and my future children to a lifetime of purity including sexual abstinence from this day until the day I enter a biblical marriage relationship."[19]

---

or hermeneutical justification for this problematic interpretation. Kostenberger, *God, Marriage, and Family*, 24.

17. Tangenberg, "Women's Mentoring on Christian Campuses."

18. Freitas, *Sex and the Soul*, 92.

19. For more on the pledge, see Tina Seller's article in this volume.

Specific gender roles after marriage continue to be pressed in evangelical circles through all possible media, as reflected by this woman's experience:

> There is more pressure within evangelical circles for a woman to be the traditional "Becky-homecky." In sermons, in evangelical publications, in Christian bookstores and certainly on the airwaves, the message comes through that a woman's highest callings are to build up a man and to raise children, which translates into staying at home with the kids. . . . Even some of the prominent women in evangelical circles who have active public ministries lambaste that very activity.[20]

Complementarianism is now so dominant in some sectors of American evangelicalism that it has supplanted even the inerrancy of Scripture—the belief that the original documents (autographs) of the Bible were without error—as a litmus test of evangelical fidelity. For example, in her study of women in evangelicalism, Julie Ingersoll demonstrates that the pivotal question for screening potential faculty members shifted from inerrancy to complementarianism in the mid-1990s. For that reason, a faculty member hired in 1992 was told by the seminary president that an affirmative position on women in ministry would have prevented his being hired three years later. As Ingersoll explains, "Inerrancy is no longer the central issue. Southern Seminary has moved from considering a candidate's views on inerrancy to making hiring decisions solely on the basis of a candidate's views on that issue [women as pastors]."[21]

What happens, then, for contemporary women who believe God has called them to a ministry outside of woman's separate sphere? For complementarians, such a call, *when interpreted correctly, appropriately, biblically*, would never lead a woman beyond her separate sphere of helper to a man in leadership. As the Danvers Statement declares, "In both men and women a heartfelt sense of call to ministry should never be used to set aside Biblical criteria for particular ministries (1 Tim 2:11–15, 3:1–13; Tit 1:5–9). Rather, Biblical teaching should remain the authority for testing our subjective discernment of God's will." A few lines later, the Danvers Statement labels a woman's resistance to accept "limitations on their roles or to neglect the use of their gifts in appropriate ministries" as nothing less than sin.

---

20. Creegan and Pohl, *Living on the Boundaries*, 110.
21. Ingersoll, *Evangelical Christian Women*, 53.

Women Called to Preach

Despite the separate spheres or complementarian ideology, women are called to preach. This call from God irrevocably transforms their prescribed plans and propels them into preaching, evangelism, pastoring. Again, this is nothing new. As one woman commented recently, "I think there's plenty of historical precedent for evangelical women being called to ministry beyond their homes and families. The call to follow Jesus has to ultimately supercede commitment to home and family."[22]

For Iva Durham Vennard, the call from God came unannounced, even unwanted initially. She planned to finish her senior year at Swarthmore College on a full scholarship. Before embarking in this direction, she attended a revival meeting where she became reacquainted with a preacher who had known her from a young age. She recorded in her autobiography that he expressed disappointment in her educational plans. "When I knew you a few years ago, I thought you were one young woman who was going to be spiritual; and more than that—a spiritual leader. But I see you seem to have gone mostly 'to top.'" His remarks "awoke once more the old gnawing restlessness and dissatisfaction of soul," and she felt under conviction about her educational ambitions.[23] After a night of prayerful searching, she declined the scholarship to Swarthmore. Opportunities immediately materialized for her participation in evangelistic meetings, first as a singer, then as preacher. At first, she hesitated because "she just did *not* approve of women preachers. It was all right to speak, to lecture, to give messages, but to come out in the open as a *woman preacher*—that did not appeal to her at all."[24] Eventually, she relented and enrolled in a Methodist deaconess training school. After graduation, she was appointed as a Methodist deaconess evangelist, and she held evangelistic meetings in churches throughout New York State, often performing her trademark soliloquy, titled "Experiences of a Deaconess Guitar." Speaking as if from her guitar's perspective, she opened the soliloquy with this statement:

> I suppose in the other days when my strings knew so well the jingle of gay college tunes, that people thought me a very frivolous instrument, and little did they predict a really useful future for me. When I entered this new life I had no idea how thrilling

22. Creegan and Pohl, *Living on the Boundaries*, 106.

23. Bowie, *Alabaster and Spikenard*, 46.

24. Ibid., 54.

it would all be, but this was the reason of it. A great change had come over "my lady." She found my soul, and for love of her I was glad to become a deaconess guitar. We have good times together, my lady in her black garb, and I. I've been dedicated to the glory of King Jesus, and it is so beautiful to belong to God![25]

While thus engaged, she received an "illumination" from God to found a training school for deaconesses with a distinct focus on evangelism, which eventually resulted in Epworth Evangelistic Institute. In the midst of these plans, she fell in love with Thomas Vennard. Throughout their long courtship, she made clear to him again and again her unwavering commitment to Epworth; she even put wedding plans on hold until the school was well established. His response every time, one that never wavered throughout twenty-five years of marriage, was simply, "I am willing to be your background of support." In a letter to her during their engagement, he wrote, "I may be the janitor of an institution of which you are principal founder and controlling head."[26] His pledge was prophetic: although he had been the lead architect for Louisville's Seelbach Hotel, he made a career-ending decision to relinquish his position in a Chicago architectural firm in order to oversee the renovation of her school's main building to keep the construction costs as affordable as possible. A mutual friend likened his support to lending strength to "the hands of his wife in the educational program to which the Lord had called her."[27]

Like Vennard, most women preachers and evangelists were married with children. In a study of eighteen American women evangelists, I found that all but two were married, twelve birthed at least one child, two adopted children, and only one remained single and without children.[28] Otherwise, these women experienced what women commonly do—marriage, keeping a home, pregnancy, childbirth, infant and child mortality, and child rearing. Then suddenly, a divine call, as they interpreted it, broke into their home and compelled them to leave and begin preaching the gospel. At this juncture, the mundane yet monumental question arose: how? What had to happen at home in order that the wife, the mother, the daughter, could leave? Because women were expected, according to the separate spheres ideology, to find their full-time

25. Ibid., 74.
26. Ibid., 112.
27. Ibid., 109.
28. Pope-Levison, *Turn the Pulpit Loose.*

occupation and satisfaction in the home, in the private sphere, they had to face head on this pivotal conundrum.

For some, the back and forth between God's call and family responsibilities was so wrenching emotionally and physically that they fell dangerously ill; it was only when they promised to follow God's command that they recovered. This happened to Aimee Semple McPherson (1890–1944), evangelist and founder of the International Church of the Foursquare Gospel denomination, whose call to preach occurred in the midst of marital difficulties and a life-threatening illness. In her autobiographical description of the tumultuous time, we can discern her illness as a liberation from the separate spheres ideology that clashed against her sense of God's call. On the one hand, the traditional voices swirled in her head—a woman should be happily occupied in her home and with her family. As she wrote in her autobiography, this voice made comments like,

> Now, see here, my lady, this will never do! What right have you to fret and pine like this? Just see those shining, polished floors, covered with soft Axminster and Wilton rugs. Just look at that mahogany parlor furniture and the big brass beds in yonder, the fine bathroom done in blue and white, the steam heat, the softly-shaded electric lights, the pretty baby's crib with its fluff and ribbons, the high-chair and the rocking-horse. Why aren't you glad to have a home like this for the babies, as any other mother would be?

On the other hand, God's voice, as she interpreted it, repeated the mantra, "Go! Preach the Word!" As she underwent several operations, the battle over separate spheres raged until she neared death's door.

> Just before losing consciousness, as I hovered between life and death, came the voice of my Lord, so loud that it startled me: "NOW—WILL—YOU—GO?" And I knew it was "Go," one way or the other: that if I did not go into the work as a soul-winner and get back into the will of God, Jesus would take me to Himself before He would permit me to go on without Him and be lost.
>
> Oh, don't you ever tell me that a woman cannot be called to preach the Gospel! If any man ever went through one-hundredth part of the hell on earth that I lived in, those months when out of God's will and work, they would never say that again.

With my little remaining strength, I managed to gasp: 'Yes—
Lord—I'll—go.' And go I did![29]

As wives, evangelists had to anticipate and handle their husbands'
reactions, which ran the full range from completely supportive to
adamantly opposed. Anchoring one end of the spectrum was Thomas
Vennard, who willingly sacrificed his career to Iva's evangelistic work.
Similarly, Methodist evangelist Phoebe Palmer (1807–1874) preached
for twenty years on her own while her husband, Walter, managed their
household and kept up his medical practice. Later they teamed up for an
extended, four-year evangelistic tour of Great Britain. However, not all
husbands accommodated so easily to their wives' public ministry. The
short-lived partnership of Kent and Alma White (1862–1946) ended in
rampant rivalry and bitter accusations. Even though Alma preached her
first sermon in Kent's pulpit, and they preached together at evangelistic
meetings for several years, their rapport disintegrated, as she became
the more successful preacher. Eventually they separated and were never
reconciled. Aimee Semple McPherson's dilemma, cited above, arose because her second marriage to Rolf McPherson limited her evangelistic
work. According to her report, she clarified before they married that the
"work of the Lord" was her first priority. However, Rolf never adjusted to
Aimee's itinerant lifestyle, as she crossed the continent from one shore to
the other, preaching from her gospel autovan, and their marriage ended
in divorce.

Husbands of course were not the only consideration; many evangelists were also mothers for whom child care concerns were paramount.
While situations varied depending on the number and age of the children and the willingness of relatives, friends, and husbands to cooperate,
mothers agonized over leaving their children for their evangelistic work.
When Alma White left her two-year-old son, who was recovering from a
serious illness, in the care of her own mother, she was still plagued with
worry. "To leave him in care of others was almost like taking a mother's
heart from her body, but the Lord had spoken and it would have been
perilous to disobey. It was no more than He required of others, and why
should I have any controversy."[30] Thus, for these women evangelists and
preachers, obedience to God's call to preach the gospel challenged a strict

29. McPherson, *This Is That*, 71–76.
30. White, *Truth Stranger than Fiction*, 48.

adherence to separate spheres and called them outside the domestic realm, and family life had to adjust in some way or another.

Strategies to Sidestep Separate Spheres

Most women evangelists and preachers in the last century devised creative strategies to maintain to some extent the prevailing separate spheres ideology while they pursued the call to preach the gospel. These strategies developed along three lines: (1) they utilized traditional notions of femininity to justify their preaching; (2) they maintained the separate spheres ideology in all areas except preaching; and (3) they considered women's preaching to be an exception, not the norm.

The first adaptation of the separate spheres ideology was to capitalize on essential, traditional characteristics of femininity as the very basis for justifying their call. Mary Lee Cagle (1864–1955), a Church of the Nazarene minister, highlighted a characteristic considered quintessentially female—being talkative. She then proceeded with the assertion that women should certainly preach the gospel because they are the ones who know best how to talk.

> Why did God give women such a talent to talk, if not to be used for Him? If God did not intend for women to use their tongues for Him He certainly did give the devil a great advantage in the beginning, for women can talk. The men are generally our superiors; but there are some things that we can excel them in. And one of them is talking. . . . It is no wonder to me why the devil has tried and in a large measure succeeded in keeping women from using their tongues for God, for he knows that if the women get filled with the Holy Ghost and turn their tongues loose on him he will have to hunt cooler quarters, or in other words will have to vacate.[31]

Even though Cagle held on to the traditional notion of male superiority over women, she encouraged women to use their innate talkativeness to preach and evangelize in public, from the pulpit or wherever a crowd gathered. Cagle, along with several other women evangelists, preached in Arkansas, Kentucky, Tennessee, and Texas, and then organized churches associated with the denomination she founded, the New Testament Church of Christ. When that denomination merged with the

31. Cagle, *Life and Work of Mary Lee Cagle*, 171–72.

Church of the Nazarene in 1908, women comprised 13 percent of ordained ministers, a statistic due in large measure to Cagle and her sister
evangelists.

A second adaptation to the separate spheres ideology was to apply
it in every arena but one—preaching. Phoebe Palmer argued that only
for the sake of preaching the gospel would God call women beyond their
traditional sphere. She explained, "We believe woman has her legitimate
sphere of action, which differs in most cases materially from that of man;
and in this legitimate sphere she is both happy and useful."[32] However,
she was adamant that women must be actively engaged in evangelism;
in fact, she blamed the church for burying women's preaching gifts in a
potter's field.

> Again we repeat that it is our most solemn conviction that the
> use of a gift of power delegated to the Church as a specialty of
> the last days has been neglected,—a gift which, if properly rec-
> ognized, would have hastened the latter-day glory. We believe
> that tens of thousands more of the redeemed family would have
> been won over to the world's Redeemer if it had not been for the
> tardiness of the Church in acknowledging this gift. . . .
>
> We believe that the attitude of the Church in relation to this
> matter is most grievous in the sight of her Lord, who has pur-
> chased the whole human family unto himself, and would fain
> have *every possible agency employed in preaching the gospel to
> every creature.* He whose name is Faithful and True has fulfilled
> his ancient promise, and poured out his Spirit as truly upon his
> daughters as upon his sons.[33]

In her four-hundred-page book, *Promise of the Father*, Palmer root-
ed this argument in Joel's prophetic text, repeated in the Pentecost story,
that when the Spirit was poured out, *all flesh*, including women, would
prophesy: "And it shall come to pass, after those days, that I will pour out
my Spirit upon all flesh, and your sons and your daughters shall prophesy" (Joel 2:28–29; Acts 2:17–18). Looking to the future, she predicted:
". . . when the residue of the Spirit is poured out, and the millennium
glory ushered in, the prophecy of Joel being fully accomplished in all its
glory, then, probably, there will be . . . such a willingness to receive profit
by any instrument; such a spirit of humility, in honor preferring one

---

32. Palmer, *Promise of the Father*, 1.
33. Palmer, *Selected Writings*, 39. Emphasis added.

another, that the wonder will then be, that the exertions of pious females to bring souls to Christ should ever have been opposed or obstructed."[34]

Several generations later, in a baccalaureate sermon preached at a LIFE Bible College commencement, McPherson also used the Joel 2/Acts 2 texts as the biblical justification for women's preaching. In her sermon, she employed illustrations showing men and women in traditional gender roles, thus demonstrating her acceptance of the separate spheres ideology. For instance, she preached about the "rugged" father who provides "advice and counsel" as well as "bread for the larder," and the mother who "rocks the little ones." Even the biblical women she cited as prooftexts to support the Joel prophecy were presented with conventional female traits: Miriam and music, Rebecca and motherhood, Mary and her "precious" virginity, even Dorcas and sewing. "I can see the Dorcases down through the years—that dear little Dorcas of the Bible days who sewed, toiled, and labored so faithfully."[35] Nevertheless, she set aside the separate spheres ideology in her call for women as well as men to preach the gospel: "There are some who believe that a woman should never witness for Jesus Christ—that her lips should be sealed. This is not according to the Word of God. 'Your sons and your daughters shall prophesy!' In this day, God has a real message for the women as well as the men and He is using them to help gather in the wheat, for the fields are ripe unto harvest and the time grows short."[36] Thus McPherson, like Palmer, prompted women to transcend their separate sphere for the sake of the gospel.

A third adaptation was to consider women preachers as an exception. Such an argument was advanced in the eighteenth century by John Wesley, the founder of Methodism, when he witnessed the effectiveness of women in his movement as Bible teachers, class leaders, even preachers.[37] Nearly two hundred years later, Kathryn Kuhlman spoke of her own

34. Ibid. Palmer's influence can be traced directly to several notable nineteenth- and twentieth-century women, such as Catherine Booth, cofounder of the Salvation Army with her husband and mother of Evangeline Booth; Frances Willard, author of *Woman in the Pulpit* and long-time president of the Woman's Christian Temperance Union; and evangelist Amanda Berry Smith.

35. McPherson, "To the Servants," 5–6.

36. Ibid., 5.

37. In a letter to Mary Bosanquet Fletcher, who reported receiving a call to preach in a dream, Wesley used the term "extraordinary call" to suggest that sometimes, in extraordinary circumstances, God could call women. In 1771, he gave Fletcher and Sarah Crosby official permission to preach based upon their "extraordinary call." He defended the right of women to preach at the conference of 1784, and in 1787 the

"exceptional call," and by it she meant that she was the exception because men did not obey God's call.

> I'll tell you something very confidentially—the true conviction of my heart. I do not believe I was God's first choice in this ministry, in the ministry He has chosen for these last days. It's my firm conviction. You'll never argue me out of this conviction, never. I'm not quite sure whether I was God's second choice, or even His third choice. Because I really believe the job I am doing is a man's job. I work hard. Few people know how hard I really work—sixteen, seventeen hours a day. I can outwork five men put together, and I'll challenge you on this. Only those who know me best know how little sleep I get, the hours I put into the ministry. Those who attend our services know I am on the stage, behind the pulpit, three and a half to four and a half hours. I never sit down.
>
> I believe God's first choice for this ministry was a man. His second choice, too. But no man was willing to pay the price. I was just naïve enough to say, "Take nothing, and use it." And He has been doing that ever since.[38]

These women became incredibly successful evangelists and entrepreneurs. Phoebe Palmer launched Five Points Mission, one of America's first urban mission centers, in 1850 in a New York City slum. She was also a prolific writer, authoring several bestselling books, and editor, for under her leadership the circulation of *The Guide to Holiness* rose from 10,000 to 40,000. McPherson founded not only a church in Los Angeles, Angelus Temple, whose 5,300-seat auditorium filled up three times every Sunday for services, but also she launched a denomination that continues today, the International Church of the Foursquare Gospel. Even her political impact was such that in the 1934 California gubernatorial campaign, she catalyzed her followers to help defeat the Democratic candidate, Upton Sinclair, whom she believed supported atheism and communism. Kuhlman broadcast her radio program, "Heart-to-Heart," for over forty years, and her long-running television program held a regular spot on CBS. Nevertheless, despite their accomplishments, the separate spheres ideology remained stubbornly intact and influential.

---

conference granted official authorization to women preachers. Wesley's decision revolved around what seemed to be the evidence of God's blessing on the preaching and teaching ministry of women in his reform movement.

38. Kuhlman, *Glimpse into Glory*, 30.

Vennard's Strategy: Disregarding Separate Spheres

Iva Durham Vennard chose a different strategy, one that disregarded separate spheres altogether. Because this ideology had long restricted women's activities in the church, she insisted that the time had arrived for women to step up and out in Christian service.

> The nineteenth century will stand out in history as "the discoverer of woman" and it is for the womanhood of this twentieth century to prove what this discovery shall mean. *No longer cramped by the old time notions of a woman's very narrow sphere,* our girls today find wide open doors for culture and education and travel. They may enter business if they choose, and the professions are inviting them. But in no realm of activity does the door swing wider than to Christian service.
>
> The Church is recognizing the necessity of the labor of trained, capable, spiritual women, and today she offers a magnificent opening for her consecrated daughters.[39]

Vennard devoted every area of her life—family, church, vocation—to developing "consecrated daughters" to preach the gospel. She and Thomas, her spouse, worked together on the educational institutions to which they both believed she was called to lead. She was clearly in charge as principal; Thomas helped her as needed with construction projects or other menial tasks. After their son's birth, Iva not only founded a new educational institution, but she also led it as principal for thirty years. To help the family cope with the multiple, pressing demands, they invited people, like Iva's mother and several former students, to live in and help with child care and household duties.

In terms of women in the church, Vennard actively and fully supported women's ordination. She joined the American Association of Women Preachers and served on its executive board when asked by the organization's founder, the Rev. Madeleine Southard, a Methodist minister. In addition, Iva herself was issued a local preacher's license by her Methodist minister in Austin, Illinois.

Yet the arena in which she instituted the most far-reaching support for women beyond separate spheres was her two educational institutions, Epworth Evangelistic Institute and Chicago Evangelistic Institute. For instance, Epworth's curriculum reinforced women's preaching. In a required textbook for theology classes at Epworth, *Binney's Theological*

39. Vennard, "Appeal to Young Women," 8.

Compend, the final section, titled "Woman's Sphere in the Church," presented women's preaching as congruent with biblical teaching. First, the author dismissed the traditional separate spheres arrangement of women relegated to household domesticity. Woman's sphere, he argued, was "not limited to the duties of the family or household, since she is often by nature and grace pre-eminently adapted for a wider service."[40] Continuing on, the author tackled this commonly quoted biblical text in which the apostle Paul supposedly prohibited women from religious leadership: "As in all the churches of the saints, women should be silent in the churches. For they are not permitted to speak, but should be subordinate, as the law also says. If there is anything they desire to know, let them ask their husbands at home. For it is shameful for a woman to speak in church" (1 Cor 14:33b–35). In his comment on this text, the author denounced its universal application to all women everywhere and for all time.

> To say that his [Paul's] prohibition applies alike to all times and conditions of society, is to say that the prudential regulations of a degraded heathen people, eighteen hundred years ago, are universally binding, and that Christianity in this respect has wrought no change in the world it came to reform. Paul surely had a different estimate of woman's service. Rom. Xvi, 1–7, 12–15. His first public discourse in Europe was at a meeting of women, and his first convert and host was a woman. Acts xvi, 9–15.[41]

Then, in a broad, sweeping statement, the author sanctioned not only women engaging in public prophesying, preaching, and teaching, but also women serving in positions of "the higher ministerial duties, as appears from the rank next after apostles."[42]

Epworth graduates took this message to heart. In the school's newsletter, the "Personals" column was replete with reports from alumna holding evangelistic meetings and pastoring churches. There was a report in the 1905 newsletter about Miss Rebecca Bell, who "visited Epworth a

---

40. Binney and Steele, *Binney's Theological Compend*, 192. This textbook was also widely used by many Methodists for decades. "At Binney's death in 1878, it was said that his *Compendium* had reached a circulation of forty thousand copies in the English language alone. By 1878 it had been translated into six languages including Arabic, Chinese, German, Swedish, Bulgarian, and Spanish" (Hartley, *Evangelicals at a Crossroads*, 194).

41. Binney and Steele, *Binney's Theological Compend*, 193.

42. Ibid.

few days before going South for a three months' revival campaign. Her first engagement is with Rev. Wm. R. Chase's church in New Orleans, La," and Mrs. Cooper, "a Deaconess who has been acting as Pastor of the Methodist Episcopal Church of Harrisonville, Mo., by appointment of the Presiding Elder of that District, spent the week after Conference resting at Epworth."

After Vennard resigned from Epworth Evangelistic Institute, she began again the next year, opening a second religious training school, Chicago Evangelistic Institute (CEI), in 1910. This school was coeducational and nondenominational, opening its doors to ninety-two male and female students representing seventeen states, two foreign countries, and fourteen denominations. By inculcating at this second school the same priority to train students in evangelism, Vennard forged unparalleled opportunities for women in the early twentieth century, at a time when mainline Protestant denominations were still dithering over the licensing and ordination of women.

CEI commenced instruction with seventeen faculty members—ten women and seven men. Only two of the men worked at CEI full-time; five were local ministers who taught part-time. Always in the majority, women faculty taught most of the courses, including Bible and theology, and women students matriculated every year in higher numbers than male students. Posed pictures of student groups in CEI yearbooks bear out this last statistic, particularly a photograph of thirty-one students where women outnumber the men three to one. Students were accustomed to seeing women in positions of religious leadership, because CEI alumnae—pastors, evangelists, missionaries, and Bible teachers—regularly returned to campus as chapel speakers and classroom lecturers.

As the finale to the academic year, students competed for awards in preaching and exposition. Women students often won first place in these competitions. In 1940, for instance, only one award went to a man; women collected every other award, including Best Sermon in Defense of the Christian Faith.[43] For the practical work portion of the school's curriculum, students ran the radio ministry, preached from the gospel auto, or worked in city missions, depending upon talent and interest, not gender, which meant that women students regularly preached in Chicago churches and missions and held revivals across Illinois as members of CEI's evangelistic teams.

43. Vennard, "Highlights of the Year," 19–20.

A quintessential CEI graduate was the Reverend D. Willia Caffray. After a decade working as a deaconess and an itinerant evangelist, she enrolled as a postgraduate student at CEI, where she and Vennard became close associates and dear friends. Caffray went on to become an international missionary evangelist, preaching in over fifty countries on fourteen trips spread over thirty years. Along with her staggering accomplishments in evangelism, she also pressed forward the fledgling movement towards women's ordination in the early twentieth century. In 1919, she signed on as a charter member of the American Association of Women Preachers. In addition, Caffray relentlessly tracked Methodism's halting progress in women's ordination, and she was among the first women to receive a Methodist local preacher's license—only seven minutes after new guidelines went into effect. Finally, in 1929, she was fully ordained as a minister of the Methodist Episcopal Church.

Conclusion

In a century's worth of perspective, little has changed with regard to the power of the separate spheres ideology and its contemporary instantiation, complementarianism. With the exception of Martha Moore Avery, each woman cited in this essay faced opposition and antagonism from church members and leaders for their preaching; nevertheless, they developed strategic ways to sidestep the separate spheres. Vennard, in particular, was deemed a danger by male church leaders due to her unwillingness to sequester deaconesses within women's separate sphere. Her "war story" replicates those that fill Julie Ingersoll's book, *Evangelical Christian Women: War Stories in the Gender Battles*—stories that are simultaneously past yet very present, a century removed yet a century reminiscent. Still, evangelical women today, in greater numbers, persevere in order to follow God's call despite the discouraging reception they often receive within the church. As one woman explained, "Pioneers don't tend to have large cheering sections. Often more people are standing by—shaking their heads—than encouraging and cheering one on. And as for me, I've found it often necessary to stop and rest, gauge the territory, try to get some perspective, gather my energies and my will to go on."[44] But on she goes in the steps of such luminaries as Phoebe Palmer, Kathryn Kuhlman, and Iva Durham Vennard.

44. Creegan and Pohl, *Living on the Boundaries*, 115.

Bibliography

Ames, A. H. "Lucy Webb Hayes National Training-School." In *Nineteenth Annual Report of the General Board of Managers of the Woman's Home Missionary Society of the Methodist Episcopal Church, for the Year* 1899–1900, 137. Cincinnati: Western Methodist Book Concern, 1900.

Avery, Martha Moore. "Spread of Social Disorder." *America* 14 (November 6, 1915) 78.

Bebbington, David. *Evangelicalism in Modern Britain: A History from the 1730s to the 1980s.* Boston: Unwin Hyman, 1989.

Bendroth, Margaret Lamberts. *Fundamentalism and Gender, 1875 to the Present.* New Haven, CT: Yale University Press, 1993.

Binney, Amos, and Daniel Steele. *Binney's Theological Compend Improved.* 2nd ed. Cincinnati: Curts & Jennings, 1875.

Bowie, Mary Ella. *Alabaster and Spikenard: The Life of Iva Durham Vennard, D.D., Founder of Chicago Evangelistic Institute.* Chicago: Chicago Evangelistic Institute, 1947.

Cagle, Mary Lee. *The Life and Work of Mary Lee Cagle: An Autobiography.* Kansas City, MO: Nazarene Publishing House, 1928.

Clark, Stephen B. *Man and Woman in Christ.* Ann Arbor, MI: Servant, 1980.

Creegan, Nicola Hoggard, and Christine D. Pohl. *Living on the Boundaries: Evangelical Women, Feminism, and the Theological Academy.* Downers Grove, IL: InterVarsity, 2005.

Freitas, Donna. *Sex and the Soul: Juggling Sexuality, Spirituality, Romance, and Religion on America's College Campuses.* New York: Oxford University Press, 2008.

Grudem, Wayne and John Piper, editors. *Recovering Biblical Manhood and Womanhood: A Response to Evangelical Feminism.* Wheaton, IL: Crossway, 1991.

Harrison, W. P. "The Methodist Deaconess." *Southern Methodist Review* 4 (July 1888) 415.

Hartley, Benjamin L. *Evangelicals at a Crossroads: Revivalism & Social Reform in Boston, 1860–1910.* Durham: University of New Hampshire Press, 2011.

Ingersoll, Julie. *Evangelical Christian Women: War Stories in the Gender Battles.* New York: New York University Press, 2003.

Kostenberger, Andreas J. *God, Marriage, and Family: Rebuilding the Biblical Foundation.* 2nd ed. Wheaton, IL: Crossway, 2004.

Kuhlman, Kathryn, with Jamie Buckingham. *A Glimpse into Glory.* Plainfield, NJ: Logos International, 1976.

McPherson, Aimee Semple. *This Is That: Personal Experiences, Sermons, and Writings.* Los Angeles: Bridal Call Publishing House, 1923.

———. "To the Servants and the Handmaidens; Baccalaureate Sermon." *Bridal Call* 13 (February 1930) 5–6.

Meyer, Lucy Rider. "The Mother in the Church." *The Message and Deaconess Advocate* (October 1901) 5.

Minutes of the Forty-Third Session of the St. Louis Annual Conference of the Methodist Episcopal Church, Held in Mountain Grove, MO, March 22 to 26, 1911. Warrensburg, MO: Perry E. Pierce, 1911.

Noll, Mark A. *America's God: From Jonathan Edwards to Abraham Lincoln.* New York: Oxford University Press, 2002.

Palmer, Phoebe. *Promise of the Father, or, A Neglected Speciality of the Last Days.* Boston: Henry V. Degen, 1859.

―――. *Phoebe Palmer: Selected Writings.* Edited by Thomas C. Oden. Sources of American Spirituality. New York: Paulist, 1988.

Pope-Levison, Priscilla. "A 'Thirty Year War' and More: Exposing Complexities in the Methodist Deaconess Movement." *Methodist History* 47:2 (January, 2009): 101–16. Online: http://archives.gcah.org/xmlui/handle/10516/221.

―――. *Turn the Pulpit Loose: Two Centuries of American Women Evangelists.* New York: Palgrave Macmillan, 2004.

Sapiro, Virginia. *Women in American Society.* 2nd ed. Mountain View, CA: Mayfield, 1990.

Tangenberg, Katy. "Women's Mentoring on Christian Campuses: Balancing Tensions of Faith, Feminism, and Femininity." Paper presented during the 2010 Lilly Summer Seminar.

Taves, Ann. "Women and Gender in American Religion(s)." *Religious Studies Review* 18 (October 1992) 263.

Vennard, Iva Durham. "An Appeal to Young Women." *Inasmuch* 2 (November 1906) 8.

―――. "Highlights of the Year: Doctor Vennard's Family Letter." *Heart and Life* 26 (July 1940) 19–20.

White, Alma. *Truth Stranger than Fiction: God's Lightning Bolts.* Zarephath, NJ: Pentecostal Union, 1913.

4

Conversations and Intersections

A Third-Wave Feminist Approach to Gender, Christianity, and Theology

CARYN D. RISWOLD

Conversations & Definitions

TWO CONVERSATIONS ABOUT GENDER and Christianity I had on the micro-blogging website Twitter in late 2009 frame a discussion of the space between feminism and Christianity and illuminate the theological intersections that they invite. I initially ventured on to Twitter as a way to promote my then-new book, *Feminism and Christianity*, to a broader audience and to experiment with public conversation on issues about which I regularly teach and write. I use Twitter as a public space, like a conference hall or a campus event, where I write and "retweet" (repost something that another person has written) things relevant to feminism and Christianity in a public online space. Conversations on Twitter are such that one person posts something (a tweet), and another person can reply to them on their own page. Tweets are limited to 140 characters, explaining the brevity of the remarks in the two conversations below.[1]

1. For more information about how Twitter works, see http://twitter.com/about. Whether or not a limit of 140 characters is conducive to actual conversation is something worth considering.

In both "conversations," I preserve misspellings as they appeared online and reformatted the tweets so that they are easier to read, like dialogue. My Twitter name is @feminismxianity, and I describe myself on my profile as a feminist theologian in the Lutheran tradition, a scholar, professor, activist, and author.

The first conversation epitomizes responses to my claims about feminist theology I tend to hear from women exasperated with Christianity. I don't really know who @SC_Jones is, but if the information she gives on her Twitter page and linked website is to be trusted, and given her tweets I think they are, she is a middle-aged woman living in Canada who is "handling [a] mid-life crisis" by publishing an erotic memoir. Her views of Christianity are immediately clear.

> @feminismxianity: Feminism too quickly ignores christianity

> @SC_Jones: Feminism has every justification for ignoring Christianity, due to its long history of misogony.

> @feminismxianity: Ignoring christian misogyny does not make it go away! Feminism fights back!

> @SC_Jones: Ignoring Christian misogony may not make it go away, but getting into bed seems like surrender.

> @feminismxianity: Not advocating feminism get in bed with christianity (interesting image, tho) rather that it sit down at the table 2 talk truth

> @SC_Jones: Considering history of misogyny I despise all established male religions and wait for apologies.

> @feminismxianity: While you wait, we will work

> @SC_Jones: Sadly, my wait for the male religions to apologize for misogonist history is likely to be long.[2]

The comments made by @SC_Jones in this brief exchange encapsulate many sentiments I hear from feminist friends and colleagues, students, activists, bloggers, and public commentators, who really see no good reason for talking about or engaging with Christianity. They take seriously the harm that churches and their theology have done to women in particular. In addition, another and more subtle reaction I hear from feminists about Christianity is to dismiss it as irrelevant. It is simply another

2. Online: http://twitter.com/feminismxianity and http://twitter.com/SC_Jones. October 2009.

patriarchal institution to be circumvented, offering nothing meaningful for women and men in the twenty-first century. All of these concerns must be addressed in a conversation about gender and Christianity today.

The second conversation is with @benmordecai. I don't really know who this person is either. If the info he gives is to be trusted, and given his tweets and his linked webpage I think it is, he was, at the time of this interchange in the fall of 2009, a twenty-one-year-old engineering student at the University of Georgia, an aspiring pastor, and engaged to be married. Again, social location matters. As a heterosexual young Christian male, who I presume to be white (from the picture he posts online), @benmordecai inhabits several positions of privilege that inform his particular relationship to Christianity as a belief system with all the right answers already in place; in other words, he seems quite satisfied with Christianity.

> @feminismxianity: Christianity is always reforming ~
> so feminism should be part of reform

> @benmordecai: Reformation describes a change back to the
> original, not from the original.

> @feminismxianity: Exactly my point. What is yours?

> @benmordecai: Adding 20th century ideas to Christianity is not
> reformation.

> @feminismxianity: Adding ideas to christianity has always hap-
> pened - pretending to live in the first century is silly.

> @benmordecai: Ahh! The truth comes out! You *are* interested
> in adding 20th century ideas to Christianity.

> @feminismxianity: Who isn't? Why so afraid of new ideas? Lets
> see: ending slavery = good idea. Not biblical. Jesus didn't
> teach about everything.

> @benmordecai: Another man I'm sure y'know- "I am bound by
> the Scriptures I have quoted, and my conscience is cap-
> tive to the Word of God."

> @feminismxianity: EXACTLY.[3]

3. Online: http://twitter.com/feminismxianity and http://twitter.com/benmorde-cai. December 2009.

In this "conversation," @benmordecai effectively repeats expressions I hear from many Christian friends and colleagues, students, theologians, pastors, bishops, and others who really see no need for Christianity to take feminism seriously. Many see feminism as he does, as a modern unbiblical invention that contradicts their presumption that nothing has changed or can change from biblical times. There is also another, I think more insidious, response; that is, they think that feminism is not needed anymore. If their denomination ordains women, permits women to read in church and assist with Communion, or allows women to vote and work outside the home, they conclude that gender equality has been reached. As with the previous conversation, all of these issues must also be recognized when talking about Christianity and gender.

In relation to each of these interlocutors, I sit in a different position of authority. To @benmordecai, I am older and a professor who is representative (to him) of a liberal agenda. In relationship to @SC_Jones, I am likely younger and (to her) representative of a patriarchal tradition. From this vantage point, I contend that both @SC_Jones and @benmordecai are missing important conversation that can happen in between their two positions. My location in between them leads me in this essay to explore theological proposals to address many of their suspicions. Four terms frame my proposal for a third-wave feminist approach to inhabit that middle ground: feminism, Christianity, third wave, and intersectional.[4] Considering them in pairs sets up my theological considerations to follow.

Feminism and Christianity

> *Feminism:* A worldview that criticizes sexism and patriarchy and advocates for the equal humanity of women and men.

> *Christianity:* A religion based on the core belief that Jesus is the Christ, the Messiah promised to deliver God's people from sin and death.

Defining these two basic terms is complicated because each has multiple permutations historically as well as today,[5] and each is misunderstood and caricatured by people who have never engaged in any serious and

4. I first articulated these precise definitions in *Feminism and Christianity*, 123–26.
5. I discuss these complexities more at length in *Feminism and Christianity*, 3–15.

meaningful work about them. I offer these definitions simply to be clear about what I mean when I use them, both when I respond to @benmordecai that Christianity benefits when it listens to feminism and when I suggest that @SC_Jones does not have to accept the misogyny that Christianity has supported.

The issues about gender and Christianity identified by these two conversation partners are not new, and the fact that these conversations and questions linger is both the legacy and limitation of previous generations of feminists. First-wave feminist engagement with Christianity appears in texts like Sarah Grimke's *Letters on the Equality of the Sexes*, written in 1838 to the Boston Female Anti-Slavery Society, and Elizabeth Cady Stanton's *The Woman's Bible*, published in two volumes in 1895 and 1898. It is also evident in theological narratives from women like Jarena Lee, who described her call to preach in her 1836 autobiography, and Sojourner Truth, who in 1851 asked the provocative theological question, "And how came Jesus into the world? Through God who created him and the woman who bore him. Man, where was your part?"[6] The first wave of feminism is largely associated with efforts toward achieving the vote for women, though the means to accomplish it divided groups of women particularly around issues of race[7] and religion.[8] The vote was achieved, some feminist theological work occurred, but substantial changes related to gender and Christianity remained for a future generation to realize.

The second wave of feminism focused on legal and structural reforms for women that grew out of the 1960s civil rights movements, such as advocating for laws protecting women from sexual assault and workplace harassment, ensuring women's access to education and sports, and making available safe and reliable birth control. Feminist engagement with Christianity in the mid to late twentieth century pivoted around moments like the groundbreaking work of Valerie Saiving's article on "The Human

6. Truth, "On Woman's Rights."

7. Post-Civil War politics included efforts to secure the vote for black people and the vote for women, and some rhetorical battles between leaders in both movements took shape. For discussion of some of this, see the PBS documentary *Not for Ourselves Alone: The Story of Elizabeth Cady Stanton and Susan B. Anthony*, and book of the same name by Ward and Burns. Discussion of similar race and gender dynamics in the Clinton-Obama presidential Democratic primary can be found in Guy-Sheftall and Cole, *Who Should Be First?*

8. Stanton and Anthony famously clashed about whether or not to take on the religious and biblical arguments against women's suffrage. See Ward and Burns, *Not for Ourselves Alone.*

Situation: A Feminine View" in *The Journal of Religion* in 1960, Mary Daly's moving *Beyond God the Father* in her 1973 book with that title, and Rosemary Radford Ruether's constructing feminist theology in *Sexism and God-Talk* in 1983. In many ways, then, feminists have answered the question of whether or not Christianity is irredeemable because of its misogyny, as suggested by @SC_Jones. While some feminist scholars would in fact agree with her that Christianity is hopelessly patriarchal,[9] I would not. I contend instead that Christianity begs for sharp feminist criticism and reconstruction.

Likewise, the case for feminism's ongoing contributions to Christianity, questioned by @benmordecai, was also made by second-wave feminist theologians: churches and theologies are now more open to and reflective of the human community because of feminist activism. Many mainline Protestant traditions voted to ordain women in the middle and late twentieth century. In addition, a widely influential body of literature by female scholars moving beyond gender to incorporate issues of race and class[10] emerged from this era. These include womanist theologians like Jacquelyn Grant in *White Women's Christ, Black Women's Jesus*, and Delores S. Williams in *Sisters in the Wilderness*, as well as mujerista scholars Ada Maria Isasi-Diaz and Elsa Tamez, who construct theology and ethics from the perspective of Hispanic women in *En La Lucha* and *The Amnesty of Grace*, respectively. Each of these books helps to create new spaces of academic discourse and empower women's grassroots organizing.

All of this work from the first and second waves continues to be relevant for the transition into a third wave of feminism because the two Twitter conversations reveal that some basic questions about gender and Christianity are ongoing. This influential body of feminist literature has neither solved problems of racism and sexism in Christianity nor convinced everyone of the essential importance of feminism for the ongoing reform of tradition.

Third Wave and Intersectionality

Third wave: Feminism populated by women and men who came
of age during and after the second wave of feminism, after Title

9. The most famous radical feminist critic of Christianity in the twenty-first century is Mary Daly, especially when she moved "beyond" God and Christianity after 1973.

10. This generation effectively began to name the racial dynamics that the first wave was ill-equipped to confront.

IX and after Roe v. Wade, with legal access and protections
already-achieved; Feminists who learned about gender equality
alongside racial equality and the social construction of sexuality, who embed commitments to global issues and systemic
analyses of privilege.

Intersectional: A methodological commitment to understanding that all people live at the intersection of multiple identities
including gender, race, class, sexuality, age, ability, and many
other things.

Third-wave feminist theology inhabits the complicated middle ground
between feminism and Christianity that has been vacated because groups
of people decided that engaging with the other is no longer necessary.
As illustrated above, this happens for multiple reasons. Some Christians,
like @benmordecai, refuse to interact with feminism because they see it
as a contemporary ideology that pollutes a pure biblical religion. They
find cultural reinforcement from media figures like Rush Limbaugh, who
popularized the term "feminazi" in the early 1990s.[11] From the other
direction, people like @SC_Jones pronounce a verdict on Christianity as irredeemably misogynist and find affirmation for their position
from radical feminist critics like Mary Daly. They are further confirmed
in their suspicions when Christianity's public and political face is often
portrayed only in the mobilization against gay marriage and women's
reproductive rights. Feminists like @SC_Jones find no constructive use
for religion in their lives and work and wonder why they should bother
with a religion that in some of its manifestations declares women to be
second-class citizens.

All of these voices have something important to contribute to this
conversation about gender and Christianity. We learn that we still need
to name the great harm done by Christians to marginalized people, including women, gays and lesbians, slaves, and native peoples around the
globe. For this reason, an intersectional approach is important in third-
wave feminism because it recognizes that race, class, gender, and sexuality flow together in every human person, informing their experience of
Christianity. We also learn that we still need to name and harness the
power that Christianity possesses culturally and politically; it shapes the

11. The Wikipedia page for this term features a picture of Rush Limbaugh, since
he popularized the term on his conservative radio talk show. Limbaugh credits Tom
Hazlett with coining the term in his 1992 book *The Way Things Ought to Be.* The
Merriam-Webster dictionary dates its origin to 1989, consistent with this claim.

lives of women and men whether they want it to or not. For this reason, Christianity must remain an object of inquiry. It remains a tradition with weight and substance that cannot be simply ignored.

Further, the way in which third-wave feminism engages Christianity makes a difference for its relevance to feminists as well as Christians in the twenty-first century. Black feminist scholar Patricia Hill Collins first and most effectively articulated the concept of intersectionality in her work in the late 1980s and early 1990s. She showed how feminist analysis of human identity needed to move away from being "additive" and toward being "intersectional."[12] It's not that I am a woman now, and then I am white over there, and later I will be heterosexual, and tomorrow I will be middle-class, and then I am able-bodied some of the time. I am all of these things at once. While some if not all of these aspects may shift over time, especially as related to class status and embodiedness, the point is that I will always have a race, a class, a gender, a sexuality, and a body that have meaning attached to them by me, a meaning constructed within a society. Each aspect is also affected by the others. Because I am white, I am more likely to be able-bodied and educated. Because I am a woman, I am more likely to be sexually assaulted. I can't not be white when I am being a woman.[13]

We all live at intersections and what follows is an offering for conversation about gender and Christianity in the vacated middle ground between @benmordecai and @SC_Jones. I will first situate the discussions about human intersectionality in a theological framework and then conclude with a proposal for holding Christian claims about revelation and truth in tension with socially constructed realities.

Intersectionality and Christian Theology

Language about human identity as intersectional sounds very contemporary and quite theoretical. On the contrary, we can find several themes in the classical Christian tradition to show how very practical it is. I will focus first on a theological thread, affirmations about Christ's humanity and divinity, and an anthropological thread, claims that a human being

---

12. Collins, *Black Feminist Thought*, 207.

13. Another term used to describe this phenomenon of human experience and identity is "confluence," which gives the verbal sense of how all of these things constantly flow together.

is both saint and sinner. A brief exploration of these themes contribute important elements to conversations about gender and Christianity today.

Jesus as Christ: Human and Divine

Two contemporary theologians present new offerings for Christology that mine traditional claims about Jesus' "twoness" for contemporary relevance. Lutheran feminist theologian Mary Streufert offers a way of thinking about Christ that builds on our embrace of his humanity and divinity to blur our categories of gender, while Brian Bantum, Christian scholar of race and theology, accomplishes a similar task with racial identity. In the areas of gender and race, the middle ground between categories is precisely where we are invited to stand today, because it is the space where many of us and our neighbors live. This middle-ground approach recognizes the growing number of those who check more than one box for "race" on the US census,[14] the emerging data on the numbers and types of intersex babies (as many as one in one hundred births),[15] and the work of organizations like the Transgender Law Center for "non-discriminatory education, health care, employment, or business environment" and the free expression of multiple gender identities.[16] Where it seems like Christian theology would be far removed from these realities, Streufert and Bantum show us otherwise.

For both theologians, making sense out of identities that do not fit in only one "box" is possible, not despite, but *because of* Christian theology, as Streufert contends, "The lead to make this apparently outrageous claim comes from Chalcedon itself, for it was through this council that the paradox of the divisionless divine *and* human God was affirmed."[17] In this statement, Streufert refers to the formula that emerged from the Council of Chalcedon in 451, claiming that Jesus Christ is fully human and fully divine, two natures united in one person, "without confusion or change, division or separation."[18] This formula itself defies logic. It is what my students and I like to call "theological math," the only kind of

14. Associated Press, "Multiracial People Are Fastest Growing Group."

15. Intersex Society of North America, "How Common Is Intersex?"

16. See the Transgender Law Center website at http://www.transgenderlawcenter.org.

17. Streufert, "Person of Christ," 141.

18. Migliore, *Faith Seeking Understanding*, 164.

math that allows a person to claim easily that 2 = 1, yet it has become the bedrock of much Christian theology.

Streufert builds her christological proposal in part on the work of Eleanor McLaughlin, who suggests that "we have to argue what seems apparently as nonsensical as the Chalcedonian paradox of full divinity and full humanity in one person. How is Jesus Christ a person whom we can experience as either man or woman?"[19] Streufert concludes that "to see Jesus Christ as fully male and fully female carries significant anthropological, christological and ecclesiological implications . . . [W]hen we think about what it means to be human from a Christian perspective, made in the image and likeness of God, we are freed from thoroughly polar understandings of human biology and gender meanings (what it means to be 'a man' or 'a woman')."[20] The emphasis on freedom arises from the gift of thinking intersectionally in Christianity. We are freed from "box-thinking" about Jesus as the Christ and about ourselves. We are multiple things in our own bodies, and we are all of these things in community with each other. Because of this, critical questions emerge, such as: How do we understand ourselves? How do we live together well? Bringing these questions into conversation with the Christian tradition uncovers new possibilities that neither reinforce the misogyny of tradition nor violate the integrity of the religion. Twoness is not a concept foreign to Christian theology; in fact, it is central to it.

Bantum similarly deconstructs rigidly constructed categories of racial identity in his book *Redeeming Mulatto: A Theology of Race and Christian Hybridity*. He states plainly that "Christ is mulatto. He is the mysterious union of God and humanity born of the Spirit and Mary."[21] Then he describes the ways in which this union disrupts categories that human beings become comfortable with, whether they be divine and human, or black and white. Like Streufert, Bantum argues that the logic that allows Christians to grasp the mystery of the Chalcedonian formula gives them freedom to break out of disruptive and limiting categories of human identity. Further, he suggests that "Christ's personhood [is] whole, as two parts irrevocably present constituting the wholeness of a person."[22] He deliberately uses the word "mulatto" in this theological proposal, because that word itself represents an effort "to referentially maintain whiteness

19. McLaughlin, "Feminist Christologies," 129.
20. Streufert, "Person of Christ," 147.
21. Bantum, *Redeeming Mulatto*, 112.
22. Ibid., 115.

through a classificatory system of descent."[23] To redeem the word is to redeem the concept, and it is through what he calls Christ's "mulattic personhood" that the world itself is redeemed. Bantum argues that the "unity of personhood" in Christ not only reconciles God and humans, but it "also explodes the grammar of humanity that is from within."[24] This metaphor of "exploding the grammar" is another way to describe moving beyond humanly constructed categories and boundaries.

These two theologians demonstrate how to talk about gender and Christianity in ways that show the resonance of the Christian theological tradition with contemporary questions about the fluidity and intersectionality of human identity. Both draw on classic Christian theological logic to make sense of contemporary human experience.[25]

Human as Being: Saint and Sinner

One other example of "twoness" that illustrates intersectionality's resonance with Christianity revolves around the consideration of human nature itself. Looking at claims about human persons made by Paul in his letters and by Martin Luther in his reformation writings completes this discussion. That these two are classic Christian sources demonstrates again how connection to the tradition can in fact advance third-wave feminist theological claims.[26] In the letters of Paul collected in the New Testament, we do not find a fully developed theory of the human person, but we do find him playing with the categories of human persons that existed in his time. In Romans and Galatians in particular, he fills in his theology of justification by grace through faith. In Romans 3:22–23 he suggests that both sin *and* faith remove all human categories and distinctions: "the righteousness of God through faith in Jesus Christ *for all who*

23. Ibid., 116.

24. Ibid.

25. This work is being done even more explicitly by those embracing queer and postcolonial theory, for example, Marcella Althaus-Reid, Robert Goss, and Mary Elise Lowe. These theories reject fixed categories of meaning and identity, growing out of the work of feminist theorists like Judith Butler, who began arguing in *Gender Trouble* in 1990 that our categories of "man" and "woman" were a flawed binary that are to simple to fully represent the reality of being human. See Goss, *Queering Christ*, and Althaus-Reid, *Queer God*. For an introduction to these approaches, see Lowe, "Gay, Lesbian, and Queer Theologies."

26. It should also be noted that the person whom @benmordecai quotes in his effort to correct me at the end of our December 2009 Twitter exchange is Martin Luther.

believe. For there is *no distinction,* since *all* have sinned and fall short of the glory of God; they are now justified by his grace as a gift, through the redemption that is in Christ Jesus" (emphasis added). Along with his assertion in Galatians 3:28 that "There is no longer Jew or Greek, there is no longer slave or free, there is no longer male and female; for all of you are one in Christ Jesus," Paul holds in tension the reality of sin in human life and his claim about being made right with God through the person and work of Jesus the Christ. Sin remains, and righteousness is real; both are true for those who believe. Further, fundamental to his theological framework is the notion that human categories of identity, like ethnicity and sex and law-keeper, did not matter when it came to a relationship with God.

Paul's writings can help free twenty-first-century Christians from the constructed binary of gender and the limitations of racial categorizing, and this is further enhanced by Martin Luther's discussions of the human person as *simul justus et peccator,* simultaneously saint and sinner. When commenting on Paul's letter to the Romans, Luther wrote that the human being "is at the same time both a sinner and a righteous man; a sinner in fact, but a righteous man by the sure imputation and promise of God that He will continue to deliver him from sin."[27] Here is another offering from the Christian tradition of a thoroughly gospel-centered attempt at conceptualizing "twoness," multiple identities existing inside the same person. Queer Lutheran theologian Mary Lowe suggests that the "paradoxical freedom in Luther's *simul* provides the freedom necessary to be converted from distorted beliefs and behaviors in unjust discourses and sinful structures."[28] Like Streufert, Lowe emphasizes freedom from distortions and limitations. Here we see how the conversation between the Lutheran tradition and contemporary discourse about structural sin helps us to move toward justice and away from structural sins of racism, sexism, and classism.

This entire discussion about intersectionality and Christian theology weaves together cutting-edge issues like gender identity and a multiracial America with resources from church tradition. For those of us in the twenty-first century who want to engage in conversation standing between feminism and Christianity, between cutting-edge discourse about gender and resources from a tradition, these are some models and resources.

27. Luther, "Lecture on Romans," 260.
28. Lowe, "Sin from a Queer, Lutheran Perspective," 79.

Given the theological approaches described here, I could continue the two Twitter conversations that began this essay by asking @benmordecai to consider whether in fact some concepts that feminist and other contemporary theologians generate are alien to the Bible and the Christian tradition. For instance, are not intersectionality and fluidity embraced in the orthodox understanding of the person of Christ and Paul's foundational claims about human being? Additionally, I could ask @SC_Jones to reflect on the powerful attempts at constructing Christian theology happening with the creativity of people like Streufert, Bantum, and Lowe. These theologians demonstrate that Christianity is a complicated tradition with surprising theological resources that move far beyond misogyny and division. So to @SC_Jones, I ask: Do the misogynist patriarchal interpretations of the past have to continue to hold sway in this religion? To both interlocutors I raise this challenge: Consider what we gain when we stand in the space between the two, and what we lose when we ignore the relevance of the other.

Revelation and Social Construction

The last two questions I will consider are absolutely fundamental to addressing the resistance to conversation from @benmordecai and @SC_Jones; these questions are the following: Is Christianity a fixed, revealed set of truths not to be tampered with? Is it a flawed patriarchal religion that has outlived its relevance?

By answering yes to those questions, my Twitter partners, though holding radically different beliefs about gender and Christianity, make exactly the same mistake: they view Christianity as fixed, unchanging, immutable. @benmordecai thinks it is fixed in the first century and closed to new insight from human experience. @SC_Jones thinks it is fixed in the mistakes it has made in its treatment of women. In response, I say that both are mistaken, in part because of my own situatedness within the tradition of understanding the church as *semper reformanda*, always reforming. Post-Reformation ecclesial traditions claim that this medieval Latin phrase describes not only what happened to the church with the era known as the Reformation, but also explains something important about the very character of the church. Lutheran ethicist Larry Rasmussen, writing to criticize the timidity of his church's approach to a social statement on human sexuality in 2005, reflects the spirit of what it means to be an always-reforming church: "Where is the spirit of the 'protest-ants' who urged believers to reread the Scriptures and tradition through different lenses and write new confessions that protesting Christians would stake their lives on?"[29] He further describes what it means for him to be Lutheran, one branch of the post-Reformation Christian church: "a Spirit-braced reform movement in and for the church catholic, a movement taking on the hard issues with the joy, humility, and bold freedom of forgiven and forgiving sinners."[30] Rasmussen's statement sets out a theological articulation of what it means for a religion not to be immutable and thus echoes the call to freedom that Streufert and Lowe also noted as essential to their reading of the same tradition.

In addition, there is a sociological articulation of this dynamic worth describing, which leads to a final question about the role of claims of revealed truth in Christianity. Scholars of religion have been influenced by theories of social construction, articulated cogently by sociologist Peter Berger in his 1967 book *The Sacred Canopy*. The threefold process of social construction applies to most every aspect of reality, including religion. First, human beings "externalize," which means that they create institutions, ideas, and values in the world. Second, those things are "objectivated," which means that they take on an objective reality of their own which then confronts human beings as fact. Third, human beings "internalize" those things, usually forgetting that they had any part in constructing them to begin with. Berger refers to this latter dynamic of forgetting as "alienation."[31] An example of the threefold process of social construction is the following scenario: Human society decided for many reasons over thousands of years that male-female monogamous marriage represented the best option for family stability.[32] Male-female monogamous marriage is now viewed as an inescapable fact of reality, informed by biology and widespread experience of its benefits. Human beings assume now that male-female monogamy is an inescapable fact of nature which they accept and participate in usually without question.

I chose this example deliberately, because it is one that presently receives a lot of question and critical attention, even reform. Even though scholars can show quite easily that male-female monogamy is a social

29. Rasmussen, "Yet Another Chance to Be Lutheran."

30. Ibid.

31. The process is discussed at length throughout Berger, *Sacred* Canopy, esp. 4–19.

32. Scores of social historians have written about the history of marriage, and the presumptions about it that tend to inform this ideal. See for example the writings of Stephanie Coontz, Joanne Ferraro, and Peter Wallenstein.

construct that does not always mesh with reality, it is nevertheless lifted up as an ideal that many people still hold on to, despite widespread divorce and infidelity. Further, it has an objective reality afforded to it especially by religion. When religion enters the process of socially constructing institutions like marriage, they are given divine justification. Many Christians, evangelicals and Catholics in particular, argue that marriage was created by God for human beings, and our participation in it is a matter of faithful obedience to God. Baptist New Testament scholar Andreas Kostenberger sums up this view by saying that "God's ideal for marriage as articulated in Genesis 1–2 nonetheless continued to set the standards for the responsibilities and roles of husbands and wives toward each other in the subsequent history of humanity."[33] Leaving the critique of Kostenberger's biblical exegesis for others to carry out, what is important here is that his view relies on the idea that God revealed a model of marriage once and for all, recorded for us in Genesis 1–2. Similarly, Roman Catholic theologian Christopher West markets and popularizes John Paul II's theology of the body for Catholics, which promotes a gender ideology similar to Kostenberger's. However, instead of grounding it in Genesis, like Kostenberger, West connects it to Christ and the church itself: "the original union of man and woman in marriage—inasmuch as it points us to Christ's love for the Church—is the foundational way in which God reveals his plan of love to the world. If Christ's love for the Church is the summit of the mountain, we could say that God's original plan for marriage is the trail-head."[34] Both West and Kostenberger maintain a fixed understanding of the Bible, religion, and gender roles in marriage. These views would likely satisfy @benmordecai because they would not admit any socially constructed reality in our understanding of marriage or of religion itself.

@SC_Jones, @benmordecai, West, and Kostenberger all commit the same error: they see the Christian religion as fixed and immutable. This is why works like those from Rasmussen and Berger must be admitted to the conversation. They shift our focus to help us perceive that something more fundamental than the details of a theology of gender is at work. The very way in which we understand religion itself, and the Christian religion in particular, matters. If it is socially constructed, *semper reformanda*, then past mistakes can be named and corrected. If we are in fact all participants in the *trado*, the handing over that makes tradition, then we have a responsibility to handle it responsibly.

33. Kostenberger, *God, Marriage, and Family*, 38.
34. West, "Can One Be Catholic."

Then the question arises: Can an effective balance between the socially constructed, always-reforming idea of religion and its claims to revealed truth be struck? My response is affirmative. Such a balance starts by understanding the fact that even though something is socially constructed, it does not mean that it is not real, and in fact valuable and important. Social construction also need not stand in opposition to revelation. Revealed truths from God, however and whenever they happen, only do so in the milieu of human society. Thus, they have to be made sense of within that society, by flawed creatures who see only partial realities and perhaps barely glimpse transcendent mysteries. Roman Catholic feminist theologian Elizabeth Johnson describes how "the unfathomable mystery of God is always mediated through shifting historical discourse."[35] This does not mean that it (God) is not real; this does not preclude its power. It does acknowledge the inevitably flawed aspect that is human society and history. More specifically, on her topic of language about God, Johnson says that "words about God are cultural creatures, entwined with the mores and adventures of the faith community that uses them."[36] Seeing this should empower us toward naming "the unfathomable mystery" all the more by listening to more than one version of one person's experience of God at some point in ancient history.

Even the lauded twentieth-century Swiss pastor and theologian Karl Barth understood the distinction between revelation and religion, arguing that religion is the human attempt to reach God, which will always fail. He insisted that religion stems from unbelief, whereas revelation comes from God.[37] Though Barth's neo-orthodoxy does not dispose his theology toward social constructionism, his basic recognition that religion is a flawed something that humans do is an important point of resonance. Protestant and Catholic, contemporary and traditional, feminist and neo-orthodox Christians alike can appreciate the fact of religion's constructed nature. For people today who are interested in conversations about gender and Christianity, this can be a common ground on which to stand. It is ground that some will not want to inhabit, however, as there are many individuals disinterested in the conversation. Unfortunately, I suspect this includes my Twitter interlocutors around whose challenges I have framed this discussion.

35. Johnson, *She Who Is*, 6.
36. Ibid.
37. Barth, "Revelation of God."

Conclusion

For those of us committed to the intersections I outline and the result-
ing conversations that can happen in them, we begin by acknowledging
our very powerful role in interpreting texts, constructing institutions, and
shaping societies. From there, we have much to discuss and accomplish
around issues of gender and Christianity. I would like very much to see
@benmordecai and @SC_Jones taken seriously in whatever it is that we
decide to talk about, because their questions and suspicions remain alive
and well, though I doubt either will be convinced by my proposals here. In
fact, in January 2010, @SC_Jones responded to someone else's tweets by
describing her criticism of Christianity in this way:

> @SC_Jones: If we can't blame god "for what man has wrongfully
> chosen to do in his name", who the hell can we blame?

If we can see religion as something still under construction, then we can
and should in fact blame "man."

Additionally, I had a follow-up Twitter exchange with @benmordecai
in August 2010 (now newly married!) when he responded to one of my
many tweets on the summer's legal developments regarding gay marriage.

> @benmordecai: Why is it that you only talk about liberal politics
> and not Jesus' death on the cross for the sins of the world?

We did then have a brief conversation before he simply moved on to tweet
Bible verses hashtagged with #jesusquotes.[38] For me, discourse about
Christianity necessitates talking about life in this world, including the politics of race, gender, class, and sexuality. That is what a third-wave feminist
approach to these conversations entails. For @benmordecai, #jesusquotes
are apparently enough. For the rest of us, there is still work to be done:

> @benmordecai: Why not proclaim what Jesus did and said? Jesus
> said, "My kingdom is not of this world." #jesusquotes

> @feminismxianity: well that's great, I happen to love & live in
> this world, as did he; justice in it matters

---

38. Hashtags are "a community-driven convention for adding additional context
and metadata" to tweets. A hashtag is created by anyone just by adding the hash (#)
symbol in front of any word or phrase. It becomes a hyperlink to other things tweeted
with that tag. See http://twitter.pbworks.com/w/page/1779812/Hashtags.

Bibliography

Althaus-Reid, Marcella. *The Queer God*. New York: Routledge, 2003.

Associated Press. "Multiracial People Are Fastest Growing Group." May 28, 2009. Online: http://www.msnbc.msn.com/id/30986649.

Bantum, Brian. *Redeeming Mulatto: A Theology of Race and Christian Hybridity*. Waco, TX: Baylor, 2010.

Barth, Karl. "The Revelation of God as the Abolition of Religion." In *Christianity and Plurality: Classic and Contemporary Readings*, edited by Richard J. Plantinga, 225–42. Oxford: Blackwell, 1999.

Berger, Peter. *The Sacred Canopy: Elements of a Sociological Theory of Religion*. New York: Anchor, 1967.

Collins, Patricia Hill. *Black Feminist Thought: Knowledge, Consciousness, and the Politics of Empowerment*. New York: Routledge, 1991.

Goss, Robert. *Queering Christ: Beyond Jesus Acted Up*. Cleveland: Pilgrim, 2002.

Guy-Sheftall, Beverly, and Johnetta Betsch Cole, editors. *Who Should Be First?: Feminists Speak Out on the 2008 Presidential Campaign*. New York: SUNY Press, 2010.

Intersex Society of North America. "How Common Is Intersex?" Online: http://www.isna.org/faq/frequency.

Johnson, Elizabeth. *She Who Is: The Mystery of God in Feminist Discourse*. New York: Crossroad, 1992.

Kostenberger, Andreas. *God, Marriage, and Family: Rebuilding the Biblical Foundation*. Wheaton, IL: Crossway, 2004.

Lowe, Mary Elise. "Gay, Lesbian, and Queer Theologies: Origins, Contributions, and Challenges." *Dialog* 48/1 (Spring 2009) 49–61.

———. "Sin from a Queer, Lutheran Perspective." In *Transformative Lutheran Theologies: Feminist, Womanist, Mujerista Perspectives*, edited by Mary J. Streufert, 71–86. Minneapolis: Fortress, 2010.

Luther, Martin. "Lecture on Romans." In *Luther's Works*, edited by Jaroslav Pelikan, vol. 25. American ed. St. Louis: Concordia, 1959.

McLaughlin, Eleanor. "Feminist Christologies: Re-Dressing the Tradition." In *Reconstructing the Christ Symbol: Essays in Feminist Christology*, edited by Maryanne Stevens, 118–51. New York: Paulist, 1994.

Migliore, Daniel. *Faith Seeking Understanding: An Introduction to Christian Theology*. Grand Rapids: Eerdmans, 2004.

Rasmussen, Larry. "Yet Another Chance to Be Lutheran." *Journal of Lutheran Ethics*, July 2005, n.p. Online: http://www.elca.org/What-We-Believe/Social-Issues/Journal-of-Lutheran-Ethics/Issues/July-2005/Yet-Another-Chance-to-Be-Lutheran.aspx.

Riswold, Caryn. *Feminism and Christianity: Questions and Answers in the Third Wave*. Eugene, OR: Cascade, 2009.

Streufert, Mary J. "The Person of Christ from a Feminist Perspective: Human and Divine, Male and Female." In *Transformative Lutheran Theologies: Feminist, Womanist, Mujerista Perspectives*, edited by Mary J. Streufert, 135–49. Minneapolis: Fortress, 2010.

Transgender Law Center. Online: http://www.transgenderlawcenter.org.

Truth, Sojourner. "On Woman's Rights." As reported by Marcus Robinson. 1851. Online: http://www.sojournertruth.org/Library/Speeches/Default.htm.

Ward, Geoffrey C., and Ken Burns. *Not for Ourselves Alone: The Story of Elizabeth Cady Stanton and Susan B. Anthony*. New York: Knopf, 2001.

West, Christopher. "Can One Be Catholic and Support Same-Sex Marriage?" Online: http://www.christopherwest.com/page.asp?ContentID=139.

PART TWO

Gender, Race, and Society

5

In Defense of *The Bell Jar*

Exploring Vocation, Sexuality, and Gender

THERESA FITZPATRICK

IN RECENT DECADES, TELEVISION and film characters such as Kat Strat-
ford in *10 Things I Hate About You*, Mallory Knox in *Natural Born Kill-
ers*, Veronica in *Heathers*, Meg Griffin in *The Family Guy*, Lisa in *The
Simpsons*, and both *Gilmore Girls* have added to *The Bell Jar*'s reputation
as a "handbook" for angst-filled, white, middle-class, twentieth-century
teenage females.[1] In most of these instances, nothing is actually said
about the novel itself; its mere presence in the hands of these women—all
young and headstrong, some dark and troubled—gives the impression
that the book somehow contributes to female anger and depression. *The
Bell Jar*'s preponderance of pop culture images, "insofar as they are tied
to the question of who reads Plath's writing and why," Janet Badia argues,
"have been central to determining everything from the novel's literary
and cultural value, to Plath's status in the literary canon, to acceptable
modes of reading the story the novel tells."[2] Such stereotypes can easily be
used to deny the novel's continued relevance in the literature classroom.
Failing to acknowledge the sophistication of *The Bell Jar*'s readership—
one including but not limited to adolescent females—too easily dismisses

1. Badia, "*The Bell Jar* and Other Prose," 124.
2. Ibid., 126.

its value as a tool to ignite conversations about vocation, gender roles, sexual double standards, and identity in a college classroom.

As a teacher of a freshman-level, general education literature course, I know students often stumble into this required class already annoyed for having to take (and pay for) a course that "has nothing to do with their major." Students who like to read have often tested out of my course, and those who don't read aren't likely to be English-major types, excited about our semester-long journey into the heart of Shakespeare and other such impossible-to-understand, no-connection-to-my-life nonsense. They are a group who can smell perceived irrelevancy from miles away and are well prepared to handle the ensuing fifty-minute discussion armed with the welcome distractions of smart phone and e-reader. What they don't know, however, is that while their current concerns and struggles come in packages most adults can't even pronounce let alone recognize, none of them are actually new, which is why *The Bell Jar*, a bildungsroman set in the summer of 1953, can galvanize a meaningful conversation about being twentyish, fiercely sexual, and identity-obsessed in 2012.

Much of the novel's appeal and relevance stems from the fact that the most attention-grabbing of all topics—sexuality and vocation—are central to the experience of both Esther Greenwood (the novel's protagonist) and most every college-age student of any decade. In addition, the novel also allows for students' urgent wish to talk through where the personal and the intellectual intersect. It is this personal aspect of learning, according to Donna Freitas, that needs to find its way back into the classroom: "Much academic work, however esoteric, has practical relevance to the way we live our lives. Why restrict students from asking, alongside their professors, how relevant this intellectual material is to their lives?"[3] In her book *Sex and the Soul*, Freitas compiled information from online surveys and personal interviews, asking college students (on both secular and religious campuses) about sex, romance, religion, and spirituality on the contemporary college campus. Among her many conclusions stands the idea that the "thick wall between the classroom and everything else" is detrimental to students, intellectually and personally.[4] She argues that it is essential for the classroom to be expanded into a space where we discuss what were formerly considered "private matters." To provide students a place to explore their big questions within the context of an academic classroom is exactly what *The Bell Jar* helps to accomplish. In fact, the frank cynicism

3. Freitas, *Sex and the Soul*, 226.
4. Ibid., 224.

and self-absorption of Esther Greenwood resonate easily with college students, who, almost sixty years later, see their *real* selves in her interior monologue as opposed to an idealized version of how they *should* be.

Vocation

When the reader first meets Esther Greenwood, she is on the verge of her final year in college and in the midst of a life crisis. She discovers this while discussing future plans with her internship advisor (the powerful, female editor, Jay Cee), realizing that what she has always envisioned for her life might no longer be her desire: "What I always thought I had in mind was getting some big scholarship to graduate school or a grant to study all over Europe, and then I thought I'd be a professor and write books of poems or write books of poems and be an editor of some sort. Usually I had these plans on the tip of my tongue. 'I don't really know,' I heard myself say. I felt a deep shock, hearing myself say that, because the minute I said it, I knew it was true."[5]

Esther's recognition that she has no idea which direction she wants her life to go completely shatters her (as yet unchallenged) worldview and contributes to her downward spiral into a severe clinical depression. If her life's "calling" was no longer a fixed absolute, what else was variable? Security? Relationships? Social norms? Religious faith? Sharon Deloz Parks refers to these moments as "metaphorical shipwrecks," which may take the form of "the loss of a relationship, violence to one's property, collapse of a career venture, physical illness or injury, defeat of a cause, a fateful choice that irrevocably reorders one's life, betrayal by a community or government, or *the discovery that an intellectual construct is inadequate.*"[6] In Esther's case, her success as a student and young writer had always been the sure foundation for her future plans. When she began to question this foundation, everything else around her became subject to question as well—a "shipwreck" moment.

Similarly, for many college students the urgent mission to justify their education is a shipwreck moment. More than trying to "pick out" a career, they face the daunting task of mapping out their adult life before it has even begun and contend with the earth-shattering feeling that they don't know *what* they want. Asking college freshmen what they want

---

5. Plath, *The Bell Jar*, 32.
6. Deloz Parks, *Big Questions, Worthy Dreams*, 28. Emphasis added.

to be when they grow up often results in a collective blank stare. What might have been clear to them a year ago (that dream to be a teacher, police officer, lawyer, or journalist) is likely to be challenged as they see all the options that are available. Often their college major does not even dictate a specific career path (a major in psychology, for example, could take one in any number of directions). Therefore, college students should instead focus on "vocation," or to use a more spiritually charged term, "calling." Deloz Parks understands these terms to mean something well beyond one's job or career. She writes, "It is a relational sensibility in which I recognize that what I do with my time, talents, and treasure is most meaningfully conceived not as a matter of mere personal passion and preference but in relationship to the whole of life."[7] Rather than asking students simply, "What do you want to be when you grow up?" she has in mind questions such as, "Who are you now and who would you like to become?" and, "What impact do you want to make on the world?"

Such questions arise naturally sparked by the subject material of the novel, particularly when Esther famously describes her paralysis of choice using the image of a fig tree from whose branches dangle life's options:

> One fig was a future husband and a happy home with children, and another fig was a famous poet and another fig was a brilliant professor, and another fig was Ee Gee, the amazing editor, and another fig was Europe and Africa and South America, and another was Constantine and Socrates and Attila and a pack of other lovers with queer names and offbeat professions, and another fig was an Olympic lady crew champion, and beyond and above these figs were many more figs I couldn't quite make out.[8]

Knowing that she can only choose one, Esther hesitates, and the longer she does so, the more figs shrivel up and fall from the tree. Most scholars focus either on the exceptionality of her choice crisis, considering the historical setting of the novel (she is both socially and educationally privileged), or her belief that she can only choose one path, considering the gendered societal constrictions of 1950s America: "the problem is not that she lacks choices or even that none of the options appeal to her; the problem lies in her desire to have what society tells her is impossible"—two (seemingly) mutually exclusive things.[9] While contemporary

7. Ibid., 148.
8. Plath, *The Bell Jar*, 77.
9. Badia, "*The Bell Jar* and Other Prose," 133.

students are not limited by what society tells them they can or cannot do (notice below that students of *both* genders express this same concern), they read this excerpt as an affirmation of the struggle to define their vocation in the midst of an unending list of choices. At the same time, they feel strongly the perceived need to master one skill quickly in order to compete in today's dizzying job market. Like Esther, they are both privileged and burdened with many options, not necessarily because of economic status, gender, or intellectual capacity, but because of the time and place in which they live.

Freitas observes that today's student "has a myriad of thinkers, models, traditions, and cultural possibilities at her fingertips and can choose any one that feels right at the moment—even if no one else chooses it. All these options, all this freedom, simply add to the confusion for many college students."[10] As one of my students confessed during an online discussion of this passage from *The Bell Jar*, "this is totally me, friends call me Jill of all Trades. It is a plague more often than not . . . :)." The smiley face icon downplayed the seriousness of this statement where she refers negatively to her experience. The following exchange occurred during the same chat session:

> Student A (male)>> College is a nervous time for anyone at that point.
>
> Student B (female)>> You cannot run through all the possible paths you might want.
>
> Student C (male)>> Yup you pick one and become really good at it or you won't get a job.
>
> Student D (male)>> I feel like that was the case with me in [high school].
>
> Student E (male)>> Yea so I went with what I was best at and enjoyed.
>
> Student F (female)>> But what if I never found out what I liked because I had to spend all my time on one thing? I had and have regrets about the choices I made til this day.

Students C and F share the common concern with "Jill of All Trades," the need to master one and only one skill and forsake any other interests in order to be successful in a highly competitive world. For both Esther and

10. Freitas, *Sex and the Soul*, 70.

these students, an added stress to the already expensive search for a vocation is the feeling that they must choose a career soon, they must love it, and they must learn (quickly) to excel at it.

Sexual "Purity"

Esther's vocational shipwreck in Jay Cee's office triggers another series of difficult realizations concerning sex, "purity," and double standards. All of Plath's obsessive purity language at the beginning of the novel, simultaneous with Esther's vocational questions, cannot be accidental. Her descent into depression, confusion, self-doubt, and attempted suicide begins exactly when her certainty about her life goals and moral code become shaken or questioned—a position familiar to the average student in my classroom. Esther admits, "When I was nineteen, purity was a great issue," and she *does* obsess over it.[11] To her, both symbolic and sexual purity represent a comfortable place to withdraw when such questioning becomes difficult to handle, explain, and accept. For example, while in New York City, after observing her blonde bombshell friend Doreen on a particularly wild night out of drinking and sex, Esther returns home and takes a long, hot, cleansing bath. Using religious imagery, she explains the purifying effect of the hot water: "I don't believe in baptism or the waters of the Jordan or anything like that, but I guess I feel about a hot bath the way those religious people feel about holy water. . . . The longer I lay there in the clear hot water the purer I felt, and when I stepped out at last and wrapped myself in one of the big, soft white hotel bath towels I felt pure and sweet as a new baby."[12]

Her purification ritual resets both her brain and sense of identity. In response to Doreen's party-girl behavior—a direct challenge to her purity "reset" button—Esther recedes back to her earlier self, invoking her decision to be more like her "pure" friend, Betsy. "I made a decision about Doreen that night. I decided I would watch her and listen to what she said, but deep down I would have nothing at all to do with her. Deep down, I would be loyal to Betsy and her innocent friends. It was Betsy I resembled at heart."[13] Esther's purified self chooses the innocent farm girl

---

11. Plath, *The Bell Jar*, 82.

12. Ibid., 20.

13. Ibid., 22.

over the party girl, thus resembling the comfort of home life rather than the corrupt big city.

One might assume that modern college students would not relate to Esther's somewhat prudish reaction, but this is not necessarily the case. Many vocalize sympathy for Esther, seeing the excesses of her friend and wanting nothing to do with them. This response concurs with Freitas's findings among American college students' attitudes toward modern sexual ("hook-up") culture. She claims that "most students distance themselves from what they regard as an overly casual attitude toward sex" and "indicate dissatisfaction about campus culture when it comes to peer attitudes about dating, hooking up, and sex."[14] Similarly, Esther's purifying hot bath provides separation from Doreen's behavior and signals her firm decision not to aspire to be like her promiscuous friend.

While Esther is often unable (or, according to Badia, "unwilling") to make crucial life decisions, her symbolic purification brings her renewed assurance, and she can once again control her surroundings.[15] Her specific views on sexual purity, however, are more complex. As a 1950s-era female, she was inundated with literature like the *Reader's Digest* article her mother gave her, "In Defense of Chastity." Written by "a married woman lawyer with children," the article warned women to remain pure for a future husband who would want to be the more sexually experienced partner. By giving into a man's advances before marriage, a woman risks losing his respect and, even worse, pregnancy out of wedlock.[16] However, Esther's ability to accept the purity ideal is challenged by her next shipwreck moment, when she learns that her current boyfriend, Buddy Willard, is not a virgin. As Esther grapples with this knowledge, she realizes "that she is subject to societal double standards" that allow Buddy to "construct his own sexual identity while she cannot."[17]

> Actually, it wasn't the idea of Buddy sleeping with somebody that bothered me. I mean I'd read about all sorts of people sleeping with each other, and if it had been any other boy I would merely have asked him the most interesting details, and maybe gone out and slept with somebody myself just to even things up, and then thought no more about it.

14. Freitas, *Sex and the Soul*, 156, 158.
15. Badia, "*The Bell Jar* and Other Prose," 132.
16. Plath, *The Bell Jar*, 81.
17. Badia, "*The Bell Jar* and Other Prose," 134.

> What I couldn't stand was Buddy's pretending I was so sexy
> and he was so pure, when all the time he'd been having an affair
> with that tarty waitress and must have felt like laughing in my
> face.[18]

Plath's manner of framing this double standard sparks a variety of responses in my students. Generally, they contend at first that this is a dated perspective, using phrases like "back then," "in the old days," or "not a problem anymore," implying that sexual double standards no longer exist. Yet, as we delve deeper into the discussion, they frequently contradict themselves, as evident in this student's discussion board posting: "It's funny how in some places in the world women are still just around to satisfy men sexually. When I was reading the part about the college boys I kept thinking to myself, this reminds me of high school, or even fraternity boys that I have met. Life hasn't changed much, in that sense." In the first sentence, she uses the phrase "in some places in the world"—placing the conflict far away—but soon after, she comes to the conclusion, "Life hasn't changed much."

In reality, life *has* changed—quite a bit. Laura Sessions Stepp, in her 2007 book *Unhooked*, presents recent studies showing that teenage females now equal their male counterparts not only in the onset of sexual activity, but also in reported incidents of one-night stands and unromantic sexual relationships. Stepp comments that young women often feel empowered by the unattached, seemingly "dateless" freedom of the hook-up culture and are more likely to engage in random sexual activity than ever before. In light of these statistics, the tables of sexuality seem to have turned dramatically. However, according to Stepp, it is the young men who reap the most benefits from this shift. Not only do they enjoy "more immediate access to sex without having to work for it," but also, as one college senior quipped, "Because girls are more assertive, it's easy for us to be assholes."[19]

While modern young females might relish more sexual freedom, another one of my students completely disagreed that gendered standards of purity have changed:

> The subject of women being seen as whores if they have sex
> before marriage is very relevant today. The thought of a woman
> having sex without being married isn't as shunned upon as it

18. Plath, *The Bell Jar*, 71.
19. Stepp, *Unhooked*, 38.

was in the 1950s but it's definitely not something that impresses men. Not to say a woman who has sex before being married means you're a whore, because I'm pretty sure the women who have sex before marriage outweigh the women who save themselves for marriage. What I am saying is, if a woman is still a virgin when she's married it's very much so considered an accomplishment. This comes from the view that women should be pure and innocent. Untouched and waiting for her only one man to take her virginity.

The confusion represented by this student's words cannot be overlooked. Just as Esther vacillates between valuing and disregarding sexual purity, this (female) student both recognizes the hold it has over young women today ("having sex without being married . . . definitely not something that impresses men," "if a woman is still a virgin when she's married it's very much so considered an accomplishment"), and identifies its implausibility ("I'm pretty sure the women who have sex before marriage outweigh the women who save themselves for marriage").

After Esther learns of Buddy's sexual experience, she seeks the advice of older females in her dorm to determine if she is overreacting. Their dismissive attitude transforms Esther's initial shock into melancholy. If the double standard remains unquestioned, then there is no hope for her to be anything other than, using Mrs. Willard's definition of a wife, "the place the arrow shoots off from": "Back at college I started asking a senior here and a senior there what they would do if a boy they knew suddenly told them he'd slept thirty times with a slutty waitress one summer, smack in the middle of knowing them. But these seniors said most boys were like that and you couldn't honestly accuse them of anything until you were at least pinned or engaged to be married."[20]

Freitas encountered a version of this double standard during one of her interviews at a secular college when she learned about the "yes girls." Though she never met a self-confessed "yes girl," she ascertained that they were a pack of females who would allegedly do anything (sexually) with any male. While evidence supporting this gossip was slim to none, Freitas uncovered the underlying inequality in how males and females are viewed on campuses in terms of sexual experience:

> Although the yes girls were famous, I never met anyone who was friends with a yes girl, or who simply hung out with one on occasion. Neither did I speak with anyone who had any firsthand

20. Plath, *The Bell Jar*, 71.

proof that these girls were as "slutty" as everyone made them out to be. That didn't stop anyone from sticking a derogatory label onto them and gossiping about what they supposedly do, and with whom. Sexually active heterosexual men are exempt from this scrutiny.[21]

Freitas as well as Plath both beg the essential question: why are women still judged harshly for the same behavior for which men are praised? And, perhaps more importantly, why do we as a society put up with it?

When I ask my students about this obvious double standard, I receive a mixed response. While they agree that the overarching concept is still very true—judgment falls more harshly on women for "sleeping around" than men—men are not necessarily off the hook. One of my more talkative male students commented, "Ok, yeah. There is a double standard, but still . . . being a man-whore is *not* a good thing. Really. It's not something we all aspire to be. Girls think those guys are gross." Freitas's research takes this comment one step further by showing that the majority of male students she interviewed "complained that expectations to display masculinity through multiple sexual conquests—to be 'players'—were cramping their ability to develop a romantic relationship with just one woman."[22] Another study cited by Stepp finds that young women between the ages of eighteen to twenty-four actually feel less pressure to have sex than their male counterparts.[23] Although at first my students claim that the sexual double standard is "no longer a problem," extraditing it to the distant realm of the 1950s, through class discussion of the novel and their personal experience, they eventually discern its impact on their view of sexuality.

Gender Roles

Esther's anger at Buddy produces a liberative effect in that she no longer feels bound to the cultural ideal of female purity; in other words, she contends that she should be free to express her sexuality: "Finally I decided that if it was so difficult to find a red-blooded intelligent man who was still pure by the time he was twenty-one I might as well forget about

21. Freitas, *Sex and the Soul*, 143.
22. Ibid., 101–2.
23. Stepp, *Unhooked*, 37.

staying pure myself and marry somebody who wasn't pure either."[24] Her anger also leads her to further question how marital happiness could possibly exist in such an unequal world: "Then when he started to make my life miserable I could make his miserable as well." This comment further proves Esther's belief that, as in the fig tree image, her wish to be more than one "fig," so to speak, will be mitigated by the housewife standard. Similarly in Buddy's mind, Esther's vocation as well as her sexuality is limited to just one fig, the one devoted to marriage and family. Buddy upholds this belief when he, while laughing, assures her that the desire to become a poet will disappear once she has children.[25] He, on the other hand, has no concerns about being both a physician and a father because there is nothing "mutually exclusive" about these roles.

In one particularly interesting discussion board posting on this topic, a student used the double standard as a transition into a discussion of marriage and gender roles—something that was *not* present in my initial question to the class:

> I agree completely with that "double standard" about how men and women are viewed about not having sex before marriage. I have also experienced first-hand about the husband and wife roles in the family. In both my sets of grandparents, my Grampas were the ones who provided for the family (one was a chemist and the other was a dairy farmer). One of my Grammas had a job as a bank teller, but she stopped working once she had kids. As far as I know, my other Gramma never had a job outside the home until most of the kids were out of the house, and then only part time. Now, my Dad has always been the one going to work to provide for our family. For about eleven years, my Mom had a job, but her job was a daycare that she ran from our house, so even what she did for a living still involved taking care of children all day. As for me, once I start having kids, I have no intention of working.

Her sincere response led me to believe that Esther's frustrations are entirely lost on this student. Earlier in her posting, she agreed that, as far as "sex before marriage" is concerned, the double standard is alive and well—men can, women shouldn't—but that is where the problem ends. The roles set in motion generations before work well, and she intends to continue them without question. Rather than any confusion over

24. Plath, *The Bell Jar*, 81–82.
25. Ibid., 93.

sexuality *or* vocation, this student unquestioningly accepts the traditional example. What she failed to do in her answer, however, was externalize the sexual double standard in order to perceive the way in which her *un*questioning of the status quo contributes to its perpetuation, and none of her classmates challenged her to do so.

While Esther's depression, suicide attempt, and subsequent stay in a mental institution cause Buddy to comment, "I wonder who will marry you now, Esther,"[26] his vulnerability and physical weakness call into question his ability to uphold his place as the strong, virile adult male. When Buddy first learns that he has tuberculosis and calls Esther at school, she "had never heard him so upset."[27] Taking after his father, he adopts the idea that anything but robust health is "psychosomatic" and due to a weak will. By admitting he needs treatment for a debilitating illness, he either challenges his understanding of male strength or views himself as a failure, both of which create a shipwreck parallel to Esther's. His conundrum is not easily solved. As one student in my class observed, Buddy seems "deflated" at the end of the book when he must step aside due to his fragile lungs and allow Esther to dig his car out of the snow, a job he clearly views as his. Recognizing that Buddy is also a victim of gendered stereotypes, that he feels the need to be the strong, experienced male with all the answers, helps to engage male students in the conversation in more than just a defensive stance.

Nevertheless, raw feelings do surface when discussing Plath's message about the male gender, like the following exchange in a chat conversation where one male student in particular read her position as hostile to men:

FitzPatrick>> Is there a message there about gender roles?

Student A>> Yes.

Student B>> Absolutely.

Student C>> Yeah.

FitzPatrick> >Go for it.

Student D>> Yes.

Student E>> Yes.

Student A>> That guys are supposed to be superior.

26. Ibid., 241.
27. Ibid., 73.

Student D>> They are bad.

As indicated by Student D's response, many of my male students feel like they become the object of anger when issues of inequality or gendered double standards enter the conversation.[28] Of course, the pop culture images referenced in the introduction help to plant such an idea in the collective mind, but that is only half of the story. For example, the passage concerning Esther's reaction to Buddy's sexual experience produces some interesting responses on his behalf: "What is he supposed to do?" asked one of my (male) students. "He obviously feels the pressure to be the experienced one in the relationship. If he had approached Esther as the one who was clueless about sex, it would have turned everything upside down. He would have been humiliated, you know? Back then, he was supposed to be the one who knew about the world . . . to teach her."

A close examination of Buddy Willard's character before and after his time in the tuberculosis sanatorium brings to light that he is also deeply affected by social pressure to be "the man." Before he goes away, he and Esther are expected to marry. He responds to Esther's desires to live in both the city and the country and to be both a poet and a mother (seemingly "mutually exclusive things") by saying that she "has the perfect set up of a true neurotic."[29] He also calls poetry, what Esther loves to write, "a piece of dust" and boasts of his perfect health and future medical career.[30] In light of these representations of arrogance and ignorance, Student D's response above is quite appropriate as Plath seems to give Buddy no redeeming qualities. However, after his return and Esther's mental breakdown, they both realize that marriage is no longer what they want. Buddy reluctantly allows Esther to dig his car out of the snow, which inspires nothing but "great, amiable boredom" in Esther, and he also worries that he was responsible for driving two of his former girlfriends "crazy."[31] His idea of the man's role is challenged by his own illness and the feeling that he caused *their* illnesses. Therefore, in his own shipwreck moment, he becomes unsettled and worried about his place, like Esther when she discussed her

---

28. Badia presents this same classroom conflict in her article "The 'Priestess' and Her 'Cult.'" When encountered with such statements as "Plath was a feminazi," she tries "to resist the temptation to correct their views on Plath and urge them instead to consider why they are so invested in seeing her in a particular way." Badia, "The 'Priestess' and Her 'Cult,'" 169.

29. Plath, *The Bell Jar*, 93.

30. Ibid., 56.

31. Ibid., 239.

vocation with Jay Cee. Even though the romantic spark has long since disappeared between them, Buddy becomes more tender toward Esther because he "gets it" now.

After the "guys are bad" remark, I asked my students to reflect further on these passages, and their comments, including some personal reflections, demonstrate a shift in perspective:

Student A>> I think that Plath is just as sympathetic to Buddy as she is to Esther.

Student B>> Really?

Student A>> But sympathy doesn't seem to help him at all.

Student C>> *

Student D>> I think he is a very sad character in the end.

Student D>> Kind of—deflated?

Student B>> I agree with that.

Student C>> While she is growing in strength.

Student B>> But in the beginning he's "so amazing."

Student E>> I agree.

Student A>> It's because of the standards he is told he must uphold.

Student D>> I totally get this—guys are still the ones who are supposed to have everything figured out. It's kinda stressful.

FitzPatrick>> There are more victims than just "Esther"

FitzPatrick>> or just "women."

Student C>> *

Student B>> :)

FitzPatrick>> It's an entire way of thinking that Plath is combatting.

Student D>> And we *still* haven't figured this all out???

As made clear by this chat segment, Student D's earlier frustration with Plath's male bashing morphed into a frustrated realization that our culture still encourages harmful gendered stereotypes for both men *and* women. Both genders encounter shipwrecks as they maneuver through a myriad of choices, both seek to find a clear vocation, both must reconcile their understanding of gender roles, sexuality, and relationships, and both encounter enormous obstacles and frustrations along the way.

Conclusion: Connecting the Personal and the Intellectual

Despite its dated language and context ("What the heck is *shorthand*????" asks at least one student every semester) and its reputation as a book for dark-and-angry young females, *The Bell Jar*'s relevance for addressing issues of vocation, sexuality, and gender has not disappeared. However, exploring this relevance requires courage from the professor to allow personal stories into the classroom, thus enabling students to make connections with their own fears and aspirations. This does not turn the classroom into a "therapy session" (as one of my colleagues feared); rather, it deepens their personal experience of character, narrative voice, theme, motif, and symbolism. In turn, students must also be courageous in their willingness to share their stories. Admittedly, this happens more easily in an online course, thus the reason for many of the above quotations coming from online chat sessions. The facelessness of online discourse opens the door for them to take more risks, especially when it is *required* that each of them "speak" twice per chat period. When they are freed from being stared at or challenged face-to-face by another student, they are more willing both to posit ideas and admit when another student has convinced them of something new. This same result can be achieved through extensive journaling, though the prompts must be thought provoking enough to probe beyond easy answers ("How do you feel about Esther's reaction?" will do absolutely nothing, while, "How is Esther's reaction to Buddy similar to her reaction to Jay Cee?" yields interesting results). Students should also be encouraged to contribute their journal responses in the classroom, perhaps chosen by the instructor and shared anonymously so that all may respond to the idea.

While Esther's vocational and sexual struggles in particular help students connect the intellectual (what keeps the discussion focused and challenging) to the personal (what makes the discussion real and relevant), once the connections are made, it is important to acknowledge that her series of shipwreck moments eventually lead her to shore. Further, the suffering that results from such moments is not—for Plath, for Deloz

Parks, or for our students—the main conclusion. Beyond the questioning, there is self-discovery and "transformation. We discover a new reality beyond the loss."[32] Though we are not privy to the outcome of her hospital evaluation, Plath leaves her readers with Esther's encounter with the asylum's board of directors, which provides a more intimate look into her thoughts as she chooses strength and self-meaning rather than depression and suicide. "I took a deep breath and listened to the old brag of my heart: 'I am, I am, I am.'"[33] In conclusion, by using Plath to tear down the "thick wall between the classroom and everything else,"[34] students in can connect what they study (the intellectual) with the motivation behind their life choices (the personal).

Bibliography

Badia, Janet. "*The Bell Jar* and Other Prose." In *The Cambridge Companion to Sylvia Plath*, edited by Jo Gill, 124–38. New York: Cambridge University Press, 2006.
———. "The 'Priestess' and Her 'Cult': Plath's Confessional Poetics and the Mythology of Women Readers." In *The Unraveling Archive: Essays on Sylvia Plath*, edited by Anita Helle, 159–81. Ann Arbor: University of Michigan Press, 2007.
Deloz Parks, Sharon. *Big Questions, Worthy Dreams: Mentoring Young Adults in Their Search for Meaning, Purpose, and Faith.* San Francisco: Jossey-Bass, 2000.
Freitas, Donna. *Sex and the Soul: Juggling Sexuality, Spirituality, Romance, and Religion on America's College Campuses.* New York: Oxford University Press, 2008.
Plath, Sylvia. *The Bell Jar.* New York: Harper Perennial, 2005.
Stepp, Laura Sessions. *Unhooked: How Young Women Pursue Sex, Delay Love and Lose at Both.* New York: Riverhead, 2007.

32. Deloz Parks, *Big Questions, Worthy Dreams*, 29.
33. Plath, *The Bell Jar*, 243.
34. Freitas, *Sex and the Soul*, 224.

6

Multiplying Masculinities

An Overview of Contemporary Theories of Masculinity

DAVID G. ALLEN

ACROSS THE GLOBE, UNATTAINABLE visions of masculinity maim our sons, brothers, fathers, and partners.[1] In Western nations, for example, males graduate from high schools less often than their female counterparts.[2] At the same time, masculinity prompts violence against our sisters, daughters, mothers, and partners—within intimate relationships as well as in the contexts of crime and militarization.[3] Contemporary masculinity studies endeavor to understand these patterns and to develop alternative ways to consider what it means to "be a man."

In this chapter, I provide an overview of these contemporary perspectives on masculinity. Because the body of literature is large, complicated, even contradictory, my goal is to navigate you in this field, to suggest themes and directions to which you can pay attention. Overall, I focus on work that concerns itself with the trends in my opening paragraph: analyses that support an imagined future of increased equality, health, and non-violence.

1. Barker, *Dying to Be Men*; Nayak and Kehily, *Gender, Youth and Culture*.
2. Epstein et al., *Failing Boys?*; Kimmel, *Guyland*.
3. Katz, *Macho Paradox*.

Although it may seem odd that masculinity studies is the progeny of feminism and women's studies, historically this development makes a lot of sense. As Hegel noted, people who suffer oppression need to understand the world of the oppressors much better than the reverse. Since, in most social systems, men—or as I will argue a bit later, "the masculine"—occupy positions of dominance and unearned privilege in comparison to women (or "the feminine"), the study of how gender has shaped social opportunities has fallen largely to women. In a similar way, people of color have had the burden of analyzing how racial and ethnic systems have disadvantaged them. In recent decades, however, a broad range of largely male academics and activists have drawn on feminist legacies to generate the field of masculinity studies.[4]

Because our culture tends to understand masculinity as determined by biology, as "natural," the language of masculinity studies can seem convoluted and cumbersome. My opening sentence is deliberately challenging: we think of boys and men injuring and killing themselves and others—that this is a (perhaps unfortunate) consequence of being biologically male. The perspective I'm taking here—a fairly mainstream one within masculinity studies—argues that trying to live up to socially constructed images of masculinity is damaging and destructive to boys and girls, to men and women. This is not an anti-male orientation (I am one, after all), but a call for deeper understanding and better alternative approaches to being a "real man." It is not our genes or chromosomes or hormones or penis that cause this destruction; it is trying to live up to inherited, social ideas about masculinity.

Theorizing Masculinity

Masculinity is an *interpretive judgment*, not an inherent quality based upon physiology. *Masculinity* is a *social construction*, not a physical characteristic based upon anatomy. In fact, *gender* is a cultural *construction*, not an aspect of being human that is based upon biology. What we and others "see" as masculine—or feminine—varies across time and location. To be seen as masculine or feminine requires a lot of work, labor that begins very early on in life and is continually renewed. *Real* boys become football players. *Real* girls become cheerleaders. Unfortunately,

4. Kegan, *Masculinity Studies and Feminist Theory*; Schacht and Ewing, *Feminism and Men*.

the boundaries of successful masculinity have become increasingly restrictive. There is a sort of sadness about how small a box people who want to be masculine must fit into. We also know from daily conversation that masculinity is not "owned" by male bodies; people who are socially identified as women can be seen as, or have some of their behavior interpreted as, masculine. *Real* girls can now be great soccer players, for instance. And the emergence of queer and transgender analyses have further undermined the stability and consistency of gender interpretations—making it clearer that genders are fluid and not always obviously aligned with body types. I am gradually, and very unevenly, trying to train myself out of assuming I can read the gender of my students off their bodies and instead to ask them what pronoun they prefer I use.

If masculinity is an interpretive judgment, of what is it a judgment? In most cases, it is advisable to think of masculinity as an assessment of *performance*.[5] We "do" rather than "are" masculine: real men don't eat quiche or hold each other's hands. Much of the labor of youth is learning how to "do" masculinity—and to suffer the misfortune of getting it wrong.[6] Or more accurately, we learn how to behave in ways that one's significant others, who change over time, "see" one as sufficiently masculine. Clearly I am taking a fairly extreme social constructionist perspective here, and I will address some of the limits and puzzles that perspective creates for me below. Yet overall, we *become* gendered (and raced and classed) individuals over time; depending upon where and when we do it—do gender, do masculinity, do femininity—our performances vary. This becomes crystal clear to me when I move from a university setting into prisons, where I do research. I am often interpreted as "gay"—meaning not sufficiently masculine—by prisoners, while in the context of my position in women's studies I am seen by some in academic circles as excessively masculine and overly heterosexual.

This variability in interpretation points to a fundamental theme in masculinity studies and feminism: gender and sex are distinct categories. One's gender is usually organized around one's biological sex—and we tend to link masculinity to certain physiological traits—but the relationship is highly variable. Since I am most interested in social justice, in imagining and working for a world that is less violent and more fair, even more loving, it is more useful, in my opinion, to focus on what is

5. Watson and Shaw, *Performing American Masculinities*.
6. Pascoe, *Dude, You're a Fag*.

changeable. And the data, including neurobiological data, suggest a great deal of what we see as "naturally" masculine is changeable and malleable.

Now that I have defined gender over against sex and masculinity over against maleness, let me mention a few caveats about my position. Any performance, gendered or not, requires certain bodily capacities. So I do not mean to suggest that "anything is possible." I do not think anyone could have gotten a very successful athletic performance out of me, but I do believe my older sister could have been an awesome jock if Title IX had existed earlier. To the extent that we link interpretations of "masculinity" to particular physical performances (or skin colors), not everyone can achieve them. And in most of our daily lives, we are comfortably complicit with a binary gender assignment that we believe can be read off someone's body. When I encounter an individual with broad shoulders, narrow hips, and a deep voice, I automatically assign a male pronoun. Masculinity "coheres" around some bodies more easily than others. Men of Asian descent, with smaller stature and less facial hair, are often stereotyped as feminine.

Trans-sexuality is a second caveat—a metaphysical puzzle, actually. There are powerful narratives of people who knew at a young age that their bodies and their genders were not aligned. Boys wanted to do "girl things," like playing with dolls, and resisted others' efforts to "correct" them. People report having this awareness that they are not the gender their families want them to be very early, as school-age children if not before. Often this misalignment and the pressures to deny or reverse it are the source of much misery, suffering, and even suicide. How does a social constructionist like me explain this without dishonoring those narratives? How can it be that a ten-year-old has somehow been socialized into a gender identity that belies his/her body? I don't know. So I sit with it, learn from the trans-sexual community, and still find the goal of gender justice better served by a social perspective than any other I know of at the moment.

Looking across the last thirty years or so, we can discern surprising consistency about what a "real man" is. Compare, for example, the following summaries, from 1974 and 2008, respectively:

> The male machine is a special kind of being, different from women, children, and men who don't measure up. He is functional, designed mainly for work. He is programmed to tackle jobs, override obstacles, attack problems, overcome difficulties, and always seize the offensive. He will take on any task that can

be presented to him in a competitive framework, and his most important positive reinforcement is victory.[7]

More recently, a leading scholar of masculinity described the dominant model with these catchphrases:

- Boys don't cry
- It's better to be mad than sad
- Don't get mad, get even
- Take it like a man
- He who has the most toys when he dies, wins
- Just do it (Ride or die)
- Size matters
- I don't stop to ask for directions
- Nice guys finish last
- It's all good[8]

Notice that these overviews summarize *performances*—someone has to behave in certain ways to meet most of these criteria. Ask yourself whether Jesus would have qualified as masculine in light of these criteria. Where are love, mercy, tenderness, generosity? Where is the performance of cheek turning? Of night-long prayer? Of sitting quietly and listening to women?

Another problem with this list of criteria is that it disqualifies men who are allegedly emasculated by consequences beyond their control—in particular, economic success. As I write this, in the midst of a major economic recession, almost a fifth of Americans live in poverty; 10 percent are "actively" unemployed and even more are either chronically underemployed or have abandoned searching. In these conditions, men who tie their masculinity to performances such as earning money, as being a breadwinner, discover that their identity *as men* is at risk because of their economic lack of well-being.

I began with these descriptions of masculinity because the approach I am taking treats "masculinity" *as representation* rather than an inherent trait. Any particular behavior is masculine only if it is interpreted as such. As a young man living in Colorado, my long hair was often

7 Fasteau, *Male Machine*, 21.
8. Kimmel, *Guyland*.

unfavorably contrasted to the crew cuts favored by athletes. It was not masculine enough. Now, jocks often have hair longer than mine was in the 1970s and gay men are favoring shorter hair. Masculinity is a set of social representations that are mutually dependent upon other sets, in particular, of course, representations of femininity but also of sexuality, family, rationality, and a host of others.[9] These representations are not neutral accounts; they are social performances. That may be an awkward way to put it, I know. But the view I hold is that when one is using language (representations), one is *doing* something, participating in social arrangements, in power. "He's a real man" is a compliment, linked to social and political prestige.

Masculinity studies pose another set of questions about these visions of masculinity: *Whose* descriptions are these? Where do they come from? At whom are they directed? Why do they exist at all? What purposes do they serve? Much of the contemporary literature on masculinity addresses these very questions and the consequences of answering them in particular ways:

- How did we get here? How did this form of masculinity emerge historically?

- How do we learn it? What are the social processes that teach us what it is to be masculine?

- Who is "we"—that is, which social groups tend to fit this model?

- What are the consequences? What are the social, interpersonal and individual results of adhering to this model or resisting it?

- What are some alternatives?

A key virtue of these questions is creating distance, the space to question, to reflect. Most of us fall into a gender category without much thought. Of course, we struggle to do masculinity in the best way we can, to meet expectations we hold of ourselves and others ask of us. But the origin and consequences of "doing" masculinity that way rarely come up. I firmly believe we have more freedom and more life possibilities if we pause to ask them and discuss the answers with others. Even if we return to embrace our current perspective, we do so with greater understanding and, perhaps, greater kindness.

9. Murphy, *Studs, Tools, and Family Jewels.*

Masculinity and Identity

The utility of these questions can be illustrated by turning to the notion of 'identity.' One's identity is basically a story one tells about oneself, about the kind of person one is, one's preferences, tendencies, aspirations. So if "masculinity" is an important part of my identity, if the stories I tell about myself (to myself and to others) involve taking up a certain definition of masculinity, then I will endeavor to *perform* in ways that are consistent with that definition. Usually we have variations to choose from. My father was unusual in giving me very few messages about masculinity; the main ones were "Don't hit your sisters" and "Play sports." He was gentle and quiet, and he never encouraged aggression. Still, for years I tried to live up to media and peer influences by performing "risk taking" (climbing mountains, driving fast) or "emotional distance" (never acknowledging or revealing emotions, avoiding any display of vulnerability) only to find that these performances were in conflict with others (e.g., a fragile body, a preference for intimacy). And I received prodigious feedback about how others read my efforts. As chair of a women's studies department, and as a nurse, I am still getting feedback! When I worked in hospitals, I was often asked if I was a "male nurse." My usual reply was, "Last time I looked." My women colleagues were not asked if they were "female nurses"—precisely because *performing as a nurse* is read as feminine and thus more "naturally" aligned with their bodies than mine.

Our histories are complex and contradictory; we have available many ways of thinking about social life and our places in it. The first challenge is *finding* these alternatives; the second is trying to figure out what sorts of lives they enable and what options they constrain. If I performed masculinity in women's studies in the ways I did when working in construction in Colorado, my colleagues would be extremely wary of me. For those of us worried about male children, masculinity studies has a lot to offer.

Representations of masculinity are not democratically produced or individually created. In modern social life, they are largely produced and circulated through institutions. Two institutions that I'll pay particular attention to are education and media. They are the source of the most readily available, widely circulated representations of masculinity. Historically, religion was a major force, and for some communities still is. Evangelical Christian pastors often speak about the lessons of Christianity for masculinity. Most boys spend far more time with media such as video games and popular music than listening to sermons, so my examples will draw heavily from media studies.

The people who control media institutions (Disney, for example) are neither demographically nor politically "representative" of Americans.[10] They generally come from privileged backgrounds and are white—as are the members of the U.S. Senate, for example. Intentionally or not, the representations they (re)produce carry the marks—the values, preferences, worldviews—of their creators. A question masculinity studies encourages us to ask is, "Whose world are we producing when we take up any particular representation as 'our own'?" When boys and men consume and rehearse the forms of masculinity circulated in video games or television or pornography (which on average we spend six to nine hours a day doing), what social world are we endorsing?[11] These are not simple questions, or even singular ones. The executives of Disney are not the same people as the executives of the major pornography producers/distributers or fashion magazines.[12] But the analytic advantage of masculinity studies lies in making these questions more answerable and reminding us that none of us can step outside of these cultural institutions.

Hopefully, these brief examples convey the sense of why I find this focus on representation so fruitful. It doesn't deny or minimize the social prevalence or impact of dominant masculinity; rather, it makes that masculinity more *visible* and allows us more analytic space to explore its significance and alternatives. But it also lets us explore how masculinity can be performed by people we don't consider male. In other words, it separates masculinity from male bodies and loosens the assumptions that all men are "masculine." Or that no women are.[13]

10. While I usually use "American" as synonymous with "in the United States," our friends in Canada, Mexico, or South America are adamant that it is not!

11. One can easily see the influence of second-wave feminism here: feminists contested children's books, textbooks, and medical literature because these media (re)produced social advantages for men and concomitant *dis*advantages for women.

12. Cook, "Western Heterosexual Masculinity"; Jensen, *Getting Off*.

13. Both of these last two points are part of what is sometimes called the "critique of essentialism"—meaning a rejection of the perspective that there are some core traits (essences) characteristic of all men (or women, or African Americans, etc.). Whether everyone in a social category shares some trait becomes an empirical matter rather than a definitional certainty.

Disciplining the Normal: Acquiring "Proper" Masculinity

This heading is intentionally ambiguous. Usually we think of applying discipline to the *ab*normal. My use of the term "discipline" comes from the Foucault-inspired literature that looks at how modern societies are governed less by the threat of external punishment than by self-monitoring: watching and adjusting our own performances. The criteria we use to assess ourselves is "the normal." Again, feminism provides a model here by noting how few actual women match the representation of "normal" women in the media—who have been air-brushed, digitally or otherwise "enhanced." Masculinity literature documents how, as market capitalism has turned toward men, the range of "normal" masculinity for boys and men has narrowed. We now monitor and consume products to manage our body shape to a degree unimaginable a generation ago. And much of the pain of boyhood is driven by the fear of not being "normal" (cool) and subject to bullying.[14] Indeed, bullying underlines one of Foucault's points: the state and its institutions (e.g., schools, prisons) don't intervene in bullying until it crosses some threshold to become "assault." If a boy cries or complains about being bullied, he might be told to "man up."

The modern "liberal individual" is actually mass-produced and requires a lot of work. One is born undifferentiated, as a group/family/community member, and then gradually acquires an individual identity. As I noted earlier, the "factories" charged with mass-producing our individuals are families, schools, religions, and market capitalism, particularly the media. The masculinity literature traces the overlapping representations of masculinity produced by these institutions. Their goal is to create a self-regulating person who doesn't require a lot of external maintenance. Because these institutions participate in reproducing social stratification, a range of normal masculinities is offered to different populations of boys. Those who are expected to become financiers and those expected to be laborers usually experience different educational environments.[15] As boys take up these masculinities and learn to think and talk about themselves in these terms, masculinity becomes a core component of our identity narratives and thus a predictor of our behavior. Despite my father's optimism (he continually enrolled me in Little League), it didn't take long for me to abandon any identity as a jock. After enough broken bones and stitches, I largely moved away from talking about myself as a physical risk-taker.

14. Swain, "Masculinities in Education."
15. Willis, *Learning to Labor*.

Abandoning isn't enough, however: we need to find replacements. My father's gentleness and the peace/civil rights movements of the sixties and seventies enabled me to develop different stories about the kind of man I wanted to be.

These factories, to continue the metaphor, have to work with the raw material of bodies. Our bodies become symbolic artifacts—texts—in the social struggles around masculinity. Genitalia and skin are the primary symbols of what we should become.[16] But bodily texts aren't always clear. For example, there are intersex bodies that have both male and female features. Often someone (a physician, a parent) decides what the child should become. Because we so heavily link sex and gender in this culture, it takes effort to untangle them.[17] While not as difficult as in the Spanish and French languages, where every object is either masculine or feminine, the fact that English has binary his/her personal pronouns makes respectful acknowledgment of variability difficult. Think of how hard it is to address or speak about someone's infant before you know if it's a "him" or "her." In my classes, I can make this observation one second and refer to a student as "he" based only on "his" body in the next. Language disciplines all of us.

Transgender and Policing the Margins

One way to see how dominant masculinity is sustained is to look at how the "margins are policed." While gay men are seen as men—just men who prefer other men as partners—transgendered individuals can be more puzzling, more challenging. As a way of performing socially, transgendering can be defined as a process of "moving across (transferring) from one preexisting gender category to another . . . living between genders . . . or living 'beyond gender' altogether."[18] A therapist once told me that many relationships are ruined when someone—she was careful not to say "you"!—tries to manage anxiety by controlling another's behavior. Similarly, social anxiety manifests in informal social control: who needs disciplining and in what direction? Violence against gays and the discomfort

16. Stecopoulous and Uebel, *Race and the Subject of Masculinities*.

17. Green, *Becoming a Visible Man*; Plummer, "Male Sexualities."

18. Ekins and King, "Transgendering."

associated with[19] people who challenge our binary gender categories are signs of anxiety, of fear.[20]

Gay and transgendering lives are associated with a host of controversial, anxiety-riddled issues, particularly in the context of the relationships between gender and Christianity. I won't go into most of these because I haven't space to treat the differences fairly. So I'll just outline a central conceptual and theological puzzle that surfaces within the masculinity literature. What is/should be the relationship between identity and desire, between how we think about ourselves and the people we desire? And what is, or should be, the relationship between desire and love? The process of learning a gender—in our case, to be masculine—includes learning to desire appropriate, "normal" objects. Here again, we return to the critical distinction between gender and sex.[21] Arousal as a physiological event is linked to biological reproduction. When we get an erection, the process *feels* innate. But history and cross-cultural literature teach us that the *object* of arousal, what turns us on, is highly variable. Biologically, there is no reason to prefer skinny women or even naked ones. Every part of our culture teaches us to prefer some images and performances over others. Dominant masculinity disciplines us into desiring what we are not, namely, the female and feminine. Indeed, the ubiquitous condemnation of anything, from a haircut to a tennis shoe, by an adolescent boy is often calling it "gay." The vast pornography and advertising industries constantly teach us what is desirable. And here the distinction between desire and love can become very troubled: Dominant masculinity loves men, seeks their approval, but desires women. Even the apparently straightforward representations we receive are complex, more complex than we may care to admit in the binary world many of us have inherited.

The stories of transgendering individuals reveal complicated, shifting relationships among desire, love, and identity. If I have a male body, but a female gender identity, I may love men and/or desire women. Bisexuality is another narrative that loosens the assumed ties between identity, love, and desire. Because identity narratives and the social formations they reproduce are so fundamental to our lives, challenging the "givenness," the inevitability or naturalness, of these categories and relationships can turn

19. Originally I wrote that this discomfort was "produced by . . ." But it's produced by the fear within the dominant.

20. DuKeseredy and Schwartz, "Masculinities and Interpersonal Violence"; Mason, *Spectacle of Violence*; Tomsen, *Violence, Prejudice, and Sexuality.*

21. Green, *Becoming a Visible Man.*

our inherited views of the world on their head. The masculinity literature encourages us to think and work through these challenges rather than reject or react to them. The lives of different masculinities have something to teach us all.

Violence as Disciplining

The associations between masculinities and violence[22] are the stuff of both daily conversation and extensive academic exploration. My brief foray will address only two aspects: (a) violence against the feminine (e.g., intimate partner[23] violence) as reinforcing a fragile self; and (b) violence as a way of policing the margins and as identity performance—creating and living up to a narrative, if you will. These are not distinct: identity requires exclusion—we define ourselves against what we are not—and the most threatening quality for masculinity is the feminine. But I think it's useful to separate these practices analytically.

(a) *Violence against the feminine.* The daily humiliation, stalking, beating, raping, and killing of women can be seen as (among many other things) performances that reveal the vulnerable and defensive nature of masculinity. Because hegemonic masculinity is defined *against* the feminine and requires boys to reject the very qualities of emotional and material nurturing that have sustained them (the source of which is usually the mother), defending against those emotions is a never-ending project.[24] On the one hand, being heterosexual is a fundamental requirement of hegemonic masculinity.[25] Women (the feminine) are an object of desire and a threat to separateness. Deep connectedness undermines the separateness demanded of the masculine. In no way am I minimizing the role that this violence plays in sustaining masculine privilege—indeed, any threat against that privilege may increase violence. But much of the violence seems either in

22. A definitional caveat: my analysis is going to reproduce something I disagree with—the limitation of "violence" to interpersonal and (largely) physical forms. By any measure, the (largely white and wealthy) men who perpetuate environmental racism, limit access to healthcare, and create structural unemployment (not to mention military adventures) produce more death and morbidity than those who commit homicide and assault.

23. I prefer "intimate partner" violence, although it too is imprecise. But "domestic" violence suggests, falsely, a location and a subordinate role.

24. Chodorow, *Reproduction of Mothering*.

25. Mason, *Spectacle of Violence*.

excess or unrelated to any particular material or social threat. And insofar as this violence is often private ("domestic"), it is unlike other aspects of masculine performances for which the audience is other men.

(b) *Violence as an identity performance.* As I have repeatedly emphasized, the primary audience for masculinity performances is other men. And the competition to be seen as sufficiently masculine involves the humiliation and exclusion of "less masculine" others. This is the heart of bullying.[26] Why should this exclusion involve violence (in contrast to, say, shunning or verbal rejection)? Much of the masculinity literature points to the role of mass media. Just as media have a profound influence on what girls view as necessary to become "feminine," so video games, athletics, and films continually link masculinity to violence. In one study, almost all the (limited) time young boys spent with their fathers was watching "action" films or media events such as professional wrestling. Again, as with Barbie dolls, Ken and other masculine dolls have become increasingly unrealistic in terms of body proportion, such as unachievable biceps, and the increasing size, number, and intensity of weapons. Boys are schooled into the violence they take up and this is the masculinity practice most responsible for the premature death and injury of our sons and brothers.[27]

Historical Perspectives

Just as social constructionism and contemporary tensions around what counts as masculine create distance and analytic perspective, so do historical investigations of American masculinities. From the outset (however one defines that—from pre-European contact to the creation of a nation-state) masculinity has always been plural. A great deal of labor goes into reducing and contesting that plurality—the disciplining practices we discussed earlier. Most of us have inherited understandings of masculinity that became relatively dominant in the eighteenth and nineteenth centuries, so I'll draw my very brief examples from that period.

First, I return to the question of sources—of *whose* understandings of masculinity have carried the day. From the colonial period until perhaps the late eighteenth century, representations of American masculinity come to us from traveling Europeans, politicians, and religious figures.

26. Jimerson, Swearer, and Espelage, *Handbook of Bullying in Schools.*

27. DuKeseredy and Schwartz, "Masculinities and Interpersonal Violence"; Katz, *Tough Guise*; Katz, *Macho Paradox.*

Almost without exception, these were propertied (wealthy), white, heterosexual men. And from the beginning, these writings were explicitly political and polemical; they were participating in a project to *produce* citizens. Indigenous and African masculinities barely appear except as the other to the white male citizen.[28]

Although he leaves many of these privileged locations unmarked, I find the taxonomy Kimmel developed in *Manhood in America* useful for tracing the three lines (variability, economy, and Christianity) of discourse that still shape our understandings. The *genteel patriarch* has faded. Once seen as the pinnacle of society, the genteel patriarch was characterized as displaying a dignified aristocratic manhood by adhering to an upper-class code of honor that was deeply tied to tradition and community commitment rather than individual advancement. Christianity was taken for granted. Character and service to others were distinguishing features because wealth could be assumed. Their "exquisite tastes and refined sensibilities" could be read off their bodies—these were not hard, weather-beaten men. And their bodies could be "sensitive" because they were propped up by deep dependencies on the labor of women, servants, and slaves. Although most wealth in contemporary America is inherited, not earned, we have come to see inherited wealth as somewhat effeminate (think about the ways G. W. Bush was caricatured as having been born on third base but thinking he hit a triple).

If the genteel patriarch has faded discursively, if not materially, then the *heroic artisan* has almost disappeared. Originally self-employed in a craft shop or farm, the artisan was represented as a hardworking man who was virtuous, honest, "stalwart and loyal to male companions." He was seen as a more vigorous form of manhood than the patriarch even if his farm and shop were often inherited and his "independence" was dependent on women and government (e.g., for roads). The artisan was undermined by economic changes—industrialization, urbanization, and lack of a collective base to resist the degradation of his working conditions. In a shift from *social* to *contractual* relations with economic centralization and industrialization, he became a laborer working for a wage. In discussing globalization, we'll see similar patterns in "developing" countries as capitalism centralizes and displaces local, sustainable economies.

The "stalwart" phrase above points to a vital theme mentioned earlier: masculinity is performed for other men. It is primarily a *homosocial* orientation. Men are always measured (and measuring themselves) against

28. Nagel, "Nation"; Wallace, *I Am a Man*.

other men. The exclusion of women as a significant audience—although not an insignificant prize—underlines masculinity as a *project of privilege*. Just as poor white men can say, "At least I'm not black," all men can say, "At least I'm not a woman." Ironically, as women gain economically and politically, they are increasingly represented in the media as fragile and the objects of both desire and violence. Currently there is a fascinating struggle between the material (women working more, beginning to narrow the wage gap, gathering more college degrees and honors) and the representational as media and other outlets try to "keep them in their place." The personal and social anxiety created by the perceived erosion of masculine privilege accounts for a great deal of political and personal violence.

The masculinity fiction we are most familiar with is the *self-made man* (a term coined in 1832). I call it a "fiction" because social independence is a fiction—our very selves are social and our material lives are inextricably bound to others and to collective resources. But as a fiction, "The central characteristic of being self-made was that the proving ground was the workplace. . . . If manhood could be proved, it had to be proved in the eyes of other men."[29] While described as competitive and aggressive in the workplace, he's also seen as temperamentally restless, chronically insecure and desperate to achieve a solid grounding for a masculine identity. The welding of Christianity to capitalism added a painful twist to this insecurity. If one believed that "No man can be obedient to God's will as revealed in the Bible without, as the general result, becoming wealthy,"[30] then economic failure was also *moral* failure.

The linking of economic success, moral worth, and masculinity in the nineteenth century created a set of material and discursive conflicts that haunt contemporary manhood. The fundamental dilemma comes from linking one's masculinity to economic conditions that are beyond one's control. The vast majority of men have minimal influence on the economy (as our contemporary recession has made quite apparent). That's challenging enough. But when one allows one's identity as *masculine* to be dependent upon the economy then, in effect, ones masculinity is out of one's control. As we'll see, there are at least a couple ways out of this dilemma: one is to become less invested in one's masculinity as central to one's identity; another is to define one's masculinity in ways that are more

29. Kimmel, *Manhood in America*, 26.
30. Ibid.

consistently achievable—returning to notions of character, service, and relationships as anchors of masculinity.

This economist masculinity highlights some sites of social struggle that continue to color American masculinity. First, our highly stratified and shifting economy needs different forms of masculinity that become embodied distinctions. Currently this is most visible in the politics of immigration and labor. We "want" brown masculinity to do certain forms of work but not to leak into other social (citizenship) and economic (property ownership) domains.[31] If the public sphere of brutish competition required one form of masculinity, life in the domestic sphere demanded another. The exaggerated separation of "public" and "private" narrowed the range of available genders for both men and women. But it's no easy task to be one kind of man in one space and a different one elsewhere. If work demands that I am hyper-competitive, judgmental, cool, and uncaring for others, how do I shed those qualities when I am with my wife and children? Contemporary studies of masculinity and fatherhood highlight this tension.

Thus, as Thoreau noted, the "mass of men lead lives of quiet desperation." We can see three main strategies for coping with this desperation. The strategies have endured even if the content and terrain have shifted over time. Kimmel describes them as:

- *Self-control*: Men sought various forms of discipline that would inure them to both the brutality of the workplace and the potentially feminizing space of domestic life.

- *Escape*: For a while we had actual geographical frontiers where white men could "choose" the "savage life." Others escaped through fantasy (books, Wild West shows) and, of course, the local bar.

- *Exclusion*: All categories of men could use theological and biological arguments to reduce competition by women (and men of color) and deal with their anxieties by projecting onto others their fears of inadequacy.

Before moving away from the history of masculinities as a strategy for understanding the sources and possibilities of contemporary masculinity, I want to reiterate the themes I opened with. (1) Knowledge of history helps to "denaturalize" and multiply masculinities both across time and within any given period. But history is also a disciplinary project (hence the political struggles around K-12 history books' exclusion of women and

31. Flores and Benmayor, *Latino Cultural Citizenship*.

people of color). We need to remember there were always competing narratives of what it meant to be a citizen, a human being, a man. (2) There are immense consequences—psychic, interpersonal and social—from linking masculinity and identity to material success. (3) As Christianity itself becomes aligned with the values of market and consumer capitalism, it adds to dilemmas of trying to be a "good man," a supplier, a provider.

Masculinities and Globalization

Thus far my analysis has fallen into a common trap by staying within the confines of a single nation-state. The discussion of history hinted at the limitations of this focus since the emergence of American masculinities that were white, propertied, and Christian was part and parcel of nation building. We were endeavoring to distinguish ourselves from our British ancestors and from indigenous and imported African masculinities. Contemporary masculinities are more obviously a globalized process. The U.S. is the major exporter of masculine representations through media while simultaneously trying to "police" variability within its borders. One can point to English-only, immigration, gay-bashing, and White Supremacy movements as efforts to limit access to privileged masculinity. They also allow one to see the different "others" against which the dominant is defending itself—language is used as a stand-in for ethnic and cultural difference, nationality, homosexuality, Judaism, Catholicism, and men of color.

Actually, it is probably more accurate to describe masculinities anywhere as *transnational* rather than "global."[32] This term has emerged precisely because there is so much unequal movement of both material men and masculine representations across nation-state boundaries. This flow produces challenges and changes everywhere. People create solidarities across a range of differences—in North America there were unexpected alliances among both labor and business leaders in Mexico, the US, and Canada in response to NAFTA. This flow in turn can lead people to create an imaginary past with purportedly purer, cleaner paradigms. Our miniature history lesson should remind us, however, that the past was always multiple and in flux. We never were a nation of only white Christian men.

As with all the topics in this chapter, there is a large literature on globalization and gender. I've chosen the tiny portion I'm highlighting to provide another destabilizing, analytic perspective—one that helps us see

32. Swarr and Nagar, *Critical Transnational Feminist Praxis*.

that masculinity is always "under construction," subject to multiple influences and yet participating in global patterns of masculine privilege. At the same time, my focus occludes myriad differences and exceptions.

Transnational analyses of masculinity examine multiple forms of movement across borders. These get reflected in our immigration laws—compare the efforts to control "undocumented" Mexicans with the privileged immigration of Indian technology workers. While masculinity remains a hegemonic position, movements of people, representations and material goods, lead to shifts in masculinities. One of the most marked shifts is toward service work—away from manufacturing and agriculture. The economies of a number of countries are dependent upon men moving abroad to do service work in more wealthy regions.[33] Although it is tempting to think of those shifts occurring "elsewhere," globalization also realigns forms of masculinity *within* the U.S. This can be seen at both ends of the economic spectrum. Scholars have identified something called "transnational business masculinity," for example.[34] In contrast to the historical linkage of masculinity and nation-state citizenship, this newer form of masculinity is highly mobile and holds only very conditional loyalties. In fact, these men may literally hold multiple citizenships. The economic privileges create emotional isolation and social distance, often associated with the commodification of sexuality as anything becomes available "for a price."[35] Simultaneously, the widening gulf between this extremely privileged, flexible masculinity and working-class men has created what are sometimes termed "struggle masculinities." In colonized countries, the "struggle" is often literal, physical violence. While it is here, too, more often it appears as a struggle over identity that is, ironically, articulated in nationalist terms. The clearest examples are the White Supremacist movements referred to earlier. Here the masculinities are defined against non-citizens as well as against non-white men. Frequently there is a religious (e.g., anti-Catholic, anti-Semitic, anti-Islam) dimension. So political activism and violence against immigrants and men of color is articulated as a strategy to "regain" (white) manhood.[36] This is ironic because the primary threat to their masculinity comes from having tied it to economic measures, and the sources of economic insecurity lie much more among

33. Donaldson et al., *Migrant Men*; Parpart and Zalewski, *Rethinking the Man Question*.

34. Connel, "Globalization."

35. Connel and Wood, "Globalization and Business Masculinities."

36. Frankenberg, *Displacing Whiteness*.

the "transnational business masculinities" than with other men of color who are supposedly competing for "American" jobs.[37]

Although it is difficult to generalize about how masculinity is being reconstructed through globalization because the dynamics are so place-specific, it is helpful to understand the dimensions along which the reconstruction occurs. One of the most obvious is changes in the division of labor.[38] As different types of work become available, both overall income and a shift in the division between "public" and "private" domains can occur. The recent Shriver Report—on the occasion of more women than men being in the U.S. workforce—documents such shifts in the U.S.[39] Men are adjusting to bringing less income into the household and a shifting of domestic responsibilities—although we still do significantly less at home.[40] Clearly these changes—already underway for decades—are less dramatic than in countries where globalization has ruined local economies and required men and women to move to cities or other countries for wage income.

Realignment of labor and shifts in sources and types of income are linked to changes in power relations. Not only are genders reorganized, but traditional status positions based on age or community role can be undermined when young men earn wages in cities and return to their home communities less compliant with traditional arrangements. Mobile individuals become more adept at "code switching"—the capacity to perform different masculinities in different contexts and, indeed, with such movement, men's bodies and the narratives that give them meaning are altered. The individualist "romantic love" framework for forming intimacy and households—exported through media, religion, and other forces—may compete with kin negotiations, changes in fathering, child rearing, and other social practices.

Historically, these transitions have always been with us—especially since the onset of European colonialism. But the speed, breadth, and depth of penetration by exogenous masculinity practices has greatly intensified. Indian men come to the U.S. on special visas to work in the computer industries; they later bring wives with them. This household may choose to have children here to give them U.S. citizenship but return to India to live in newly built communities more isolated from traditional family ties

37. Hartigan, Jr., *Racial Situations.*
38. Parpart and Zalewski, *Rethinking the Man Question.*
39. Boushey and O'Leary, *Shriver Report.*
40. Treas and Drobnic, *Dividing the Domestic.*

and influences. Often they bring understandings of domestic labor with them that lead to different patterns of employment in their new households.[41] It is vital to understand that these remakings don't just occur "over there," but also "at home." And as I've noted throughout this chapter, none of these changes is monolithic or unidirectional. Both local and global feminist movements, for example, have unsettled established gender relations. Many regions have experienced an upsurge of what are sometimes termed "recovery" projects—including the rearticulation of traditional and/or ancestral practices that are oriented more to communitarian than individualist ways of being. In the U.S., both the sustainability movement and the rise of religious orthodoxies can be interpreted within this framework, as can Islamist or Hindi "traditionalist" movements. Many scholars have linked the emergence of "muscular Christianity" to these cultural dynamics as an effort to reclaim "traditional" forms of patriarchy that have become less available within contemporary contexts.[42]

Conclusion: Destabilizing Masculinity

Contemporary masculinity studies emerged from feminist projects to unsettle gender-linked inequalities. By turning feminist analytics toward the masculine, these studies have emphasized the historical and social basis of any particular masculinity. The sex/gender distinction developed by feminism to resist biological explanations of gender inequalities has helped us see that, similarly, masculinity and bodies are socially correlated, not mechanistically determined. And as women-of-color theory has explicated and critiqued the implicit whiteness and singularity of "woman," masculinity studies emphasize the plurality of masculinities—historically, regionally, and contemporarily. Different social stratifications require different performances of masculinities. There is increasing recognition that masculinity is unhealthy for men and boys, not just for women who have endured its social and physical violence.[43]

From the beginning, masculinity in what is now the United States was tied to citizenship and to making citizenship exclusive. Citizenship was tied to economic well-being. So masculinity became linked to economic productivity. As globalization has intensified and highlighted the flows of masculinities across nation-state boundaries, this connection

41. Bhatt, "At Home in Globalization."
42. O'Brien, "Jesus for Real Men."
43. Barker et al., "Questioning Gender Norms."

between masculinity and economic status has led to increasing tensions for individual masculinity narratives and community arrangements. Some responses to these tensions are directed toward "reclaiming" a hegemonic status while others focus on articulating forms of masculinity that are less violent, more inclusive, and open to forming allies across genders and different forms of masculinity. This struggle—between a hegemonic, racial, and class-based masculinity and forms of alternatives and resistance—has been with us from the beginning. Only a historical perspective will be able to weigh the ebb and flow. The goal of masculinity studies is to support analytical and political space for these resistive masculinities.

Bibliography

Barker, Gary. *Dying to Be Men: Youth, Masculinity, and Social Exclusion*. New York: Routledge, 2005.

Barker, Gary, C. Ricardo, M. Nascimentob, A. Olukoyac, and C. Santosa. "Questioning Gender Norms with Men to Improve Health Outcomes." *Global Public Health* 5 (2010) 539–53.

Bhatt, Amy. "At Home in Globalization: Social Reproduction, Transnational Migration and the Circulating Indian Household." PhD thesis, University of Washington, 2011.

Boushey, Heather, and Ann O'Leary. *The Shriver Report: A Woman's Nation Changes Everything*. Washington, DC: Center for American Progress, 2009.

Chodorow, Nancy. *The Reproduction of Mothering: Psychoanalysis and the Sociology of Gender*. Berkeley: University of California Press, 1978.

Connel, R. W. "Globalization, Imperialism and Masculinities." In *Handbook of Studies on Men & Masculinities*, edited by Michael Kimmel, Jeff Hearn, and R. W. Connel, 71–89. Thousand Oaks, CA: Sage, 2005.

Connel, R. W., and Julian Wood. "Globalization and Business Masculinities." *Men and masculinities* 7 (2005) 347–64.

Cook, Ian. "Western Heterosexual Masculinity, Anxiety and Web Porn." *Journal of Men's Studies* 14 (2011) 47–63.

Donaldson, Mike, Raymond Hibbins, Richard Howson, and Bob Pease. *Migrant Men*. New York: Routledge, 2009.

DuKeseredy, Walter, and Martin Schwartz. "Masculinities and Interpersonal Violence." In *Handbook of Studies on Men & Masculinities*, edited by Michael Kimmel, Jeff Hearn, and R. W. Connel, 353–67. Thousand Oaks, CA: Sage, 2005

Ekins, Richard, and Dave King. "Transgendering, Men and Masculinities." In *Handbook of Studies on Men and Masculinities*, edited by Michael Kimmel, Jeff Hearn, and R. W. Connel, 379–92. Thousand Oaks, CA: Sage, 2005.

Epstein, D., J. Elwood, V. Hey, and J. Maw. *Failing Boys?: Issues in Gender and Achievement*. Buckingham: Open University Press, 1998.

Fasteau, Marc. *The Male Machine*. New York: McGraw-Hill, 1974.

Flores, William, and Rina Benmayor. *Latino Cultural Citizenship*. Boston: Beacon, 1997.

Frankenberg, Ruth. *Displacing Whiteness: Essays in Social and Cultural Criticism.* Durham, NC: Duke University Press, 1997.

Green, Jamison. *Becoming a Visible Man.* Nashville: Vanderbilt University Press, 2004.

Hartigan, John, Jr. *Racial Situations: Class Predicaments of Whiteness in Detroit.* Princeton, NJ: Princeton University Press, 1999.

Jacobson, Matthew. T. *Whiteness of a Different Color.* Cambridge, MA: Harvard University Press, 1998.

Jensen, Peter. *Getting Off: Pornography and the End of Masculinity.* Boston: Southend Press, 2007.

Jimerson, Shane, Susan Swearer, and Dorothy Espelage. *Handbook of Bullying in Schools: An International Perspective.* New York: Routledge, 2010.

Katz, Jackson. *Tough Guise: Violence, Media and the Crisis in Masculinity.* Video. Northampton, MA: Educational Media Foundation, 1999.

———. *The Macho Paradox: Why Some Men Hurt Women and How All Men Can Help.* Naperville, IL: Sourcebooks, 2006.

Kegan, Judith. *Masculinity Studies and Feminist Theory.* New York: Columbia University Press, 2002.

Kimmel, Michael. *Manhood in America.* New York: Free Press, 1996.

———. *Guyland: The Perilous World Where Boys Become Men.* New York: HarperCollins, 2008.

Mason, Gail. *The Spectacle of Violence: Homophobia, Gender and Knowledge.* New York: Routledge, 2002.

Murphy, Peter. *Studs, Tools, and Family Jewels: Metaphors Men Live By.* Madison: University of Wisconsin Press, 2001.

Nagel, Joane. "Nation." In *Handbook of Studies on Men & Masculinities,* edited by Michael Kimmel, Jeff Hearn, and R. W, Connel, 397–413. Thousand Oaks, CA: Sage, 2005.

Nayak, Anoop, and Mary Jane Kehily. *Gender, Youth and Culture: Young Masculinities and Femininities.* New York: Palgrave, 2008.

O'Brien, Brandon. "A Jesus for Real Men." *Christianity Today,* April 27, 2008. Online: http://www.christianitytoday.com/ct/2008/april/27.48.html.

Parpart, J., and M. Zalewski. *Rethinking the Man Question: Sex, Gender and Violence in International Relations.* London: Zed Books, 2008.

Pascoe, C. J. *Dude, You're a Fag: Masculinity and Sexuality in High School.* Berkeley: University of California Press, 2007.

Plummer, Ken. "Male Sexualities." In *Handbook of Studies on Men & Masculinities,* edited by Michael Kimmel, Jeff Hearn, and R. W. Connel, 379–92. Thousand Oaks, CA: Sage, 2005.

Schacht, Steven, and Doris Ewing. *Feminism and Men: Reconstructing Gender Relations.* Albany: SUNY Press, 1998.

Stecopoulous, Harry, and Michael Uebel. *Race and the Subject of Masculinities.* Durham, NC: Duke University Press, 1997.

Swain, Jon. "Masculinities in Education." In *Handbook of Studies on Men & Masculinities,* edited by Michael Kimmel, Jeff Hearn, and R. W. Connel, 213–29. Thousand Oaks, CA: Sage, 2005.

Swarr, Amanda, and Richa Nagar. *Critical Transnational Feminist Praxis.* Albany: SUNY Press, 2010.

Tomsen, Stephen. *Violence, Prejudice and Sexuality.* New York: Routledge, 2009.

Treas, Judith, and Sonja Drobnic. *Dividing the Domestic: Men, Women and Household Work in Cross-National Perspective.* Stanford, CA: Stanford University Press, 2010.

Wallace, Maurice. *"I Am a Man": Latent Doubt, Public Protest, and the Anxious Construction of Black American Manhood.* Ann Arbor, MI: ProQuest, 2006.

Watson, Elwood, and Marc Shaw. *Performing American Masculinities: The 21st-Century Man in Popular Culture.* Bloomington: Indiana University Press, 2011.

Willis, Paul. *Learning to Labor: How Working Class Kids Get Working Class Jobs.* New York: Columbia University Press, 1981.

7

Discipleship and Identity

A Theological Consideration of Race, Gender, and the Human Situation

BRIAN BANTUM

Introduction

"ALTERNATIVE VOICES" was the title of the week devoted to considerations of women, African Americans, and native peoples in my un-
dergraduate American history course. At the time, this attention to
non-male, non-white voices was the mark of a progressive professor. This
pattern of incorporating "minority voices" is often repeated in introductory courses ranging from history (where a week might be spent reading
excerpts of Malcolm X or Martin Luther King) to English to theology,
my own discipline, where a week, maybe two was spent reading James
Cone or Rosemary Radford Ruether before concluding the course with
a white male contemporary writer. Typically, "alternative voices" weeks
were cast as responses or prophetic voices, but little was done in the
previous coursework to situate these readings or understand the relationships these authors had with the previous weeks' material, themes,
and concerns. Within these introductory courses, the professor rightly
sought to account for the realities of difference that academic scholarship

has so often glossed over. In the midst of giving voice to difference, however, the broad classification of difference within "alternative voices" and other similar monikers has served to collapse many differences into one another, in particular the difference of race and gender.[1]

Difference constituted by biology, race, and ethnicity has perpetually marked what it means to be human. Contemporary scholarship has seen a dramatic increase in attempts to uncover marginalization in Western society and in the West's effects upon the world. As well, minority voices have also begun to rearticulate theological, historical, and social realities from their own spaces of particularity. In theology, these voices have come to be known as "contextual theologies." However, in the midst of these emerging voices, does the similarity of marginalization take priority over the differences between differences? In what ways must we attend to the particularities of identities in order to resist their perpetual marginalization? The core question is this: can we approach racial and gender identities (and the oppressive structures that refuse them) in the same way? Or, to put it another way, should we understand the difference that constitutes male/female as analogous to white/black, Thai/Korean, or English/Ghanaian?

In this essay, I approach race and gender as different but related theological challenges. Theological reflection upon gender and race necessarily intersects because of its attention to the body in relation to God and the world. Yet, whereas gender difference structures men and women in their lives together, racial/ethnic difference structures race and ethnicity into lives apart. Thus, while the marginalization of female and darker bodies is a shared context, the particular ways this marginalization becomes instantiated within society and its institutions (and especially its churches) are very different. Leadership in the church, for example, remains dominated by men due to implicit or explicit operations of male normativity, yet these churches are constituted of both men and women. Notions of child rearing, work, friendship, housekeeping, spiritual leadership, and decision making all become subject to implicit and explicit notions of what men and women are "made for." In these spaces, women are marginalized through domestication, a power that subjugates women in relationship to men, whether in the home or the workplace.

---

1. I am seeking to articulate an understanding of the particular theological roots of racial and gender dynamics of disempowerment and oppression. It is important to note how dynamics of race and gender are not isolated moments. The grammars of race and gender have often been layered to reinforce oppressive racial or gendered norms. For an excellent account of such language, see Carter, "Race, Religion."

The marginalization of race, while similar to gender, can be seen as a mode of distancing where white communities resist the presence of different racial and ethnic communities. Here, racial difference is not subjugated within domestic spaces of the home or within a church or workplace, but in a distance where the domestic lives of whites and African Americans are geographically separate, with little interactions of friendship or co-working. Multiracial churches, for example, represent only 7.5 percent of all churches.[2] In addition, economic and educational disparities persist throughout the United States, and in recent years a de facto resegregation of neighborhoods and schools has emerged.[3]

Theological scholarship has sought to address the patterns of subjugation in the church and the world. But in the midst of these inquiries, the contextual questions of gender and racial difference have either been collapsed into one another or treated as separate questions altogether. Contextual theological scholarship has done much to express the realities, consequences, and possibilities of racialized and gendered speech in theology and society. And yet in these reflections, two fundamental questions have not been addressed in the interrelationship between gender and race:[4] How does difference structure the lives of men and women in their lives together? How does difference structure the lives of racial and ethnic peoples into lives apart?

At its heart, the intersection of race and gender lies within a common refusal of difference that must be theologically narrated to attend both to the significance of bodily particularity and being made in the image of God, the *imago Dei*. But in order to do so, we must see how the refusal of difference becomes instantiated in the radically close or domestic (the intrarelationships between men and women) and the radically distant (the interrelationships between races and ethnicities). These mutual

2. See Emerson and Smith, *Divided by Faith.*

3. Several studies indicate a slow (or not so slow) return of de facto segregation in schools. This turn was seen most clearly in the 2007 Supreme Court Case, Parents Involved in Community vs. Seattle Public Schools, which saw the cessation of mandated busing to maintain racial integration. Similar movements have been seen throughout the United States in cities such as Charlotte and Raleigh, NC. See Clotfelter, *After Brown.*

4. I should note here Womanist theology as a crucial exception to the bifurcation of race and gender. Womanist theologians have sought to articulate a space where the fullness of human thriving is possible for men and women alike. At the same time, while Womanist theologians have demonstrated how oppressive notions of race and gender have marginalized black female bodies, an articulation of how race and gender are distinct but related in the lives of non-black women remains to be explored.

movements point out particular ways in which fallen humanity has sought to dominate the world, while also indicating vital aspects of our own humanity and relationships with one another and, ultimately, God.

This essay will examine the theological positioning of race and gender through four particular emphases: 1) difference as a theological category and problem, 2) refusal of difference in race and gender, both of which manifest in distinct but crucial ways, 3) race and gender as problematically yolked in the modern situation, and 4) a theological reconception of human difference articulated in the person and work of Christ.

The Problem of Difference and the Body: Gender

The problem of difference marks all human existence and poses a distinct theological problem, namely: how does humanity account for difference between one another and between humanity and God? In contemporary theology, the problem of difference has become especially pronounced as the veil of male European superiority has been slowly torn away to reveal a seemingly endless diversity of faces and lives that academic classification and social domination covered over and silenced. Such classifications derived from a moment of encounter, whether of Adam seeing Eve or a European seeing the first African. In these encounters with difference, a vast array of classifications, associations, and related judgments worked together to understand what a people was, were, or could be.[5] Yet, this process of encounter and discernment is not a modern problem; it can be seen throughout the interrelationships of cultures and more fundamentally as a mark of humanity's createdness.

Some of the earliest Judeo-Christian accounts of humanity display the difficulty of difference. Adam and Eve, created for God and for one another, when approached by the fundamental sign of their difference and their distinction from God in the Tree of the Knowledge of Good and Evil, sought to control, to mediate this difference for themselves rather than subject themselves to it.

From the very beginning of creation, humanity is encountered by a variety of differences: differences among animals to be named, differences among species of plants that they must rely on for sustenance, differences between themselves as male and female, and finally difference between themselves and God. The constellation of differences serves not only to

5. Christian studies of such encounters include Rivera, *Violent Evangelism*; and Jennings, *Christian Imagination*.

PART TWO: Gender, Race, and Society

describe the world around them, but also to constitute human identity in the midst of these differences. Identity constituted in the dynamic movement between differences is what critical theorist Homi Bhabha refers to as the "location of culture."[6] Understood in this way, identity is not fundamentally a biological fact or a social construct, but a dynamic process in which all human beings participate. The accounts of creation found in Genesis suggest that Adam and Eve's identity is a dynamic movement within creation itself, created within a matrix of difference that they must negotiate and faithfully discern.

But within this matrix of difference called Eden, Adam and Eve are confronted by differences that in some cases they are given dominion over (animals, land), and other differences that constitute a limit, difference that marks a horizon or boundary to their identity and capacity to know (the Tree of the Knowledge of Good and Evil). In the midst of these differences, Genesis narrates the Tree of the Knowledge of Good and Evil to be a boundary that will be eventually tested and transgressed by Adam and Eve. "So when the woman saw that the tree was good for food, and that it was a delight to the eyes, and that the tree was to be desired to make one wise, she took of its fruit and ate; and she also gave some to her husband, who was with her" (Gen 3:6). In desiring the tree, Adam and Eve sought something that was beyond them, but in so doing also sought to locate themselves outside of that boundary, outside of their own createdness. The desire for the fruit of this tree, for eternal life and equality with God, would not only have consequences for Adam and Eve's abiding with God, but also become inflected in the understanding of difference between Adam and Eve.

German pastor and theologian Dietrich Bonhoeffer describes the effects of this transgression within the interrelationships of Adam and Eve as differences that became fundamentally a boundary to be destroyed, overcome. He writes, "With the creation of woman, humankind's limit has advanced into the midst of the created world. . . . Violating the Tree of Life would at the same time violate the other person . . . it is a defection . . ."[7]

6. Bhabha suggests that in the modern world we must begin to consider identity in new ways, asking, "How are subjects formed 'in-between', or in excess of, the sum of the 'parts' of difference (usually intoned as race/class/gender, etc.)? How do strategies of representation or empowerment come to be formulated in the competing claims of communities where, despite shared histories of deprivation and priorities may not always be collaborative and dialogical, but may be profoundly antagonistic, conflictual and even incommensurable?" (Bhabha, *Location of Culture*, 2).

7. Bonhoeffer, *Creation and Fall*, 118–20.

Difference, in Bonhoeffer's view, must be understood in two particular moments in the Genesis account. Difference is first a gift provided to Adam and implicitly to Eve through the creation of one out of the other. Being drawn out of Adam, Eve is of the same "kind," of the same substance, and yet Eve is not Adam. Eve mirrors, makes visible to Adam, human limitations, such as that humanity is *not* God. Thus Eve is a gift to Adam as Adam is a gift to Eve, each offering one another a visual boundary, a material cue to human limitations that mark their difference from one another and their collective difference from God. At the same time, these bodily cues of human limitation are also necessary to outline the fullness of humanity. Adam and Eve are not full without a community of persons just as they are not complete without communion with God. As long as Eve is before Adam and Adam is before Eve, each is reminded of a mutual binding to one another and to God.

However, their eating of the Tree of Knowledge fragments these mutual reminders. Bonhoeffer observes that humanity's fallen condition is irrevocably tied to a profound misapprehension of what difference is and what it is for. As he writes, "Violating the Tree of Life would at the same time violate the other." The violation Bonhoeffer refers to here is a refusal to be bound to God; seeking to be different and apart from God fragments the very binding of Adam to Eve. They can no longer see difference as a gift. This misapprehension and the consequential fall manifests in two distinct ways in the Genesis account. First, the Tree of Knowledge can be seen as a mark of distance, as that which is not and cannot be present to Adam and Eve. "But of the tree of the knowledge of good an evil you shall not eat, for in the day of that you eat of it you shall die" (Gen 2:17). Second, the tree is a tangible sign of their difference, a distance from God that is grace. And yet this distance is something to be overcome, to be obtained, utilized for a form of life Adam and Eve presume is fitting to them.

But as Adam and Eve become enveloped with what should be distant, they were confronted with one another in a new way. "Then the eyes of both were opened, and they knew that they were naked; and they sewed fig leaves together and made loin cloths for themselves" (Gen 3:7). The opening of Adam's and Eve's eyes in this moment reconstructs the domestic space and creates an estrangement within the community. Whereas Adam and Eve would once look upon one another with nothing being hidden, post-fall Adam and Eve discover one another in a new way, seeing themselves and one another in terms of what should not be known. In this transformation, Adam and Eve become domestic others to one another, persons whose lives are not intertwined in a beloved, grace-filled difference, but estranged and hidden from one another. Yet Adam and Eve constitute a community; they occupy a domestic space together. In seeking a likeness to what was beyond them, the domestic other, the local now becomes present in a shameful way that must be covered and managed. As "their eyes were opened," Adam and Eve become aware of a difference between one another that they cannot account for and thus cover themselves in shame.[8] In their dialogue with God, we see not only a difference in representation, but alienation between Adam and Eve, who once were one flesh, as they continue to place themselves within spaces of innocence, all the while subjecting the other to accusations of transgression.

Not only is there a disorienting of difference in the reverberations of the fall, but also the consequences of the fall become inhabited within the interrelationships of husband and wife. For Eve, her "desire would be for your husband, and he shall rule over you" (Gen 3:16b), and for Adam "cursed is the ground because of you; in toil you shall eat of it all the days of your life" (3:17b). The identities of male and female are thus necessarily bound to one another, no longer in love, but in subjection and toil. Far from reflecting the image of God or the ideal of male-female relationship, this reordering of male/female identity is emblematic of humanity's fall rather than humanity's nature as made in the "image of God." Exile from the garden of Eden thus becomes a geographical representation of the intimacy turned exilic estrangement that now permeates the hierarchical relationship between husband and wife, an alienation of the "near ones."

In the fall there is an inversion. There is a fracturing of what was rightfully distant and near, so that those pieces are shorn from one another and reordered, consequently reordering human life with one another and with God. Put another way, the fall of humanity reveals humanity's resistance to difference, inflected in two distinct ways: in relationship to the one who is near and in relationship to the one who is far. This pattern of encounter and refusal is one that could be said to permeate the story of Israel and humanity more generally as Israel struggles to discern its own faithfulness in relationship to those who are foreigners and strangers.[9]

8. Gregory of Nyssa suggested humanity was originally created without gender and were only distinguished as male and female as a consequence of the fall. See Harrison, "Gender, Generation, and Virginity." For a consideration of Gregory of Nyssa and contemporary questions of the body, in particular Judith Butler, see Coakley, "Eschatological Body."

9. For a powerful account of how difference becomes resisted in Israel see Williams, *Sisters in the Wilderness*. The means of power held by Sarah become inflected

Poles of domestication and distancing are not dichotomies that are unrelated to one another, but can be seen as reciprocating motions within the unfolding drama of humanity. Theologically speaking, the problem of humanity's fall is the failure of negotiating our fundamental difference from God.[10] This failure reverberates within the lives of one another as domination. Domination is on the one hand the brutal enslavement, murder, or devaluing of particular bodies; on the other hand, it is also refracted through the believer's subtle but nonetheless tragic misapprehension of difference as deviation from a constructed or false center. Such examples are too numerous to count, but one rather stark example is Augustine's subtle but damning qualification about man and woman: "Then you [God] gave form to the believing soul, the soul truly alive because by robust self-control it had reduced its impulses to good order. Its mind was now subject to you alone, and needed no human norm to imitate, for you made it after your own image and in your own likeness, and subordinated its rational activity to the sovereignty of intellect, as woman is to man."[11] In this subtle illustration of humanity's nearness yet distance from God, Augustine circumscribes the pattern of hierarchy within humanity itself as woman is necessarily bound to man, but in such a way as to be fundamentally different, subjugated, subordinated. Augustine's observations were certainly neither new to theology nor to human self-reflection, but his illustration begins to illumine how difference conceived in terms of gender articulates genders as explicitly bound to one another.

Novelist and renowned feminist theorist Simone de Beauvoir would suggest that "male and female stand opposed within a primordial *Mitsein* [being with], and woman has not yet broken it."[12] Beauvoir's observation highlights how domination and patterns of subjugation between men and women are expressed within *necessary* relations. In other words, the opposition of maleness and femaleness is articulated within an irrevocable nearness, man over woman, but always man *with* woman in either household patterns or normative narrations of vocation and place, where women's lives and behaviors are perpetually bound to male-centric norms and modes of being. Beauvoir's lament concerns the seemingly inevitable

upon Hagar, who is not only a woman, but also a subjugated woman whose very body becomes the tool of another's promises.

10. Augustine famously spoke of the root of sin as pride, but what is pride but an attempt to orient things outside of us into a relationship that is favorable to us—controlled and determined by us?

11. Augustine, *Confessions*, 341.

12. Beauvoir, *Second Sex*, xxv.

suffering within a relationship of being, which only further reiterates the fallen state of humanity whose ultimate aim is an illusory autonomy.

Feminist theologians have suggested that this pattern of domination has taken place not only within social constructions of the "feminine" similar to what we see in Augustine, but also in the ways women's lives have been narrated within particular modes of relationship with men and especially Jesus. Feminist theologian Elizabeth Schüssler-Fiorenza suggests, "Women who read the Jesus story or have a 'personal' relationship to Christ take up the position that romance novels or films offer to women in relationship with men. . . . [M]en are to be education for themselves whereas women are to be socialized for men. The tendency to conceptualize as intimate live relationship between a believing woman and the exceptional man and singular hero . . . has a long theological tradition . . ."[13]

The subjugation of women in relationship to men takes place within the orientation of women's lives (and hopes) inside of male certainty, the presuppositions of male knowledge or power that continues to permeate all facets of human society and continually circumscribes the lives of women inside of male plans or determinations. The structural realities of domination present in gender are iterated through radically interpersonal relationships between men and women on a daily basis that repeatedly order these relationships in radical connection to one another. These patterns of relation become reverberated through perpetual distortions of intimacy, such as pornography, strip clubs, the magazine and fashion industries, and on a more daily basis, questions of who adjusts their schedule in order to raise children. These iterations occur on street corners and through subtle or not so subtle eye contact, leering, "shouts of admiration," or even within common expressions of sexual intimacy in marriage where women are encouraged to meet the needs of their spouse so as not to lead their husbands into sin.

In the midst of humanity's fall, the domination of women by men and the creation of unjust structures and norms of gender and roles, undoubtedly mirror injustices bound to race. At the same time, gender difference becomes articulated in society through relationships and norms of the domestic, of intimacy that permeate the daily lives and expectations of men and women alike.

---

13. Schüssler Fiorenza, *Jesus: Miriam's Child*, 55.

The Problem of Difference and the Body: Race

While examining the interrelationships of men and women in the wake of the fall of humanity, distorted patterns of relationship work out in either frequent interaction or within homes or within communities. But in either case, the realities of gender difference become oriented within domestic realities, everyday interactions that shape the lives of men and women together. In contrast to this domesticity, difference also becomes displayed through exclusion or distance. Although human history is again replete with examples of calls for ethnic or racial purity, the rise of racial consciousness in the modern West provides a significant example of how racial difference becomes articulated through a complicated distance.

In the sixteenth century, as Europe extended its reach into the world, it began to encounter the fullness of the world's diversity. In confronting those from Africa, Asia, and eventually what would become the Americas, Europeans were confronted with a profound difference. In the "heathen" of the world, the Europeans came into contact with a people who were not only different in terms of their skin color, but also who embodied a visual marker of the European's close approximation to the image of God.[14] In this way, the encounter between peoples was fundamentally a theological moment. Theologian Willie James Jennings describes the theological significance of one such moment and its descriptive power as Gomes Eanes de Azurara (Zurara), historian of Prince Henry the Navigator of sixteenth-century Spain, documents one of the first auctions of African slaves on Spanish shores. Zurara wrote of the slaves, their diversity of color, their being auctioned, of being torn from their fathers and mothers, and of their forced baptisms and salvation. The significance of bodies (and their color) in this moment is placed within an interpretation of God's creation and redemption as Spain ventures further and further into the world, possessing more and more land. In Zurara's account Jennings observes that "land and body are connected at the intersection of European imagination and expansion. The imagined geography diminished in strength as a more authentic and accurate geography emerged. The scale of existence, however, with white (unharmed) flesh at one end and black (harmed) flesh at the other, grew in power

---

14. For helpful descriptions of the systems of classification that arose during the age of discovery and colonization, see Jordan, *White Man's Burden*, 3–25; and Sollors, *Neither White nor Black*, 112–41.

precisely in the space created by Portuguese expansion into new lands."[15] As the Portuguese extended their reach into the world, they simultaneously created a descriptive distance between light and dark bodies, allowing for the subjugation of the dark. This discursive distancing was accomplished through theological language describing African peoples in contrast to Europeans. According to the descriptive process of colonization, civilizations displayed their *imago Dei* through their "civilization," and no people were exempted from this classificatory gaze.

The history of the development of racial discourse regarding Africans and non-Europeans in the New World is certainly not a new idea, but it is important to place these broader patterns of encounter and classification in connection to the burgeoning social systems that developed within the global, colonial world. These differences bore out structurally not only within homes (not entirely at least), but also through structures of distancing, separation, and exclusion. Descriptions of Africans, especially as declensions from the white ideal, have a history as far back as sixteenth-century England.[16] And yet while maleness had been understood as an ideal or height of what it meant to be human, racial difference was now articulating and ordering social life in a different, but no less troubling way. Through enslavement and a radical discursive distancing, the relationship between white and dark bodies would be perpetually described in relationship to the other, even while the intermingling of white and dark seemed inconceivable.

The pervasive attempts to discipline and order the spatial and interpersonal relationship of light and dark could be seen through American history in anti-miscegenation laws, lynching, black codes, and Jim Crow. The directness of such attempts at distancing has become somewhat muted, but the realities of racial integration in the United States bares a discomfiting resemblance to the patterns of our past.[17] The persistent resistance to welcome racial difference into spaces of equality, intimacy, and community point to a pattern of domination that presupposed the necessity of a physical distance, of a geographical and social separation in

15. Jennings, *Christian Imagination*, 24.

16. Jordan, *White Man's Burden*, 4.

17. In addition to the patterns of distancing in education (which correspond closely to geographic proximity), Michelle Alexander also points to the high rates of incarceration among African-American men and the structural bias of the criminal justice system that renders them permanently exiled from participation within society. See Alexander, *New Jim Crow*.

order to make and maintain such differences. These patterns of distance endure in contemporary society and especially in the United States in pronounced racial and ethnic stratification and the disproportionately low rate of interracial marriage. These patterns indicate that racial difference is not approached as something to be ordered within one's life, but to be resisted and disciplined outside of one's home, from a distance (think suburbs).[18]

Black theologian James Cone sought to resist the effects of this distancing, which included perpetually inadequate education, unequal treatment by law enforcement, discrimination, and physical violence. His conception of black theology suggested the importance of resisting the temptation of black Americans to acquiesce to a conception of a white Jesus and examine instead the realities of Jesus' presence among the poor and the oppressed.[19] This radical identification, this refusal of distance between God and the destitute, was the basis of the black theology movement.

Cone's discussion of Jesus thus sought to resist the enclosure of Jesus within white autonomy and exclusion by extricating Jesus from the separation of white ideology and replacing him within the black American existence. Cone saw God not as distant from black men and women, but radically close and as such radically distant from white America. Cone's theological vision began to outline a fundamental difference between racial and gender inequality: while blacks were seen as inferior, as nonbeings within American society, white women endured subjugation within a world of privilege. This is not to say that one mode of domination was worse than another. I do not want us to lose the central strand of our question: why does domination happen within relationship for some, and why does domination result in distance for others?

But there is a third space to consider that makes visible the more complicated interconnections between race and gender and thus how the consequences of the fall are not entirely separate modes of being, but in fact collectively interpenetrate all of our daily lives. This third space of subjugation is also found within the colonial world and especially in

18. See Avila, *Popular Culture.*

19. See Cone, *God of the Oppressed.* It should be noted that Cone deviated from a more integrationist theological posture advocated by theologians such as Deotis J. Roberts, who, while equally critical of white supremacy and racism, resisted Cone's more radical claims of a fundamental distance between white and black. See Roberts, *Liberation and Reconciliation.*

the American slave system. When the importation of slaves was made illegal, the American slave system became deeply concerned with its slaves' reproductive capacities.[20] However, these reproductive capacities were not relegated only to slaves, because slave masters frequently visited the quarters of their female slaves, often bringing friends or sons. To quote Langston Hughes, the Southern sky was full of "yellow stars."[21] Thus, black bodies were the objects of violent desire while at the same time they were loathed as the very negation of white womanhood.

The black female body constituted a point that was not outside of white life. Rather, it penetrated the white consciousness, creating a boundary of what was not pure, even when the mixed child, this impurity, moved within white life, confronting its male and female inhabitants. In a similar manner, the black male body, in the years following the Civil War, would be seen as a severe threat against the purity of white womanhood. Accusations of rape and ill intent were the common (though duplicitous) reasons for the lynch mobs that sprung up throughout the United States between 1870 and 1920.[22]

The slave master's desire for his female slaves, the lynch mobs pursuing black men, these particular spaces help us to see the intersection between gender and race as the confluence of two distinct aspects of difference that amplify one another in the moment of encounter between men and women and between different races/ethnicities. Racial difference was articulated as approximating whiteness to the *imago Dei* in ways that were similar to descriptions of women as descended from men and thus ontologically bound to submissiveness.[23] And yet racial subjugations became manifest within colonial society in the form of plantations, rape,

20. Copeland, *Enfleshing Freedom*, 25–27. See also Hartman, *Scenes of Subjection*.

21. Hughes, "Mulatto."

22. See Wells-Barnett, *On Lynchings*.

23. For an example in early Christian thought, refer to Augustine's description of women cited above. The articulation of an ontological difference bound in a view of creation would be echoed by European and American thinkers throughout the sixteeth to nineteenth centuries; they drew on the language of the Great Chain of Being that classified all living things in relationship to God, with European humanity at the highest rungs of the chain. Historian Winthrop Jordan notes the care with which African bodies would be at once portrayed as more than ape-like but less than white, thus attempting to acknowledge certain bodily similarities while also inscribing particular ontological differences that would not weaken the hierarchy (and the economic and social structures) tied to those physical classifications. See Jordan, *White Man's Burden*, 194–204.

lynching, and segregation. These patterns of violence were the creation of deep cultural distances, punctuated by severe intrusions of intimate violence. White identity perpetually resisted the presence of the dark body within its domestic space, its everyday space, in any measure of equality or freedom. Its presence within the domestic was always subject to terror and control.

The American slave system created a curious set of interconnections wherein African-Americans were perpetually distanced through physical and discursive violence, and yet (in the American South) they remained in close physical proximity to their oppressors. In the wake of the Civil War, the cultural distance would come to be geographic as segregation policed dark bodies in order to preserve white bodies. In contrast, the subjugation of women has taken place within the intimate spaces of homes and family enclaves and persists in the everyday interactions of working, shopping, playing.

While the violence of American racial economy has waned, the power of its distancing remains. This interrelationship is further seen in contemporary patterns of interracial marriage. The Pew Research Center recently reported that interracial marriages have increased to 14.5 percent from 7 percent in 1980.[24] Do these statistics point to a profound new openness to diverse peoples and the possibility of a "post-racial" era? Closer examination of the data reveals that of the 14 percent, only 9 percent of these marriages include white men or women. Also, African-American women marry outside of their race at the lowest percentage, while Asian-American men marry outside of their race at half the rate that Asian-American women do. What do these patterns indicate? Although interracial marriage is increasing, these patterns are not equal among races; they move away from certain racialized and gendered bodies (Asian-American men and especially African-American women) while being overrepresented by others (Asian-American women.) Thus, these patterns of interracial marriage do not fundamentally disrupt patterns of racial desire, but in fact replicate patterns where black female bodies are discarded and Asian-American bodies are fetishized and desired for their exotic approximation to white female bodies.[25] Thus, interracial marriage

24. Passel et al., "Marrying Out."

25. For a crucial account of the connection between colonialism and the fetishization of African and Asian bodies, see Young, *Colonial Desire*, 98. Recent statistics on interracial marriage reveal a crucial divide in the contemporary situation, where certain notions of difference (blackness) can be seen as being resisted while other notions

is moving along gendered and (ironically) racialized lines. Put differently, racial difference and desire become narrated or worked out within gendered articulations of difference.

These pockets of racial and gender intersection reveal that difference continues to articulate itself within an economy of distance and domesticity, rendering certain bodies as undesirable or unsafe while strictly disciplining female bodies within the confines of daily suburbanized existence.[26] In this way, two distinct narrations of difference become reflected in our daily lives, either through the disciplined order of male-female relations, the racially stratified realities of modern cities, or a third space where gender and race become reciprocating realities that both order and animate desires and the distortions of difference that gave rise to such interstitial spaces in the first place.

A Theological Appraisal

But how do we begin to parse the significance of these patterns theologically? To do this, we must return again to Simone de Beauvoir's important observation regarding the difference between race and gender. Beauvoir highlighted what, in her mind, was the fundamental difference between gender and race. For Beauvoir, racial (and ethnic) identity "can point to creation of the Other by the One. Historically considered, Jews and Blacks have not always existed whereas there have always been women."[27] While her contention that all difference is created from above may be problematized by more recent considerations of how societies articulate themselves in relationship to power, her primary point is nonetheless crucial. A fundamental difference between race and gender is the enduring presence of women. Beauvoir alluded to a tension that can be more clearly seen when

---

of difference (Asianness) are disproportionately favored. Questions of assimilation and the troubling notion of Asian-Americans as a "model minority" must be worked through here, but the pattern of interracial marriage reveals that its increasing numbers do not mitigate the legacy of racial and gender differences, but it operates within patterns of difference that the modern world fosters.

26. This economy of the distance and domesticity can be seen again in the sociological phenomenon of "white flight," especially in the urban sprawl of the 1960s. As US cities increased in minority population, white flight escaped farther and farther in the name of safety or education. Suburban patterns of relationship began to shift or at least became more firmly consolidated around the nuclear family and the husband as the breadwinner, further isolating women within suburban duties and imaginations.

27. Beauvoir, *Second Sex*, xxv.

the assertion of women's seeming "transcendence," which seems almost natural, is placed in relationship to her more well-known assertion that "a woman is not born, she is made."

What are we to make of Beauvoir's seemingly contradictory remarks regarding women's historicity (or social construction) and woman as a fact (or essential)? In these two statements, Beauvoir expresses that femininity, or the characteristics (and social standing) seemingly bound to women's ovaries (and intellect), is undoubtedly the construction of a male-dominated society that has construed power, intellect, and rationality in strictly male terms that render as normative male bodies and ways of being in the world and as subordinate women's bodies and ways of being in the world. A woman's life, in Beauvoir's view, perpetually lives into these realities. In this way a woman is "made." And yet, unlike race or ethnicity, where we can point to a time when it was not, women have always existed. Women and men are different in ways that do not shift or change over time. There was never a time when there were no women.[28]

Beauvoir describes the identity of the body in relationship to these difficulties: "Nevertheless it will be said that if the body is not a *thing*, it is a situation."[29] Beauvoir's contention that the body is a situation does much to point to the various contingencies that demarcate not only female bodies, but all bodies. Her description of the way maleness inflects itself upon femaleness thus shows that this is not merely a consequence of poor choices, but a profound misapprehension of what different bodies are for: autonomy rather than community, domination rather than gift. Her observation opens up for us a pattern of differentiation within creation in the way in which the female body was drawn into a fundamental and necessary relationship with the man (domestic), while for non-white bodies distance was concretized. Cultures remained distinct. (Even in a world of burgeoning globalization, difference is drawn and disciplined to become appropriate consumption.)

The "fact" of women's bodies, of difference between men and women more generally, encounters people with the perpetual refusal of these differences. For Beauvoir, the only possibility of escape was in some construct of autonomy, which in its own way reiterated the differentiation of the fall more acutely. The conception of human possibility as an individual reality

28. Critical theorist Toril Moi offers a reading of Beauvoir that shifts away from a strict notion of gender performance advocated by theorists such as Judith Butler. As Moi explains, "For Beauvoir women exist, for Butler they must be deconstructed" (Moi, *What Is a Woman?*, 76).

29. Beauvoir, *Second Sex*, xxv.

is a tragic illusion that seeks to mitigate the radical claim of the human situation as creatures. The refusal of this fact gave rise to these patterns of domination in the first place.

Theologically speaking, conceptions of difference as domestication and distancing allow us to begin to reimagine Christ's own work and thus humanity within his salvific presence. In Christ, the domestic and the distant are drawn radically near one another. God who is fundamentally Other, who is as far from us as anything could be, is also radically near, nearer to ourselves than we can be to ourselves. Even further, Jesus ruptures these economies of differentiation in such a way that they must be overlapped, but overlapped and offered as our human situation, as the fact of our existence that must be lived into as an "already but not yet," an eschatological body as Sarah Coakley describes it.[30] Christ enters into this economy through the womb of a woman, through a radically domestic occurrence that itself was the product of a profound reordering of male-female relationships such that Joseph was to follow Mary, in a way. Even in Christ's conception, God's injunction to Adam to "rule" over Eve is recapitulated in Mary's obedience and Joseph's submission to Mary's mission and calling. In doing so, the communion of male and female as the *imago Dei* is recapitulated, and it offers those who follow Christ a radically different image of marriage and male/female relationships from the decrepit structure of male marital hierarchy.

Similarly, Christ also displays what I call the fundamentally mulattic character of Christian discipleship. That is, Christ's constitutes the re-creation of a third space. Where in the slave system the third space was one of intermixture through violence and transgression, Christ, God, becomes flesh in Mary's womb, so that Christ's constitution as flesh and spirit re-creates human identity and thus takes humanity's desire to be like God into his own body. Rather than this movement usurping power and distorting the human image, by virtue of being fully God and fully man, Christ draws humanity into a new humanity. This new humanity is characterized by what I call the "neither/nor-but," a rather awkward way of describing how difference is now reconfigured in Christ's body and humanity. This transformation is similar to the children of those transgressions in what would become a third space of the slave system.

The mixed children of the American slave system were bound to both peoples, yet they were never fully a part of white society. At the same time, through preferential treatment of masters or their own occasional

30. See Coakley, " Eschatological Body."

attempts to differentiate from the field slave, the mulatto came to occupy a nebulous middle space. Within this space, the mulatto would make clearer the illusory nature of race claims, yet continued to succumb to America's racial logic. Within this logic, whiteness remained tethered to the image of God and dark bodies were articulated as distant, separate from what it meant to be truly a child of God. Such spaces were tragic and led inevitably to death in contexts where identity is claimed to be absolute, natural; in this way, a likeness to God led inevitably to assertions of submission of the other. Yet expressing Christ as mulatto reorders racial logic by reimagining social space and the possibilities of personhood within these spaces. Christ inhabited a "mulatto" situation and consequently the human situation, because the mulatto is bound to all. As such, "'Neither/nor-but existence' is a 'mulattic' existence, drawn in the midst of negations which continually assert what it is not, but in the midst of embodying and making those boundaries apparent."[31] Racial identity that refuses difference refuses change, inherently refuses God and the nature of Christ's redemptive act of a mulatto Jesus. "This Christological claim also bears witness to the assertion of an identity within bodily space that draws the boundaries into itself, transforming conceptions of in and out, high and low, and thus blurring the ways in which we assert what bodies will and will not be and what they might be transformed into and what they cannot be transformed into."[32]

In Christ, that which was far away was brought near, that which was different and impure was *Mitsein*, to be with. Race and gender as situations, as facts of our existence that must be lived into and repented of, each articulate aspects of humanity's refusal as well as aspects of what it means to be human, to be with God. In acknowledging that we are not God, that the power of our creation does not lay within our own self-assertion, we become free to be bound to other races and ethnicities and thus become changed in the process. In acknowledging that God is with us, that God is radically near, we become free to abide with God and with God's creation in such a way that the particularities of our genders (their radical particularities, of such and such, or so and so) can flourish within daily modes of worship and life together.

The questions of race and gender are not fundamentally the same question. Thus, collapsing the realities of race and gender into one another, or keeping them perpetually apart, only serves to perpetuate the

31. Bantum, *Redeeming Mulatto*, 108.
32. Ibid., 108–9.

disconnect between gender roles/possibilities and those with whom we desire to live/those of whom we are afraid. In doing so, the church reiterates problematic modes of domestication and distance, the very structures of sin that were overturned within the household of Joseph and Mary, within the confines of a man and woman bound together to raise God. While an examination of these distinct aspects of race and gender, domesticity and distance, are not intended to exhaustively describe the human condition, it is my hope that in imagining their effects upon our lives we come to understand the fundamentally communal nature of lives as disciples, that our identities are the accumulation of a variety of identifications.[33] Our lives can at once demonstrate how persons are pressed by forces of domination even as our own lives press upon others. To universalize these patterns is to ignore their timbre and impact at different times and to varying degrees. This difficult task of description and confession is the task of discipleship, made all the more possible by articulating the realities of race and gender in perpetual conversation with one another, rather than as competing descriptions of who we are. In holding these two together, we see both their similarities and their differences, but more importantly, these insights allow us to see the particularities of Christ's work afresh.

Bibliography

Alexander, Michelle. *The New Jim Crow: Mass Incarceration in an Age of Colorblindness.* New York: New Press, 2010.

Augustine. *Confessions.* Translated by Maria Boulding. New York: Vintage, 1998.

Avila, Eric. *Popular Culture in the Age of White Flight: Fear and Fantasy in Suburban Los Angeles.* Berkeley: University of California Press, 2004.

Bantum, Brian. *Redeeming Mulatto: A Theology of Race and Christian Hybridity.* Waco, TX: Baylor University Press, 2010.

Beauvoir, Simone de. *The Second Sex.* New York: Vintage, 1989.

Bhabha, Homi. *The Location of Culture.* New York: Routledge, 1994.

Bonhoeffer, Dietrich. *Creation and Fall.* Dietrich Bonhoeffer Works 3. Minneapolis: Fortress, 1997.

Carter, J. Kameron. "Race, Religion and the Contradictions of Identity in Frederick Douglass' 1845 Narrative," *Modern Theology* 21/1 (2005) 37–65.

33. Discipleship is a following of Christ that takes up the particularities of one's life—gender, race, ethnicity, community, nation—and draws one's habits of mind, practices, and modes of life into the habits, practices, and modes of life that are perpetually present in Christ's body and in the life of the church. Further, discipleship is not only about personhood, but also the communal and institutional structures of everyday life and the ways in which Christ's followers bend into Christ those around them.

Clotfelter, Charles T. *After Brown: The Rise and Retreat of School Desegregation.* Princeton, NJ: Princeton University Press, 2008.

Coakley, Sarah. "The Eschatological Body: Gender, Transformation, and God." *Modern Theology* 16/1 (2000) 61–73.

Cone, James. *God of the Oppressed.* Maryknoll, NY: Orbis, 1997.

Copeland, Shawn. *Enfleshing Freedom: Body, Race, Being.* Minneapolis: Fortress, 2010.

Emerson, Michael, and Christian Smith. *Divided by Faith: Evangelical Religion and the Problem of Race in America.* Oxford: Oxford University Press, 2000.

Harrison, Verna E. F. "Gender, Generation, and Virginity in Cappadocian Theology." *Journal of Theological Studies* 47/1 (1996) 38–68.

Hartman, Saidiya V. *Scenes of Subjection: Terror, Slavery, and Self-Making in Nineteenth-Century America.* New York: Oxford University Press, 1997.

Hughes, Langston. "Mulatto." In *The Collected Poems of Langston Hughes*, edited by Arnold Rampersad, 100–101. New York: Vintage, 1994.

Jennings, Willie James. *Christian Imagination: Theology and the Origins of Race.* New Haven, CT: Yale University Press, 2010.

Jordan, Winthrop. *The White Man's Burden: Historical Origins of Racism in the United States.* New York: Oxford University Press, 1974.

Moi, Toril. *What Is a Woman?: And Other Essays.* Oxford: Oxford University Press, 1999.

Passel, Jeffrey S., Wendy Wang, and Paul Taylor. "Marrying Out: One-in-Seven New U.S. Marriages is Interracial or Interethnic." Pew Research Center, June 4, 2010; rev. June 10, 2010. Online: http://pewsocialtrends.org/files/2010/10/755-marrying-out.pdf.

Rivera Pagán, Luis. *A Violent Evangelism: The Political and Religious Conquest of the Americas.* Louisville: Westminster John Knox, 1992.

Roberts, J. Deotis. *Liberation and Reconciliation: A Black Theology.* Louisville: Westminster John Knox, 2005.

Schüssler Fiorenza, Elisabeth. *Jesus: Miriam's Child, Sophia's Prophet: Critical Issues in Feminist Christology.* New York: Continuum, 1994.

Sollors, Werner. *Neither White nor Black, Yet Both: Thematic Explorations of Interracial Literature.* Cambridge, MA: Harvard University Press, 1997.

Wells-Barnett, Ida B. *On Lynchings: Southern Horrors, a Red Record, Mob Rule in New Orleans.* New York: Arno, 1969.

Williams, Delores. *Sisters in the Wilderness: The Challenge of Womanist God-Talk.* Maryknoll, NY: Orbis, 1993.

Young, Robert J. C. *Colonial Desire: Hybridity in Theory, Culture and Race.* New York: Routledge, 1995.

8

Is This the New Girl Order?

Representations of Post-Feminist Identities in Sex and the City [1]

ALLYSON JULE

Introduction

SEX AND THE CITY 2 opened in cinemas across the U.S. and Canada in May 2010. By all accounts, the movie was a disappointment, particularly to film critics, who judged both the first and second *Sex and the City* movies as vapid, shallow, and even regressive regarding women's roles and sexuality in American society. However, the original TV show was, in fact, quite interesting for feminist scholars because it was challenging and provocative concerning an emerging new feminism. The original show ran on the independent cable network HBO, freeing it from the usual mainstream censors in the U.S. The TV show was an adaptation of journalist Candace Bushnell's weekly light and breezy newspaper column and semi-autobiographical best-selling 1997 book of the same name. The story itself (both in print and on screen) focuses on four women and their close, supportive friendship in the midst of sometimes distressing

1. This paper was originally conceived as a conference paper for the International Gender and Language Association (IGALA) in Wellington, New Zealand.

story lines, such as infertility, breast cancer, sexual discrimination in the workplace, and the breakdown of marriages and long-term partnerships. Each of the four main characters represents slightly different versions of femininity: the glamorous Samantha loves lots of sex with many different men; Miranda is an ambitious, determined, and hard-working lawyer; Charlotte represents an ultra-conservative and romantic character; and Carrie, the writer and main character, serves as a fun-loving and reflective combination of glamour, self-determination, and idealism. The themes and plot of each episode are framed by questions Carrie asks (as a voice-over) in her weekly newspaper columns.

Of particular concern for me is the larger hyper-sexualized culture represented in much media which surrounds my students at a Christian university. Though Christian higher education has long been concerned with maintaining some distance from popular culture (to "be in the world but not of it"; Rom 12:2), my view is that I want my students to search anywhere and everywhere for what is "true, honorable, just, pure, lovely, commendable" as a spiritual discipline (Phil 4:8). In this regard, I think TV shows inadvertently can offer relevant conversation starters to explore the life-affirming gospel message of redemption in the midst of real lives, even urban secular ones. Also, I have to admit that I was thirty-three in 1998—the same age as the character of Carrie at the time of the original broadcasts. That is to say, it feels to me that *Sex and the City* has been my generation of women's iconic show. As a social scientist, I find the show intriguing and see it as a tool for understanding contemporary society. Further, as a Christian feminist social scientist, it should be no surprise that the show holds some intrigue to me regarding emerging versions of the female self.

My intention in this essay is to explore the closure of the *Sex and the City* TV series (not the movies) from a social-semiotic perspective and point out the emerging embodiment of today's feminism; that is to say, I think *Sex and the City* offers versions of post-feminist[2] identities that matter more to today's college students than second-wave feminists might fully appreciate. More specifically, I propose that all four female characters (with the particular focus on the main character, Carrie Bradshaw) represent what Anoop Nayak and Mary Jane Kehily call the "New Girl Order," where females are seen simultaneously as controllers of their own destinies, as powerful in terms of their financial independence and sexual

2. By "post-feminist," I am referring to the multiple and diverse strains of feminist activity and study since what is known as the mid-century second-wave feminism.

freedom, but also as deeply connected with traditional femininity as particularly revealed in what they say concerning their own desires. Nayak and Kehily reclaim the term "girl" as a key identifier of a version of womanhood as sassy, sexy, and more fun than the feminists of the 1970s, often viewed as too serious. The term "woman" feels too heavy—too "feminist." In the New Girl Order, feminist sisterhood is important but so is the traditional value of domestic happiness and intimacy with a man.

The New Girl Order

It is helpful at the outset to locate the New Girl Order alongside what is commonly called third-wave feminism. As Caryn Riswold in this volume suggests, the third wave is "populated by women and men who came of age during and after the second wave of feminism," and that generation (my own) came to understand "gender equality alongside racial equality and the social construction of sexuality" as simply part of contemporary life in the Western world.[3] In particular, Christians have had to come to terms with feminism as culturally at odds with traditional gender roles previously assumed (the male to lead, the woman to follow). Riswold names this tension between feminism and Christianity today as a "complicated middle ground" that is informed by the experiences of those born and raised during and after the 1970s women's movement. Further, she suggests that this middle ground has been largely vacated because "groups of people have decided that engaging with the other is no longer necessary."[4] I propose that the terms "third wave" and "New Girl Order" are more or less synonymous. However, I see the New Girl Order as more representative of an emerging new wave of feminism: a generation whose version of female empowerment embraces traditional notions of femininity while assuming feminist freedoms.

The New Girl Order views identities as contradictory and as containing multiple selves and desires that coexist. It allows for women's financial independence, fulfilling and absorbing careers, the accompanying enjoyment of consumerism, and yet open displays of femininity (such as the wearing of sexy shoes and high-fashion clothing). In addition, the New Girl Order embraces open displays of sexual behavior (including much talk about sex and desire) without shame and accepts a range of sexualities and explorations. There also exists a strong grounding of power in female

3. Riswold, "Conversations and Intersections," ch. 10 in this book.
4. Ibid.

JULE—*Is This the New Girl Order?*

friendships while still pursuing the ultimate male-female relationship: the final romantic closure to life's various story lines. Angela McRobbie[5] alerts us to the hidden problem inherent here: that the feminine often emerges as the less attractive identity because it verges on neediness and more infantile expressions and gestures. The feminist energy of self-reliance can be sexier, more interesting, and more engaging than the stereotypical female experience.

Sex and the City portrays a glossy image of four white, privileged, self-involved American women obsessed to various degrees and for various reasons with relationships (often with men), yet it simultaneously explores and engages feminist issues such as choice, sexuality, and success. Each story line remains strongly positioned within the female friendship bond, which offers each woman support and solidarity. Here, the New Girl Order emerges for and from women who represent "the ideal neo-liberal subjects for post-industrial times."[6] In the specific location of affluent Manhattan, there exists an elevated view of women, one that displays "high esteem" because today's American white women have benefitted from feminism; as a result, they are "more flexible, presentable and capable" than ever before.[7] Such women are also newly positioned in contemporary culture as the subjects of consumption, which *Sex and the City* represents well in the fashion focus of the main characters on their expensive shoes and clothes.

Further, the New Girl Order confidently (perhaps, some would say, naively) claims and assumes equality with men. For instance, the main character, Carrie, serves as a personally empowered woman, a white thirty-something New Yorker living alone in the early twenty-first century who came of age in the 1980s; she assumes her own gender equality as a woman in a progressive world but also desires intimacy with her Mr. Right (called "Big" throughout). In fact, all four female characters (Samantha, Miranda, Charlotte, and Carrie) are celebrated as women of the New Girl Order because they each "merge the feminine and the feminist in moments of humour and pathos."[8]

While the feminist and the feminine attempt to exist together in *Sex and the City*, such presentations of women have incurred criticism from feminists. In general, feminists don't like the show. Alice Wignall, for example, suggests that the entire show was about one main

5. McRobbie, "Reflections on Young Women."
6. Nayak and Kehily, *Gender, Youth, and Culture*, 52.
7. Ibid., 67.
8. Ibid., 69.

relationship—Carrie's quest for Mr. Right, a.k.a. Big. Wignall sees this premise as problematic for feminists in large part because Big is "arrogant, egocentric and apparently unable to see a good thing" in Carrie (online).[9] Jaime Weinman heavily criticizes the show for leaving a legacy of "neurotic, sex-obsessed" women who are now less powerful (not more powerful) than they've been in years because they are now more self-absorbed and far less concerned with changing social injustices or engaging with larger civil rights (something second-wave feminism focused/focuses on).[10] The show pivots around the friendship of women, and this is perhaps the strongest feminist aspect of the show; however, all four characters focus on their relational experiences with men and their varied but similar quests to find the perfect final romantic fit.

Analysis: Modernist Text and the New Girl Order

Terry Eagleton[11] articulated modernist fiction as requiring discourses that allow for a "closing down" of story lines in order to bring some satisfying closure. This need in modernism for certainty and clarity undermines the alternative postmodern reality that real life rarely offers such endings: most of our own story lines are vague, unresolved, and contradictory. *Sex and the City* presents us with a clash of a modernist text in search of a clean ending with the post-feminist celebration throughout of various, complex, and unresolved desires, including both personal freedom and deep intimacy with another.

The scenes explored here are the final few in the story line of Carrie Bradshaw's quest for the perfect man. In the final episode (season 6, episode 8, "An American Girl in Paris, Part Deux"), there are the farewell conversations Carrie has with her Russian lover, Alex, and then with Big, who comes to Paris to claim her for himself. For the analysis, I have relied on social-semiotic methods,[12] complemented by speech-act theory.[13] I examine the ways in which Carrie, the main character, brings her story line to a close in these scenes (at least until the movie picks it up again four years later). Overall, there is a strong modernist move towards establishing closure, resolution, and a fairy-tale romantic ending, leaving the audience

9. Wignall, "Can a Feminist."
10. Weinman, "Curse of *Sex and the City*."
11. Eagleton, *Literary Theory*.
12. Kress and Van Leeuwen, *Reading Images*.
13. Austin, *How to Do Things with Words*.

with a feel-good factor and only a vague sense of some unsatisfied desire.[14] Carrie's great love, Big (unnamed until the last moment of the finale), represents both a seductive and limited romantic archetype. Joanna Di Mattia[15] discusses at length Carrie's relationship with Big, contrasting Big with other men in Carrie's life over the course of the series, particularly the all-American sensitive guy, Aiden Shaw, and the moody Russian artist, Alexandre Petrovsky. These other relationships seemed to offer other alternatives to the romantic fairy tale that Carrie is looking for, but she ultimately secures in Big by the end of the series a high romantic note.

There are moments throughout the three scenes that come across as a bit cliché, and as a result they make rather uncomfortable viewing. This might simply be that, from a feminist perspective, certain characterizations of post-feminist identities can seem shallow and unprincipled. Even if we *fully* embrace the notion of post-feminism as embracing and admitting to complexities and ambiguities, and celebrate *Sex and the City* for this, there remain aspects of the text that are problematic. Carrie's rather needy behavior in scene 25, the hotel bedroom scene, is one example. The conventional gushing love scene on the Seine is another. I argue that the reason for this sense of discomfort arises from the view that *Sex and the City* is structurally a modernist fictional text,[16] straining to represent a post-feminist version of reality, while needing to bring some closure to the story. (Could it simply have stopped midstream?) This need for closure imposes certain constraints upon the characterization and the story lines, which become evident during the closing scenes. Perhaps such tensions reflect the complexities of today's young women in search of self: the ideals may not mix with the realities.

In the final scenes, there is a strong move towards establishing closure, resolution, even a fairy-tale romantic ending, leaving the audience with a feel-good factor and reaffirming the status quo. According to Eagleton, modernist fiction relies on conservative discourses, and in particular relation to gender, *patriarchal* discourses, for such a closing down to become possible.[17] If we look at the four main plot lines generally, we see the power of patriarchal discourses serving to "consensualize the fates" of the key characters:

14. Lacan, *Ecrits.*
15. Di Mattia, "What's the Harm in Believing?"
16. Barthes, *Mythologies*; Eagleton, *Literary Theory.*
17. Eagleton, *Literary Theory.*

- Samantha loses her "masculinized" sex drive as she discovers the curative power of romantic love, ironically through the cathartic experience of breast cancer. In effect, she becomes "feminine."

- Miranda, the most career driven of the four, submits herself to the traditional notion of nuclear family life, embracing love, marriage, and parenthood.

- Charlotte, the most traditional of the four, adopts an underprivileged child from China to complete her dreams for the perfect all-American, heterosexual family in light of her husband's infertility.

- Carrie fulfills her fairy-tale dream of marrying/settling down for romantic love.

So how do the closing scenes construct multiple identities for Carrie, the lead character, but simultaneously undermine these in the quest for modernist resolution and closure to the story? Scene 25, for example, seems to be explicitly about Carrie's negotiation between two competing rather than merging identities—the feminist and the feminine. She feels that her identity needs have not been sufficiently recognized by her Russian lover, Alex, and she is unhappy about this. From a feminist perspective, Carrie appears to be discovering who she is, what she really wants in life, and her need to express this. As a result, she uses a series of self-referential statements:

I'm in this relationship too. I am a person, in this relationship.

This self-referential style alternates between the two characters as they directly address the issue of their identities throughout the scene:

Alex: I'm so sorry. I thought I was clear all along about who I am.

Carrie: Well, maybe it's time to be clear about who I am.

Carrie asserts herself strongly against the patriarchal implications of Alex's statement that his professional identity (as an artist) takes precedence over their relationship. This is the moment when she takes control of the conversation and makes a passionate declaration in support of her needs as a person:

I am someone who is looking for love. Real love. Ridiculous, inconvenient, consuming, can't-live-without-each-other love. And I don't think . . . that love is here in . . . in this expensive

suite in . . . in this lovely hotel . . . in Paris. It's not your fault; it's
. . . it's my fault. I shouldn't have come here.

Carrie's strength of feeling is indexed by a series of emotive adjectives
that accumulate in power: *real . . . ridiculous . . . inconvenient . . . consum-*
ing . . . can't-live-without-each-other. In terms of content, this utterance
encapsulates the traditional heroine's quest of romantic fiction for true
love. However, in terms of function, the utterance performs two key
speech acts. First, it declares Carrie's sense of self and demands recognition of this from Alex. Secondly, it serves to "finish" the relationship,
which is underscored a little later on by her action of leaving the room.
In feminist terms, this characterizes her as a strong, independent, and
assertive woman who takes her share of responsibility for the relationship's failure. However, in "feminine" terms, scene 25 offers a competing
identity, which ultimately undermines the feminist reading. In the early
part of the scene, Carrie is seriously annoyed with her Russian boyfriend:

> I'm in this relationship too. I am a person, in this relationship.
> Have you any idea what it's been like for me here? Eating alone
> and waiting for my boyfriend who would rather spend time
> with a light installation?

While Carrie manages to be witty about her plight, a feminine reading is
that Carrie feels insufficiently adored as a woman. Alex is not manifesting
enough devotion to her; he is not living up to the romantic stereotype
of a besotted lover. She might be a strong, independent woman on one
level, but she also demonstrates a high level of neediness on another level.
The message here is, "You don't love me enough so I'm going to have a
tantrum and then I will dump you!" McRobbie argues that Carrie comes
across here as a narcissistic, infantile, self-obsessed, and affected figure,
which rather undermines the identity of her as a strong, assertive, independent woman.[18] But this contradiction can be interpreted in various
ways. Perhaps one of the consequences of the feminine alongside a feminist identity is that more feminine characterization can appear demanding and needy. If a woman wants to be taken seriously as a person but at
the same time to be recognized as desirable to men, then her appearing to
be needy *may* be a necessary outcome. Another reading of this behavior
might be that Carrie's complex characterization is being sacrificed to the
modernist quest for a clear narrative closure.

18. McRobbie, "Reflections on Young Women."

Then there is a shift in scene 26 toward feminist versions of identity when Carrie meets Big in the hotel lobby. The narrative attempts to subvert the classic fairy-tale motif by having Big arrive in a black suit rather than shining armor to rescue the damsel in distress (Carrie lying in a crumpled heap on the floor). Carrie has already insisted to the hotel receptionist that she can pay for her own room, so she is clearly viewed as financially independent. And she is also seen to be emotionally independent. Rather than allowing Big to race up the stairs to challenge the Russian in a "pistols at dusk" showdown, Carrie struggles to gain control over the situation.

I don't need you to do this. Stop, this is totally unnecessary.

She is ironically self-aware of the part in the fairy-tale narrative she tries to resist:

I took care of this myself. I don't need you to rescue me.

She is as speedy as he is racing up the stairs; he is the vulnerable one in this scene because of his heart condition; she is the one who literally "floors" him, and they lie on the floor laughing together. In feminist terms, this act of slapstick is a semiotic index of their supposed equality in the relationship. However, the quest for modernist closure reasserts itself in scene 27, which presents the classic romantic moment on the bridge over the Seine where Carrie not only makes her lifetime commitment to Mr. Big, but also asks him passively to "take me home." Despite the equality demonstrated in the previous scene, Carrie has indeed been rescued by Big.

Perhaps the case for modernist closure invoking patriarchal norms is best demonstrated in the narrative structure of these three closing scenes, which manifest many of the features of classic realist fiction.[19] Carrie gradually moves from a state of self-delusion—loving the wrong man—to discovering the "truth": she has been in love with Big all along. With the Russian, Alex, she was simply *playing* at being in love according to stereotyped notions of romance—Paris, the fancy hotel, expensive necklace, romantic gestures. Thus, the romance with Alex can be read as a fake and could never match up to the "real thing," hence Carrie's show of neediness, perhaps. According to the fake/real-love dichotomy, she sensed that the relationship with an exotic "other" could not ultimately fulfill her, while her culturally compatible, all-American male can. With

19. Eagleton, *Literary Theory.*

Big, who is also associated with New York and her female friends who live there, she has found her "real" self. In modernist terms, she has at last discovered her "true" identity, which brings the epic narrative to a close. But her true identity is here defined in terms of learning who she really *loves*, rather than who she really *is*.

Conclusion

Sex and the City is a challenging text in its representation of multiple identities, and the modernist quest for closure requires compromises with the characters and story lines in the final scenes. In order for Carrie to discover her "true" self, she must submit herself to the towering masculinity of Big; she appears to do so wholeheartedly and with genuine relief that the quest is finally over. The question remains as to whether the show can be written off by feminists as a capitulation to patriarchy and women's deepest desire being for a man. Very briefly, I would argue that the more famous final closing scene suggests otherwise. In the final scene, Carrie walks the streets of New York first with her four friends and then continues her journey alone. She delivers a long, final voice-over describing the different types of relationships the character experienced during the series. The monologue culminates with these words:

> But the most exciting, challenging, and significant relationship of all is the one you have with yourself. And if you find someone to love the you [that] you love . . . well, that's just fabulous.

As Carrie says the word "significant," viewers see an image of her cell phone light up with a crucial piece of information: the first name of Big (John), which has been tantalizingly withheld throughout 94 episodes. Her body language shows her to be happier than at any previous point. The release of his name signifies the end of a journey. She has captured her big love and has been rescued by him in reply. In this way, the ending offers us a glimpse of the New Girl Order: there is something very much on offer in the feminist worldview but also something irresistible in the feminine desire for intimacy with another. The New Girl Order celebrates both.

Finally, in terms of students in my classroom, a discussion of the New Girl Order resonates well with them, including (and even particularly) those who consider themselves part of a Christian subculture. As human beings, we struggle with competing desires and commitments:

to be strong and self-reliant and yet able to give way to others and relate within meaningful intimate relationships. Understanding our own power of personal agency alongside an ethic of consideration for others and a desire for relationships is a paradox worth pondering. My hope is that my students can grab hold of the deep complexity of personhood. I think the New Girl Order may well be a helpful notion in the fumbling towards wholeness and relevant for today's young woman and those who love her. Each generation must grapple with its own societal realities, its own social contexts concerning gendered expectation. I believe the exploration of today's post-feminist images can be an important and helpful experience for today's young people.

Bibliography

Austin, John L. *How to Do Things with Words*. Cambridge, MA: Harvard University, 1962.

Barthes, Roland. *Mythologies*. London: Penguin, 1981.

Baxter, Judith. *Positioning Gender in Discourse: A Feminist Methodology*. Basingstoke: Palgrave, 2003.

Di Mattia, Joanna. "What's the Harm in Believing?: Mr. Big, Mr. Perfect, and the Romantic Quest for *Sex and the City*'s Mr. Right." In *Reading Sex and the City*, edited by Kim Akass and Janet McCabe, 17–32. New York: Palgrave Macmillan, 2004.

Dow, Bonnie. *Prime-time Feminism: Television, Media, Culture and the Women's Movement Since 1970*. Pittsburgh: University of Pennsylvania, 1996.

Eagleton, Terry. *Literary Theory: An Introduction*. Oxford: Blackwell, 1983.

Kress, Gunther, and Theo Van Leeuwen. *Reading Images: The Grammar of Visual Design*. London: Routledge, 2006.

Lacan, Jacque. *Ecrits: A Selection*. Translated by A. Sheridan. London: Tavistock, 1977.

McRobbie, Angela. "Reflections on Young Women and Consumer Culture." Paper presented at HM Treasury, London, AHRC Cultures of Consumption, 2004.

Nayak, Anoop, and Mary Jane Kehily. *Gender, Youth, and Culture: Young Masculinities and Femininities*. Basingstoke, UK: Palgrave Macmillan, 2008.

Weinman, Jaime. "The Curse of *Sex and the City*." *Maclean's*, April 28, 2008, 59–60.

Wignall, Alice. "Can a Feminist Really Love *Sex and the City*?" *The Guardian*, April 16, 2008. http://www.guardian.co.uk/lifeandstyle/2008/apr/16/women.film.

PART THREE

*Gender, Sexuality,
and Marriage*

9

(Theology of the) Body Language
Christopher West as Harlequin 2.0

KAREN TRIMBLE ALLIAUME

DURING MY FIRST YEAR in college in 1983, my dorm-mate Kathy approached me with a sheepish look on her face. She had been reading a romance novel, and it was giving her a strange, tingly feeling. She didn't know exactly what this feeling was, or how to deal with it, and she wanted to know if her feelings were normal. From my position as a more experienced romance reader, I tried to reassure her that they were. I started reading romance novels in high school, especially Harlequin Series romances from the late seventies and early eighties, with titles like *The Velvet Glove* and *The Long Surrender*. While I enjoyed them, I was also troubled, not so much by the sexual feelings the narratives aroused, but rather by what I thought of as the heroes' meanness. These particular romance novels featured older men who suspected young, innocent heroines of cheating on them and punished them accordingly, usually through sexual teasing. By the requisite happy ending, the hero's hostility had been explained away, revealed as evidence of his deepening love for the heroine: a grownup version of "he pulls your hair because he really likes you."

My college friend Kathy is Catholic, born and raised, and so am I, and that dorm hallway in which we discussed romance reading in low

173

voices was at a Catholic liberal arts college. In our families, there was a dearth of family sex talk, and in particular, of positive sex talk: what little knowledge we gleaned boiled down to *don't*. Don't have sex before marriage, don't use birth control even once you are married, and, much less explicitly, don't be gay.[1] Bereft of specific religious vocabulary with which to parse the goods and pleasures of sex, I found that my romance reading served as a platform from which to begin constructing a rudimentary feminist moral assessment of sexual relationships. My pleasure in reading romance novels gradually became guiltier, not because good Catholic girls didn't read sexy novels, but because the stories were premised on a relationship of gender inequality of which I couldn't, in good conscience, approve. The happily ever after ending could no longer justify for me the means (or meanness) that led to it.

In gleaning information about sex and romantic relationships from romance novels rather than our religion, Kathy and I were not so different from contemporary college students, for whom there is a "communication gap between Catholic youth and Catholic teaching" when it comes to sex.[2] Catholic college students, among the many interviewed by Donna Freitas for her 2008 book, *Sex and the Soul*, laugh at the idea that their faith has anything relevant to say to them about sex. One such student remarks, "If you consider yourself a *real Catholic* then [sex is] not acceptable."[3] Most of these students, Catholic and otherwise, struggle to build meaningful social lives in campus cultures in which hookups, sexual activity with no promise or expectation of a long-term relationship, have become the norm.[4] And what many really want, even more than good sex, is romance. In her study,

1. The official moral teachings of the Catholic magisterium (the teaching authority of the pope and bishops) restrict all moral sexual activity to marriage between a man and a woman. The definition of licit sex *within* marriage includes two aspects. First, it must be procreative, that is, open to the conception of children by the avoidance of means of artificial birth control (see Paul VI, *Humanae Vitae*, no. 11). Second, it must be unitive, fostering the mutual love and bonding between married partners. These parameters also serve as the rationale within Catholic moral theological tradition to prohibit homosexual sexual activity, both on the grounds that it cannot result in the procreation of children and that it is not unitive, because it is "objectively disordered" (see Congregation for the Doctrine of the Faith (hereafter CDF), *Persona Humana*, no. 7).The denial that homosexual sex can be unitive is used to refute the oft-made counter-argument that the Catholic Church allows men and women who are beyond the age of childbearing to marry, so why can't homosexual couples marry? The relevance of these teachings to Christopher West's work will be discussed later in this essay.

2. Freitas, *Sex and the Soul*, 195.

3. Ibid., 195.

4. Ibid., 70.

Freitas finds that both college women and men "tended to disassociate romance from sexual intimacy," and that "romance, to them, is chaste."[5] While evangelical Christian students can find accessible relationship and sex advice, couched in terms of their faith and often written by their own peers, Catholics "have to infer their ideal from movies, television shows, novels, and rumors among friends."[6]

Against this paucity of relevant and pithy Catholic-inflected sex advice, a writer like Christopher West, who offers his work as a romantic paean to the chastity extolled by Catholic tradition, easily stands out. West is the author of several popular works explicating the late Pope John Paul II's teachings on sexuality and marriage, collectively known as the "theology of the body."[7] His popular versions of John Paul's teachings about sex and marriage are appealing and effective to a young Catholic female audience longing for romance, because his rhetorical strategies fulfill the same promise of Harlequin romances: that "it is possible really to be taken care of and to achieve that state of self-transcendence and self-forgetfulness promised by the ideology of love."[8] West employs conventions of the romance genre, among other strategies,[9] to repackage traditional Catholic teachings about sex (don't have premarital sex, don't use birth control, don't be gay). Turning don'ts into I do's, West addresses women like Freitas's students who are fed up with hookups, the very same female audiences who read or watch, enthralled, as girl-next-door Bella and sexy vampire Edward meet, misunderstand, and eventually love one another in Stephenie Meyer's wildly popular *Twilight* series of novels and movies. Yet some of the same dangers that attend the fictional romance of vampire Edward and human Bella—the over-idealization of love, losing oneself utterly in a relationship, rationalizing violence—also figure in West's presentation of romance in order to make Catholic sexual morality appealing to a newer and younger audience.

5. Ibid., 106–7.

6. Ibid., 99.

7. West is a one-man industry based on these teachings: he lectures widely and has produced several books as well as study materials on the theology of the body. For a full list of these materials, see his website at http://www.christopherwest.com.

8. Modleski, *Loving with a Vengeance*, 29.

9. These other rhetorical strategies seem to be aimed more at his male audience and include the narration of his own past sexual sins and subsequent conversion from them, as well as practical everyday analogies, such as automobile maintenance, or the dangers of eating junk food versus healthy food.

The first danger, the over-idealization of love, stems from West's granting a theologically unsound ultimacy to heterosexual love that mimics rather than corrects our culture's obsession with sex.[10] The second, the loss of selfhood in defining oneself too completely through relationship, follows from the first, and pertains particularly to young women, for whom divine sanction to love one's soulmate may also seem to call for a level of sacrifice unsanctioned by a more balanced Christian perspective. The tendency to make romantic love everything can ultimately and all too easily lead to the third danger, the rationalization of male violence. Finally, West's celebration of God-given heterosexual romance presents a fourth danger, working as it does in concert with the silencing and devaluing of homosexual experience and disempowerment of LGBTQ persons. Personally, I am concerned about the harms wrought when romantic expectation is unrealistically heightened and when the possibility of relationship is utterly foreclosed, where one person's (or couple's) pleasure is celebrated at the cost of others' exclusion.

In order to explain how conventions of the romance genre function in West's work, the first section of this essay outlines several conventions that characterize the genre of romance; I will use the *Twilight* series to further illustrate them. Drawing on the insights of romance authors and feminist critics of romance to explain both the appeal of romance as well as its accompanying dangers, I then lay the groundwork for my analysis of how this appeal and danger operate in West's *Theology of the Body for Beginners*.

10. I am indebted to Cloutier ("Heaven," 18–31 and 29), as well as Cloutier and Mattison ("Bodies Poured Out," 215–17) and Mattison ("When They Rise," 33–34 and 41–43), for their helpful examinations of problems attending the appeal of West's popularizations of John Paul II's theology of the body, particularly that of over-romanticization. They persuasively argue, individually and together, that Catholics who long for perfect, intimate, intense romantic relationships have these desires stoked both by popular cultural images of romance *and* by the intense romanticism of West's construal of the theology of the body. This over-idealization of marriage through the conflation of cultural and theological romantic ideals, Cloutier and Mattison conclude, sets people up for failure when the realities of long-term relationships do not live up to the ideals (Mattison, 41; Cloutier and Mattison, 216). Like them, I am not interested in whether West is getting John Paul II right as much as in the persuasive effects of West's work on his audience (Cloutier and Mattison, 207). Unlike them, I here press those observations further by examining the precise mechanisms of this appeal through a feminist lens.

Hidden Codes of Romance, Part One: Overblown Language, Enigmatic Heroes, and a Man Just Like Mom

> It is difficult to explain the appeal of romance novels to people who don't read them. . . . In a sense, romance writers are writing in a code clearly understood by readers but opaque to others. . . . The reader trusts the writer to create and recreate for her a vision of a fictional world that is free of moral ambiguity, a larger-than-life domain in which such ideals as courage, justice, honor, loyalty, and love are challenged and upheld. It is an active, dynamic realm of conflict and resolution, evil and goodness, darkness and light, heroes and heroines, and it is a familiar world in which the roads are well-traveled and the rules are clear.[11]

In the above-quoted essay, entitled "Beneath the Surface: The Hidden Codes of Romance," romance authors Linda Barlow and Jayne Ann Krentz defend romance genre conventions against their critics, both feminist and literary. Romance, they explain, uses a type of figurative language that the uninitiated often mistake as fulsome, clichéd, or hyperbolic, such as the following passage from Barlow's *Fires of Destiny*: "Caught up in the tender savagery of love . . . she saw him, felt him, *knew* him in a manner that, for an instant, transcended the physical. It was if their souls yearned toward each other, and in a flash of glory, merged and became one."[12] This depiction of the requisite happy ending merges the sexual with the romantic, portraying "a sexual bonding that transcends the physical, a bond that . . . can never be broken."[13] This type of language is effective, Barlow and Krentz argue, in eliciting the emotional response that the reader wants and expects: her heart will pound, her pulse will race; Kathy will sheepishly approach me in our dorm hallway to ask why she's tingling. What romance readers understand, they explain, is that this language is not meant to paint a realistic picture of ordinary life, but to invite the reader into the realm described in the above quote, a "larger-than-life domain" in which opposites clash and eventually, inevitably, resolve into unity. The play of difference and oppositions remains crucial to the chiaroscuro of the romance novel. "The final union of male and female [must] be a fusing of contrasting elements: heroes who are

---

11. Barlow and Krentz, "Beneath the Surface," 15–16.

12. Barlow, *Fires of Destiny*, as quoted in Barlow and Krentz, "Beneath the Surface," 21.

13. Barlow and Krentz, "Beneath the Surface," 20.

gentled by love yet who lose none of their warrior qualities in the process and heroines who conquer devils without sacrificing their femininity."[14] Finally, as Krentz writes, "The hero must be a source of emotional and, yes, sometimes physical risk. He must present a genuine threat."[15] In on the secret of romance's specialized language, the reader of romance, along with its heroine, must also decode the hero's hidden agenda to resolve this threat and achieve the happy ending, the resolution of contrasts.

Beautiful, hostile, and enigmatic, Edward of *Twilight* is the archetypal hero that romance readers want. Bella narrates this early encounter with Edward in their high school biology classroom:

> Just as I passed, [Edward] suddenly went rigid in his seat. He stared at me again, meeting my eyes with the strangest expression on his face—it was hostile, furious. . . . I kept my eyes down as I went to sit by *him*, bewildered by the antagonistic stare he'd given me. . . . As I flinched away from him, shrinking against my chair, the phrase *if looks could kill* suddenly ran through my mind.[16]

After avoiding her for days, even attempting to transfer out of their shared class, Edward finally confesses to Bella that he is tired of trying to stay away from her.[17] His hostility was only a result of his intense attraction for her. Bella spends much of this first novel hurt and confused by Edward's behavior, only gradually peeling away the layers that reveal the true motives behind it: He's super-strong because he's a vampire. He avoids me because he likes me. He won't have sex with me before we're married because he doesn't want to hurt me.

For some feminist critics, romance novels are irredeemable. Ann Douglas, for instance, writing in 1980, saw the success of Harlequin Series romances as a backlash against feminist progress, as an attempt to reindoctrinate women readers into the prescribed roles of patriarchal marriage and motherhood just as they were beginning to step into new roles. In these "soft-porn fantasies," wrote Douglas, "women's independence is made horrifically unattractive and unrewarding."[18] For other feminist theorists of romance, the relationship between romance and

14. Ibid.
15. Krentz, "Trying to Tame the Romance," 108.
16. Meyer, *Twilight*, 23–24.
17. Ibid., 84.
18. Douglas, "Soft-Porn Culture," 26.

reader is more complex. Tania Modleski, for instance, theorizes that re-petitive romance reading functions to inoculate readers against the evils of a sexist society. It does so by reassuring them that although some men are actually brutal (vampire James really does try to kill Bella), much masculine brutality can be interpreted, like Edward's, as "a manifestation not of contempt, but of love."[19] Modleski diagnoses readers' pleasure as, at best, a coping measure allowing women to rationalize the inequalities with which they struggle in their relationships.

Janice Radway's 1984 study confirms Barlow and Krentz's asser-tion of the centrality of this reinterpretive process to romance readers' pleasure. Looking at a group of middle-class white homemakers in a Midwestern town, Radway found that the genre of romance raised these women's spirits because it "involve[ed] the reader vicariously in the gradual evolution of a loving relationship whose culmination she is later permitted to enjoy . . . through a description of the heroine's and hero's life together after their necessary union."[20] The most compelling element of the novels these readers preferred, what they enjoyed most, was the "reinterpretation of misunderstood actions and . . . declarations of mu-tual love. . . . [They] wish to participate in the gradual growth of love and trust and to witness the way in which the heroine is eventually cared for by a man who also confesses that he 'needs' her. . . . These preferences also hint," Radway concludes, "at the existence of an equally powerful wish to see a man dependent upon a woman."[21]

The fantasy of a man's dependence upon a woman is not too fan-tastical, if by fantastical we mean foreign from our culture's tendency to assign women greater responsibility and capacity for creating and main-taining relationship. On this level, it's no surprise that a man might be portrayed as depending upon a woman for love. What Radway found more surprising was that the romances her informants preferred were those that portrayed the man as the nurturing figure. For this group of women, an ideal romance novel was one in which the hero's ministra-tions to the heroine were linked analogously, by the narrator or by the heroine herself, to maternal nurturance. "Romance reading addressed needs, desires, and wishes that a male partner could not."[22] Hostile and

19. Modleski, *Loving with a Vengeance*, 33.

20. Radway, *Reading the Romance*, 66.

21. Ibid.

22. Ibid., 13.

enigmatic as he is, *Twilight*'s Edward also fits this portrait of romance hero as nurturer: he uses his strength to tote Bella downstairs to make sure she eats breakfast,[23] but also uses it to resist acting on his sexual attraction for her.[24]

Yet neither Edward's superhuman powers nor his superhuman restraint can always protect Bella from herself, for as the series continues, the danger for her increases, not only from outside threats like rival vampires, but also from Bella herself. In the second novel, *New Moon*, Edward breaks up with Bella, believing their relationship puts her in danger from rival vampires. Depressed and close to despair, Bella takes careless risks with her own safety, nearly killing herself before Edward's return.[25] Willing to throw herself away without Edward and willing to throw herself in harm's way for him, Bella stands a poster child for the potential harmful effects when one lives for the ultimacy of romance.

One must ask, though, is it really true that the pleasures of romance outweigh its dangers? Will young readers and viewers of Edward and Bella's fraught and dangerous romance also be tempted to imitate Bella's self-sacrificial and sometimes self-destructive behavior? Recalling an old friend who contemplated suicide when her boyfriend broke up with her, I can't believe that her story is unique, nor can I attribute her despair to reading romances, since she didn't. Yet if the ultimacy of romance, like the ubiquity of sex, is part of the cultural air we breathe, we need to continue to utilize, like Modleski and Radway, a feminist hermeneutic of suspicion when it comes to the ideology of romance, particularly when male violence is glorified or softened. At the same time, I believe that the relationship between reader and text, like that between any reader and text, is complex enough to make causes and effects unpredictable. This same complexity also attends readers' relationships with Christopher West's works of Catholic advice on sex and marriage. However, we must begin our reading of West by noting that while the authors of romance novels

23. "'Shall I rephrase?' he asked. 'Breakfast time for the human.' 'Oh, okay.' He threw me over his stone shoulder, gently, but with a swiftness that left me breathless" (Meyer, *Twilight*, 315).

24. "'You don't realize how incredibly *breakable* you are. I can never, ever afford to lose any kind of control when I'm with you'" (ibid., 310).

25. For instance, Bella follows Edward and gets lost in the woods and rain, curling up under a tree before she is found (Meyer, *New Moon*, 73–76). Later, she follows an impulse to approach four men standing outside a bar at night, even though she thinks she recognizes them as men who threatened her once before (108–14). Finally, she throws herself off a cliff and almost drowns (359–62).

cited above claim only the authority of their reading community, West claims that the authority of Pope John Paul II and of God stand behind his retelling of romance: the stakes for good and for ill are therefore necessarily and greatly heightened.

Hidden Codes of Romance, Part Two: Overblown Language, Divine Secrets, and Why the Pope Rocks

> I came to see that the male-female "thing" is right at the heart of the whole beauty and splendor of the Catholic faith. . . . For some reason, I was privy to a kind of divine secret that had the potential to transform the whole world, and I needed to do something about it.[26]

In John Paul's original theology of the body, given as a series of lectures at the Vatican from 1979 to 1984, the Pope unpacks his controlling concept of the spousal meaning of the body as the original, created capacity of man and woman, as male and as female, to express love for one another in a reciprocal sexual relationship. The meaning of every human body is therefore understood as spousal, as having "the power to express love: precisely that love in which the human person becomes a gift and—through this gift—fulfills the very meaning of his [sic] being and existence."[27] In other words, John Paul argues that the self-giving to which God calls every human being is expressed most fundamentally and potently through the marital sexual relationship. Many Catholics hail his theology of the body as rehabilitating the reputation of the Catholic Church from denigration to a celebration of sexuality, while others criticize its over-romanticization of sexuality as well as for construing Christian self-giving too narrowly.[28] Yet John Paul's teachings themselves are fairly inaccessible to non-specialist readers: the most recent English translation of John Paul's theology of the body, *Man and Woman He Cre-*

26. West, "Introduction," xiii–xiv.

27. John Paul II, *Man and Woman*, 185–86, 188. Emphasis original.

28. For instance, on the plus side, John Paul II's biographer, George Weigel, calls the theology of the body "one of the boldest reconfigurations of Catholic theology in centuries," "a kind of theological time-bomb set to go off with dramatic consequences . . . perhaps in the 21st century" (as quoted in West, *Theology of the Body*, 1). On the negative side, Cloutier ("Heaven," 30) criticizes the narrowness of the focus of the theology of the body on sexual acts, suggesting that "real love is messy, unclean, and most often involves interacting with social outcasts."

ated Them, by Michael Waldstein, clocks in at a grand total of 735 pages, including the introduction and other material appended to help the reader make sense of this work. This is where West comes in. His translations of John Paul's theology of the body into simple and colloquial terms, proliferated through numerous books, public lectures, videos, and podcasts, are accessible and appealing to wider audiences. Further, if Barlow and Krentz are right about romance readers' attunement to the hidden codes of romance, then some part of West's audience may already be primed to receive his message. West's use of the romance convention of fulsome and hyperbolic language will become apparent throughout as I quote from his book *Theology of the Body for Beginners*. The second romance convention he uses to great effect is that of deciphering the enigma that needs explaining. In his case, Catholic Christianity itself serves as the mysterious and misunderstood hero of the story, and sexual difference becomes the key to deciphering the mystery. Finally, West casts Pope John Paul II himself in the role of the nurturing romance hero who truly understands what women need.

The romance begins in the garden of Eden: West portrays John Paul II's interpretation of the second chapter of Genesis as the story of a man, Adam, looking for love. He finally finds it in Eve—bone of his bone and flesh of his flesh. Adam is depicted as "express[ing] absolute wonder and fascination" upon beholding Eve's body, a body that fully expresses her personhood. Their ensuing "experience of *unity* overcomes the man's *solitude* in the sense of being alone without the 'other', and not only sexual union, but spiritual union, is the result."[29] ("She saw him, felt him, *knew* him in a manner that, for an instant, transcended the physical. It was if their souls yearned toward each other, and in a flash of glory, merged and became one."[30]) Naked, Adam and Eve feel no shame (yet); in Eden their desire for one another is pure, because it is a desire for the entirety of the other. The problem, West explains, is that after the fall we all tend to confuse love and lust. How can we tell the difference? Isn't all sex just bad, as Freitas's Catholic students surmise?

According to West, it is the "often repressive approach of previous generations of Christians" that is to blame for the "cultural jettisoning of the Church's teaching on sex."[31] As we have already seen, West emphasizes

29. West, *Theology of the Body*, 24. Emphasis original.
30. Barlow, *Fires of Destiny*, as quoted in Barlow and Krentz, "Beneath the Surface," 21.
31. West, *Theology of the Body*, 15.

that Christianity does not reject the body. John Paul II provides, according to West, the "fresh theology that explains how the Christian sexual
ethic—far from being the prudish list of prohibitions it's often assumed
to be—corresponds perfectly with the deepest yearnings of our hearts
for love and union."[32] One of the mysteries that the theology of the body
reveals, when explained by West, is how to discern real from inauthentic
love and sex when you can't figure it out from feelings alone.[33] Real sex is
that expressed between married, heterosexual, monogamous spouses in
which every sexual act is open to conception. This is the sex that expresses
who you really are, even if you don't know it, and no other kind of sex
can ever be authentic, no matter how pleasurable. "The sexual embrace
is meant to image and express divine love. Anything less is a counterfeit
that not only fails to satisfy, but wounds us terribly."[34] Real, authentic sex
is good for you; false sex—which in this case includes premarital, non-
vaginal, artificially contracepted, and homosexual sexual activity—is, by
definition, not. Even marital sex that doesn't image and express divine love
can, it seems, fall short of West's definition of real sex.

West's championing of the traditional Catholic position on sex is appealing because, rather than simply denouncing nonmarital sex as lustful
and sinful (at least right off the bat), it first hastens to affirm even the
pleasures of the wrong kind of sex. He explicitly encourages readers to
sift retrospectively through past relationships to find the wheat amongst
the chaff, the spark of pure desire hidden within the falsity of lust. "Behind every sin," he writes, "behind every disordered 'acting out,' there's a
genuine human desire that's meant to be fulfilled through Christ and his
Church. As our desires become 'untwisted,' we begin to realize that we
really desire eternal love and joy."[35] West reveals the benign intention
behind the Catholic Church's forbidding of premarital sex by revealing
previous sexual experience not just as impure or sinful, but as precursor
to true love. This keeps his good news accessible to those feeling burned by
bad romance or by meaningless hookups, such as the students interviewed
by Freitas. If all that Catholic students know about Catholic sexual teaching is the list of don'ts, then West offers a peek at a tantalizing divine secret:

32. Ibid.

33. Cloutier ("Heaven," 19) observes that West appeals to younger Catholics, such
as Cloutier's own students, by utilizing the traditional Catholic sexual norms not to
forbid particular sexual acts, but as criteria for distinguishing authentic loving sexual
relationships from their many pleasurable, but ultimately unsatisfying, counterfeits.

34. West, *Theology of the Body*, 33.

35. Ibid.

Catholicism does *not* condemn sexuality and bodies, but celebrates them. The norms are the same, but the rationale behind them has changed its packaging. Real Catholic sex turns out to be the same as your parents' and grandparents' Catholic sex, but this sounds a lot better when prescribed as healthy romance and being true to yourself, than recommended as an avoidance of sin. His encomia of the joys of married sexual love become not condemnations of the past, but invitations to a hopeful future.

What then is God's plan for our future? "God wants to marry us," says West, and God wants this eschatological marital plan to be so obvious that God imprinted it in our flesh as male and female.[36] Sexual difference, therefore, is the key to unlocking this mystery, its Rosetta Stone. While he confirms rather than dismantles the list of familiar Catholic don'ts, West proposes that we have been looking at it all wrong. "Sex is not first what people *do*. It's who people *are* as *male and female*."[37] "If you are looking for the meaning of life," writes West, "it's impressed right in your body—in your sexuality! The purpose of life is to love as God loves and this is what your body as a man or woman calls you to. . . . A man's body doesn't make sense by itself, nor does a woman's body."[38] "This is what the body teaches us: we're destined for love."[39] West's romantic rhetoric of obvious yet hidden difference between men and women, stamped into our contrasting and complementary bodies, reinforces a naturalized commonsense understanding of sexual difference, while at the same time proffers the rediscovery of this difference as revelatory. Sexual love, expressed properly in marriage, is a foretaste of heaven, in which "the union of the sexes as we know it now will give way to an *infinitely greater* union."[40] This is why sex should mirror divine love—because "marital union is meant to be an icon in some way of the inner life of the Trinity!"[41] It is God's relationship with God that serves as the model to which married couples are called. Knowing the ending ahead of time (as do Christians hoping for heaven or romance readers looking forward to the requisite happy ending) allows for the proper ethical assessment of sexual desire.

By turning the negatives of Catholic sexual teaching into positives, West performs what Barlow and Krentz claim women romance readers

36. Ibid.
37. Ibid., 55. Emphasis original.
38. Ibid., 29.
39. Ibid., 121.
40. Ibid., 55. Emphasis original.
41. Ibid., 25.

want: "One of the most significant victories the heroine achieves at the close of the novel is that the hero is able to express his love for her *not only physically but also verbally* . . . Romance heroines, like women the world over, need to hear the words."[42] In declaring God's loving desire to marry us, a desire that can now be caught up with, conflated with, and identified with (the right) partner's desire for sexual union, West explains all the enigmas and leads his readers to the happy ending: You thought he hated you? He really loves you. You thought he just wanted your body? Your body expresses your person, and he wants all of you. You thought the Church didn't like bodies? The Church *loves* bodies. As West writes, "Christianity says 'the body is so good you can't even fathom it.'"[43] By the way, the confusion as to which "he" West might be talking about—God or boyfriend?—is deliberate on my part because West himself shifts abruptly between the divine and the romantic.

We can think of the interpretive lens of the theology of the body, as presented by West, in two ways. First, the effect is like putting on a pair of 3D glasses with their two different-colored lenses (male and female) that nonetheless work together to provide an accurate perspective on everything visible through them. Without these lenses, the world is flat, fuzzy, and confusing, but put them on and suddenly meaning and purpose jump out. Secondly, think of the lens as wide-angled: the theology of the body, as promulgated by West, pans out from sex to encompass life, the universe, everything. One Catholic student said that because of the theology of the body, "'it all made sense' . . . and by this, she did not simply mean the traditional sexual teachings, but rather 'everything,' beliefs about God and Christ and the Trinity and God's love."[44] The bigger picture into which sex now fits, for sympathetic readers of West, includes not just a newly perceived coherence of Catholic sexual teachings but the whole of Christian theology. As West himself puts it, "The way we understand and express our sexuality points to our deepest-held convictions about who we are, who God is, the meaning of love, the ordering of society, and even the ordering of the universe."[45]

Once this spousal meaning of the body is understood, a whole world opens up akin to the world of romance as described above by Barlow and Krentz: "free of moral ambiguity, a larger-than-life domain in which such

42. Barlow and Krentz, "Beneath the Surface," 23. Emphasis original.
43. West, *Theology of the Body*, 4.
44. Cloutier, "Heaven," 22.
45. West, *Theology of the Body*, 1–2.

ideals as courage, justice, honor, loyalty, and love are challenged and up-
held. It is an active, dynamic realm of conflict and resolution, evil and
goodness, darkness and light."[46] West's fulsome rhetoric invites his readers
into this romantic world and produces a sense of conspiratorial glee, of
being in on a secret, of spiritual adventure cobbled out of the stuff of everyday life and relationships. His readers, too, are now "privy to a kind of
divine secret that ha[s] the potential to transform the whole world."[47] West
uses both marital and martial rhetoric to support this sense of purpose-
ful adventure: once you know the (open) secret, you are conscripted into
a spiritual army. Your heterosexual marriage, or your single chastity, are
neither simply personal choices nor simply obedience to God's plan, but
a simultaneous taking up of arms. As he writes, "The battle for man's [sic]
soul is fought over the truth of his body."[48] Warriors, indeed—but gentled
by love.[49]

Christopher West's popularization of the theology of the body not
only resembles a 1970s Harlequin romance with the brutal hero treating
the heroine badly because he loves her, but also it reads like other types
of romances. For instance, West figures Pope John Paul II himself as akin
to the romance hero admired by Radway's readers, a man who attends to
and nurtures women's needs. Drawing on John Paul's pre-papacy experience as a counselor of married couples, West portrays John Paul as the
tender lover (like Christ) who refuses to scold, forbid, or condemn, but
rather wants only what's best for us, especially for women. In addition, he
offers consolation to those who have a hard time obeying sexual teachings,
emphasizing redemption over condemnation. Similarly, West comforts
those who have succumbed to the secular counterfeits of authentic love by
explaining that Christ showed compassion to sexual sinners, "especially
women, because, behind their deception, he knew that they were looking
for him, the true Bridegroom." [50] He imagines in this way the reaction
of the woman taken in adultery (John 8:2–11) to Christ's telling her "go
and sin no more": did she, West wonders, grumble, "Who is this man
to tell me what I can and cannot do with my body!"? Or, he continues,

46. Barlow and Krentz, "Beneath the Surface," 15–16.

47. West, "Introduction," xiii–xiv.

48. West, *Theology of the Body*, 12.

49. "The final union of male and female [must] be a fusing of contrasting elements:
heroes who are gentled by love yet who lose none of their warrior qualities in the
process and heroines who conquer devils without sacrificing their femininity" (Barlow
and Krentz, "Beneath the Surface," 20, and as quoted above; see n. 14).

50. West, *Theology of the Body*, 63.

"do you think, having encountered the love she was truly looking for, she left transformed, renewed, affirmed in the deepest part of her being as a woman? This is what Christ offers to us all."[51]

West portrays both Christ and Pope John Paul II as sensitive, albeit celibate, romance heroes, who understand what women really want and counsel their fulfillment. He gets a lot of rhetorical mileage from highlighting John Paul's insistence that the husband must assure that his wife has an orgasm. "Such tenderness on his part in the context of marital intercourse acquires the significance of an act of virtue," wrote the pope-to-be.[52] When West read this passage aloud during a lecture, he recalled that an astonished engaged woman once exclaimed . . . "The Pope rocks!"[53] Here then is an opportunity for West to defend Catholic teaching against feminist objections. Noting that "few men express the tenderness and virtue" called for by John Paul II, West invokes the romantic conventions of chivalry: he first apologizes to women "as a representative of the male side of the human race" for "the way male lust has wounded you," and to the men he says, "Get ready . . . I'm going to call you forth into battle—a battle that involves all the courage and stamina you can muster . . . we . . . must be men who are willing to *die* rather than ever indulge our lusts."[54]

Brighter and much less ambiguous than the ethically confused cultural world it criticizes, West's romantic vision of good sex is "a familiar world in which the roads are well-traveled and the rules are clear."[55] And one of these rules—don't have homosexual sex—remains in place not because your bodies are bad but because it won't fulfill you. Homosexuality is brushed off quickly in West's *Theology of the Body for Beginners*, dismissed in a single paragraph both as "a complex issue that we can't discuss at length here" (readers are referred to another of West's books, *Good News about Sex & Marriage*) and as simply one among many types of inauthentic, dissatisfying sex. However, even though the passage is short, focusing on West's language within it is instructive: When extolling the beauty of heterosexual sex within marriage, his prose appears lyrical and fulsome. When telling what's wrong with homosexual sex, his analogies shift abruptly to the functional. "While there is a strong push today to

51. Ibid., 63–64.

52. Karol Wojtyla (Pope John Paul II), *Love and Responsibility*, as quoted in West, *Theology of the Body*, 82.

53. West, *Theology of the Body*, 82.

54. Ibid., 83. Emphasis original.

55. Barlow and Krentz, "Beneath the Surface," 15–16.

normalize homosexuality, in reality it's another manifestation of 'flat-tire syndrome.' No matter what our particular experience of lust, we're all in need of 're-inflation' . . . No one—no matter what his or her distortions—is beyond the scope of Christ's redeeming love." [56] For the woman taken in adultery, Christ is a tender hero. For an LGBTQ person, Christ is the mechanic getting you back on the (right) road. In homosexual relationships, there will be no romance, no joy in beholding full sexual personhood, and no happy ending as in the bright and binary world of the theology of the body. This is the final way in which West's romantic repackaging of Catholic sexual morality affects its appeal, at least to heterosexual females in his audience. His celebration of the goodness of the body and of sexual pleasure stands out in stark relief against the backdrop of explicit magisterial teachings condemning homosexuality. In other words, sex seems good again, because it's still forbidden for someone.

Critics point out that John Paul II's theology of the body needs the romantic popularization of Christopher West precisely to appeal to the younger Catholic audience.[57] One commentator observes that the prose in the former Pope's original catecheses is "dense and difficult to read," and that he "only asserts and never demonstrates," thus "minimizing the contradiction between various parts of his lectures."[58] While this same commentator goes on to note, perhaps rather wistfully, that these are minor deficiencies, since "how many theological writings are not dense, repetitious, and inconsistent,"[59] ethicist Mark Jordan points out that the stylistic deficiencies of magisterial documents are not merely unfortunate infelicities of prose to be downplayed; rather they are rhetorical devices central to the message being delivered. He argues that tedium, repetition, invocation of absolute authorities, and even threats do important work in official Catholic teachings on homosexuality.[60] Further, Jordan suggests that, rather than reading these teachings for content or logic alone, "we should examine how the documents are designed to move readers—to move them to opinion, passion, or action."[61]

Jordan then draws our attention to two documents that outline official Catholic teaching on homosexuality: *Persona Humana*, the 1975

---

56. West, *Theology of the Body*, 32.

57. Cloutier, "Heaven," 24.

58. Johnson, "Disembodied 'Theology of the Body,'" 112–13.

59. Ibid., 113.

60. Jordan, *Silence of Sodom*, 23.

61. Ibid., 22.

"Declaration on Certain Questions Concerning Sexual Ethics," and the 1986 "Letter to the Bishops of the Catholic Church on the Pastoral Care of Homosexual Persons," both issued from the Congregation for the Doctrine of the Faith. The 1975 Declaration characterizes homosexual orientation in two kinds: either transitory and thus not incurable, or due to something innate, pathological, and incurable.[62] Homosexual orientation is distinguished from homosexual acts in the Declaration in that the former, if incurable, is not considered directly sinful, while the latter are always to be disapproved.[63] While some Catholic commentators applauded this distinction as providing an opening for change in Catholic sexual teachings, its rhetoric does not seem like the proclamation of good news to Jordan.[64] Rather, the Declaration's rhetorical pattern of "lament, denunciation, exhortation, and prescription" assumes what it presumes to discover by arguing from conclusion to premise.[65] In other words, homosexual acts are not condemned by the Declaration because they are found wanting when judged by the principle that all legitimate sex must be procreative. Rather, argues Jordan, the principle that all sex must be procreative is derived from the premise that homosexuality must be condemned.[66]

The 1986 Letter clarifies that the recognition of some homosexual identities as incurable (therefore not chosen, and therefore not sinful unless acted upon) is not good news for those so designated, explaining that "although the particular inclination of the homosexual person is not a sin, it is a more or less strong tendency ordered toward an intrinsic moral evil; and thus the inclination itself must be seen as an objective disorder."[67] Even more disturbingly, as Jordan points out, the Letter turns quickly from condemning anti-homosexual violence—"it is deplorable that homosexual persons have been and are the object of violent malice in speech or in action"[68]—to predicting it:

> But the proper reaction to crimes committed against homosexual persons should not be to claim that the homosexual condition is not disordered. When such a claim is made and when homosexual activity is consequently condoned, or when civil

62. Ibid., 28–29.

63. Ibid.

64. Ibid., 29.

65. Ibid., 26–28.

66. Ibid., 28.

67. CDF, "Letter to the Bishops," no. 3.

68. Ibid., no. 10.

legislation is introduced to protect behavior to which no one has any conceivable right, neither the Church nor society at large should be surprised when other distorted notions and practices gain ground, and irrational and violent reactions increase.[69]

In other words, "they" (meaning LGBTQ persons and gay rights activists) bring violence on themselves simply through asserting their rights. Apparently it's a slippery slope from here to the vaguely menacing "other distorted notions and practices" left unspecified in the document.

Here, again, is where West comes in. Read next to the stark assertions and warnings contained in these documents, West's work extolling the theology of the body appears as the kinder, gentler version. West asserts that "the Pope doesn't need to nor does he attempt to force assent to his proposals . . . the Pope imposes nothing and wags a finger at *no one.*"[70] He doesn't have to: that work is accomplished elsewhere, particularly by the Congregation for the Doctrine of the Faith. Effectively leaving homosexuality out of *Theology of the Body for Beginners* is a wise omission if one is selling romance. If West is to appeal to a generation who demonstrate higher percentages of acceptance of homosexuality as well as gay marriage[71] and who almost certainly have gay friends, then outright condemnation of homosexual sex and relationships would interrupt the romance and might even turn off some of its readers. The seductive appeal of West's portrayal of the theology of the body lies in its explicit celebration of sex within heterosexual romance, not its implicit condemnation of homosexuality. While caught up in the romance of the former, the latter is easy to ignore.

West's romantic repackaging of John Paul's theology of the body not only attracts readers more quickly than official Catholic documents to the expected ending—don't have sex except for noncontracepted, procreative

69. Ibid.

70. West, *Theology of the Body*, 16. Emphasis original.

71. Pew Forum on Religion & Public Life, "Changing Attitudes on Gay Marriage," reports that whereas in 2001 Americans opposed same-sex marriage 57 percent to 35 percent, "today, the public is about evenly split." Breaking down this support by generational cohort in its 2011 polling, Pew found that Americans born 1981 or later are twice as likely to support same-sex marriage as those born in 1928–45. Finally, Pew Research Center for the People & the Press, "Most Say Homosexuality Should Be Accepted by Society," a political typology survey released May 4, 2011, found that "among younger people in particular, there is broad support for societal acceptance of homosexuality. More than six-in-ten (63%) of those younger than 50—69% of those younger than 30—say that homosexuality should be accepted."

heterosexual sex within marriage—but also it offers a more pleasurable way of getting there, again and again, in book after lecture after podcast after blog post. His rhetorical achievement reconnects romance and sex and religion for those for whom all three have been practically, but not ideally, sundered. If it is true that young adults, especially women, do not actually have many positive experiences of sex and romance, then they may indeed be more receptive to West's interpretation, namely that their bad experiences merely point them toward more authentic ones. However, the question we need to keep asking is whether this ending is indeed a happy one. I have argued that it is not due to the exclusions attendant on its definitions of happiness, particularly for those whose hopes of romance are, according to the official Catholic teachings, truncated from the start.

Bibliography

Barlow, Linda, and Jayne Ann Krentz. "Beneath the Surface: The Hidden Codes of Romance." In *Dangerous Men and Adventurous Women: Romance Writers on the Appeal of the Romance*, edited by Jayne Ann Krentz, 15–29. Philadelphia: University of Pennsylvania Press, 1992.

Cloutier, David. "Heaven Is a Place on Earth?: Analyzing the Popularity of Pope John Paul II's Theology of the Body." In *Sexuality and the U.S. Catholic Church: Crisis and Renewal*, edited by Lisa Sowle Cahill, John Garvey, and T. Frank Kennedy, 18–31. New York: Crossroad, 2006.

Cloutier, David, and William C. Mattison III. "Bodies Poured Out in Christ: Marriage Beyond the Theology of the Body." In *Leaving and Coming Home: New Wineskins for Catholic Sexual Ethics*, edited by David Cloutier, 206–25. Eugene, OR: Cascade Books, 2010.

Congregation for the Doctrine of the Faith. "Letter to the Bishops of the Catholic Church on the Collaboration of Men and Women in the Church and in the World." May 31, 2004.

———. *Persona Humana* ("Declaration on Certain Questions Concerning Sexual Ethics"). December 29, 1975.

Douglas, Ann. "Soft-Porn Culture." *The New Republic*, August 20, 1980, 25–29.

Freitas, Donna. *Sex and the Soul: Juggling Sexuality, Spirituality, Romance, and Religion on America's College Campuses*. New York: Oxford University Press, 2008.

John Paul II, Pope. *Man and Woman He Created Them: A Theology of the Body*. Translation, introduction, and index by Michael Waldstein. Boston: Pauline, 2006.

Johnson, Luke Timothy. "A Disembodied 'Theology of the Body': John Paul II on Love, Sex, and Pleasure." In *Human Sexuality in the Catholic Tradition*, edited by Kieran Scott and Harold D. Horell, 111–21. Lanham, MD: Rowman & Littlefield, 2007.

Jordan, Mark. *The Silence of Sodom: Homosexuality in Modern Catholicism*. Chicago: University of Chicago Press, 2000.

Krentz, Jayne Ann. "Trying to Tame the Romance: Critics and Correctness." In *Dangerous Men and Adventurous Women: Romance Writers on the Appeal of the Romance*, edited by Jayne Ann Krentz, 107–14. Philadelphia: University of Pennsylvania Press, 1992.

Mattison, William. "'When They Rise from the Dead, They Neither Marry Nor Are Given to Marriage': Marriage and Sexuality, Eschatology, and the Nuptial Meaning of the Body in Pope John Paul II's Theology of the Body." In *Sexuality and the U.S. Catholic Church: Crisis and Renewal*, edited by Lisa Sowle Cahill, John Garvey, and T. Frank Kennedy, 32–51. New York: Crossroad, 2006.

Meyer, Stephenie. *New Moon*. New York: Little, Brown, 2006.

———. *Twilight*. New York: Little, Brown, 2005.

Modleski, Tania. *Loving with a Vengeance: Mass Produced Fantasies for Women*. 2nd ed. New York: Routledge, 2008.

Paul VI, Pope. *Humanae Vitae* ("On the Transmission of Life"). July 25, 1968. Online: http://www.vatican.va/holy_father/paul_vi/encyclicals/documents/hf_p-vi_enc_25071968_humanae-vitae_en.html.

Pew Forum on Religion & Public Life. "Changing Attitudes on Gay Marriage." Online: http://features.pewforum.org/same-sex-marriage-attitudes/. Pew Research Center. Accessed September 20, 2011.

Pew Research Center for the People & the Press. "Most Say Homosexuality Should Be Accepted by Society." http://www.people-press.org/2011/05/13/most-say-homosexuality-should-be-accepted-by-society/. Pew Research Center. May 13, 2011.

Radway, Janice A. *Reading the Romance: Women, Patriarchy, and Popular Literature*. 2nd ed. Chapel Hill: University of North Carolina, 1991.

West, Christopher. *Good News about Sex & Marriage: Answers to Your Honest Questions about Catholic Teaching*. Rev. ed. Ann Arbor, MI: St. Anthony Messenger/Servant Books, 2004.

———. "Introduction." In *Freedom: Twelve Lives Transformed by the Theology of the Body*, edited by Matthew Pinto, ix–xvi. West Chester, PA: Ascension, 2009.

———. *Theology of the Body for Beginners*. West Chester, PA: Ascension, 2004.

Wojtyla, Karol (Pope John Paul II). *Love and Responsibility*. Translated by H. T. Willetts. San Francisco: Ignatius, 1981.

10

Toward the Ideal of Companionate Marriage in the Plays of William Shakespeare

JAMES G. DIXON III

Let me not to the marriage of true minds
Admit impediments...

—*SONNET* 116

Dwell I but in the suburbs
Of your good pleasure? If it be no more,
Portia is Brutus' harlot, not his wife.

—*JULIUS CAESAR*

A MAN FINDS HIMSELF saddled with a shrewish wife. Her hot temper, sharp wit, and bold spirit are notorious in her community and have become an increasing embarrassment to her husband. One day he decides to teach her a lesson in an attempt to tame her unbridled spirit. In the end, he discovers the only satisfactory method is to beat her until she bleeds and then to wrap her up in the salted hide of his old faithful horse. By rubbing salt in her wounds, the husband reminds the woman of her proper role in marriage: to be meek, submissive, dependent, and obedient.

This story, circulated in a popular ballad of his time, entitled *A Merry Jest of a Shrewd and Curst Wife Lapped in Morel's Skin for Her Good Behavior* (c. 1550),[1] was one of the sources of Shakespeare's early comedy *The Taming of the Shrew*. What Shakespeare does with that source in constructing his own play reveals the revolution he is exploring regarding the nature of love and marriage. Central to this revolution is the tension he dramatizes between the traditional dynastic view of marriage, in which fathers treated their daughters as commodities to be negotiated with potential husbands, and a new, egalitarian view of love and marriage as nurtured in the rising Christian humanism of the time; this view is apparent in Puritan sermons and pamphlets of the period—what came to be known as "companionate marriage."[2] This ideal saw women and men as equal before God and therefore equally worthy to be educated to develop their full potential, with the goal of being equal partners in intelligence, wit, and responsibility.

The late sixteenth and early seventeenth centuries in England, when Shakespeare was writing his plays, was a time of turbulent political, religious, and cultural tensions. Henry VIII had broken with the Roman Catholic Church over the question of his divorce to Queen Catherine and had established his own church with a new "reformed" set of values and views on everything from liturgy to marriage.[3] The Protestant Reformation had swept through Europe mid-century, and the navy of Protestant England, under Elizabeth I, defeated the mighty Armada of Catholic Spain in 1588. In some ways, the Catholic veneration of the Virgin Mary shifted to the secularized veneration of the Virgin Queen Elizabeth, Gloriana. The new Protestant culture was busy calling into question every aspect of the hierarchical structures, including those of marriage and family, that had been associated with Catholic authority.

As Stephen Greenblatt and other New Historicists have noted, part of Shakespeare's "genius" and certainly part of his dramatic effectiveness is the way in which he captures the dynamic tensions at work in

1. See the full text of this ballad and Dolan's commentary in *The Taming of the Shrew*, 254–88.

2. Jardine, *Reading Shakespeare Historically*, 116; Bevington, "Difficult Ideal," 372.

3. It is worth noting here the irony that Henry VIII, who treated his several wives so poorly and broke with the Roman Catholic Church over his unjust determination to divorce his first wife, should be the one credited with triggering the Reformation in England and so opening the space for a new view of women and marriage to emerge in British culture. It is further ironic that such a misogynist had only daughters survive childhood, one of whom became one of the greatest monarchs in British history.

the culture in which he lived. The fact that his period was one of such productive ferment on the threshold of the modern era has contributed to keeping his plays intriguing and relevant for successive generations and cultures to the present. Harold Bloom has gone so far as to claim that Shakespeare "invented" the human as we know it, since his plays have had such currency in the modern world and his understanding of human nature has had such a formidable influence on how we think of ourselves as humans.

This paper will demonstrate that the same is true of gender, love, and marriage. Shakespeare's plays enact the tensions regarding these issues that were to a great extent produced by the religious and subsequent cultural upheavals of his time. These tensions continue to be relevant, both in conservative religious contexts[4] and in the larger culture of the Western world, in which Shakespeare continues to have a shaping influence. Part of Shakespeare's continuing success lies in what the poet John Keats called his "negative capability," his ability to negate himself as a writer to allow his characters on all sides of whatever conflict he is dramatizing to speak for themselves, without the intrusion of an author's mediating perspective. Thus the conflicts remain rather than the solutions. And when solutions are presented in his plays (e.g., marriage at the end of the comedies), they are often problematized to some degree to reveal the inadequacy and tentative character of those solutions.

The overall movement of his plays, however, and his dramatization of the conflicts of his time regarding gender, love and marriage, reveal that Shakespeare throughout his career is exploring the possibilities of a new model of marriage in the modern world. Feminist critics have been widely divided on this issue, from Janet Dusinberre's enthusiastic embrace of Shakespeare as a liberator of women to Kate McLuskie's indictment of Shakespeare as fully complicit in reinscribing the patriarchal order that he pretends at times to overturn.[5] I am drawn toward Dusinberre's end of this continuum. Shakespeare clearly was a man of his own times, formed to some extent by the patriarchal order of the centuries that preceded him. Yet as a writer of particularly keen sensibilities to the dynamic currents of his time—in this case the "controversy about women" heightened by the Protestant Reformation, the rise of Puritanism, the ascendance of Queen Elizabeth, the continued development of Christian Humanism,

---

4. This controversy is evident in such recent books as Kostenberger, *God, Marriage and Family*; and Grudem and Piper, *Recovering Biblical Manhood and Womanhood*.

5. Boose, *Family*, 615–16.

and the wildly popular genre of literature on "the formal controversy about women"—Shakespeare found a hugely productive creative space in which he could probe the possibilities of a revolution in gender relations. He is not a propagandist in the mode of George Bernard Shaw, since he explores all of the ramifications of this new model, negative as well as positive. Yet the positive glimpses he does provide of this new model have proven attractive enough to outweigh the negative in our imagination and to serve as a lasting model for a culture in transition.

Shakespeare's Cultural Background

Several examples may be sufficient to demonstrate the new wave of thinking in Shakespeare's time regarding the role of women and the nature of marriage. Earlier in the sixteenth century, Thomas More, chancellor to Henry VIII and martyr for his Catholic faith, believed so strongly in the education of women that he provided the same classical education to his daughters that he provided for his son.[6] Margaret More became especially well known for her erudition, which nudged Erasmus toward a more progressive view regarding women and education.[7] In 1568, Edmund Tilney published *The Flower of Friendship*, a fictional dialogue regarding marriage among several individuals—including Erasmus and Lady Julia (a character based on Erasmus's ideal wife in his 1523 dialogue *Conjugium*). This work extols the virtues of companionate marriage and even provides what Valerie Wayne identifies as an emergent feminist critique of humanism that pushes this ideal toward true egalitarianism in marriage.[8] This work received a second and third edition in 1571 and 1577, and Tilney was appointed the Master of Revels to the court of Elizabeth I in 1579, a position he retained until 1610. This position gave him complete

6. Thomas More deserves some credit for his progressive views regarding the education of women, but C. S. Lewis reminds us that More was also stuck in some retrograde patriarchal views. He relentlessly criticized Martin Luther for his egalitarian views on marriage. Luther, writes Lewis, "praises women repeatedly: More, it will be remembered, though apparently an excellent husband and father, hardly ever mentions a woman save to ridicule her. It is easy to see why Luther's marriage (as he called it) or Luther's 'abominable bichery' (if you prefer) became almost a symbol. More can never keep off the subject for more than a few pages." Lewis, "Donne and Love Poetry," 117.

7. Ackroyd, *Life of Sir Thomas More*, 146–49.

8. Wayne, "Introduction," 84.

jurisdiction over the production of plays during that time, which over-laps almost completely the career of William Shakespeare.

The Puritans of the sixteenth century consolidated the impulses of Christian humanism with the anti-authoritarian impulses of the Protes-tant Reformation. In *Worldly Saints: The Puritans as They Really Were*, Leland Ryken argues that "few ideas unleashed such wellsprings of feeling among the Puritans as their praise of the ideal of the companionate mar-riage." He adds that "the ideal of friendship, which in classical antiquity had been largely confined to male friends, now became transferred to the marriage relationship."[9] He cites the works of several Puritan writers and preachers of the time, including Thomas Gataker (with titles such as *A Wife Indeed* and *A Good Wife God's Gift*) and Henry Smith, the most popular Puritan preacher in London in the late sixteenth century, who wrote that a good wife is "such a gift as we should account from God alone, accept it as if he should send us a present from heaven with this name on it, *The gift of God*."[10] Henry Smith also emphasized the necessity of com-patibility, and Richard Greenham, preacher at Christ Church, Newgate, London, explained that a man could know his wife was brought to him by God if there was "'any agreeing or proportionable liking' between them, especially 'in the gifts of ye mind . . .'"[11] Stephen Greenblatt argues that "[i]t took decades of Puritan insistence on the importance of compan-ionship in marriage to change the social, cultural, and psychological landscape."[12] C. S. Lewis argues further that the Puritans combined the notion of companionate marriage with the tradition of romantic love: "the conversion of courtly love into romantic monogamous love was largely the work of English, and even of Puritan, poets."[13] And Ryken concludes that "the Puritan ideal was wedded romantic love."[14]

This is not to say that the more egalitarian view of marriage that the Puritans and Christian humanists of the sixteenth century sought was the same as what is meant by those who use the term "egalitarian" in early twenty-first-century debates concerning marriage. Even the most "enlightened" men of the time were deeply entrenched in patriarchal tra-ditions and structures. Puritans still strongly believed in the husband's

9. Ryken, *Worldly Saints*, 42–43.

10. Ibid., 43.

11. Greaves, *Society and Religion*, 139.

12. Greenblatt, *Will in the World*, 128.

13. Lewis, *Donne and Love Poetry*, 117.

14. Ryken, *Worldly Saints*, 51.

headship and the wife's subordination in legal and familial matters. But as Ryken observes, "Puritan ideas on sex and marriage had the effect of mitigating hierarchy in the direction of marital equality," and he adds that "the Puritan ideal of the companionate marriage tended to soften the claims of male dominance and to produce an enlightened version of marital hierarchy."[15] Herbert Richardson concludes that "the rise of romantic marriage and its validation by the Puritans . . . represents a major innovation with the Christian tradition."[16]

The tension regarding marriage and the proper roles of women and men was dramatized in an entire genre of literary works attacking and defending women from the late Middle Ages through the Renaissance, what Linda Woodbridge calls "the formal controversy about women."[17] In 1589, about the time Shakespeare began writing plays, Jane Anger (an allegorical name?) published *Protection for Women*, a response to some of the misogynist diatribes of the day (including one by Shakespeare's contemporary dramatist, John Lyly, in his *Euphues*).

Stephen Greenblatt has argued that Shakespeare was among the first to begin exploring the relatively uncharted terrain of companionate marriage. The following detailed and chronologically ordered analyses of Shakespeare's plays will demonstrate that Greenblatt is essentially right—though only if we acknowledge an evolution in Shakespeare's thoughts on the issue of companionate marriage. In any case, throughout his career, Shakespeare employs this controversy for dramatic purposes. Although the controversy remains unresolved by the end of many individual plays, through the body of his work Shakespeare explores the possibilities of new creative ways for men and women to experience erotic love, in anticipation of an egalitarian marriage that reflects biblical principles of friendship and mutual submission.

Tensions in the Early Plays

Let us return to *The Taming of the Shrew* to trace how Shakespeare began to challenge the misogynist diatribes of his day. The plot of Shakespeare's comedy involves the travails of a wealthy father, Baptista, wearied by the burden of marrying off his two daughters, Katharine and Bianca. Bianca

15. Ibid., 52–53.

16. Richardson, *Nun, Witch, Playmate*, 69.

17. Woodbridge, *Women*, 13.

is the quintessentially meek and submissive daughter, one who plays almost to perfection the role her patriarchal society asks of her, and so is quite attractive to a gallery of male suitors, each of whom must prove his financial worth to engage in such a potentially rewarding enterprise as wooing the daughter of a wealthy father and gaining a sizeable dowry and eventual inheritance. The elder daughter Katharine, however, is the opposite of Bianca—hot-tempered and quick-witted—and refuses to play the demeaning game of selling herself to the highest bidder. But the father refuses to marry the younger daughter until the elder has been married, so Bianca's suitors are desperate to find a man foolish enough to take the risk of wooing this "shrew." Enter Petruchio, who arrives from out of town with this plain boast: "I come to wive it wealthily in Padua;/ If wealthily, then happily, in Padua" (1.2.75–76).[18] He cares not that Kate is famous as a shrew. In fact, he relishes the prospect of "taming" her.

So far, this seems like the stuff of misogynist farces current throughout European Renaissance culture.[19] It could even be a setup for a reprise of the brutal physical abuse the husband gives his wife in Shakespeare's source material, *A Merry Jest of a Shrewd and Curst Wife Lapped in Morel's Skin for Her Good Behavior.* As is typical of Shakespeare's treatment of character, however, the rather simplistic intent of "taming" her turns into something more complex, as we see in Petruchio's first meeting with Katharine. Just before she enters, he preps himself by laying out his strategy: far from the physical abuse used by his predecessors in the misogynist farces, Petruchio lays out an almost spiritual tactic. He decides that he will present her with another mirror for herself than the dysfunctional one her society has forced upon her:

> I will attend her here,
> And woo her with some spirit when she comes.
> Say that she rail; why then I'll tell her plain
> She sings as sweetly as a nightingale:
> Say that she frown, I'll say she looks as clear
> As morning roses newly wash'd with dew:
> Say she be mute and will not speak a word;

18. *The Riverside Shakespeare*, 2nd ed. All subsequent references to the texts of Shakespeare's plays are to this edition.

19. In addition to the shrew farces common in medieval Europe, misogyny had long been a staple in the comic literature of Western civilization, from the stories of Socrates' shrewish wife, Xantippe, to the cantankerous wife of Noah in the Chester mystery plays, to the Wife of Bath in Chaucer's *Canterbury Tales*. For more on the Wife of Bath, see Mikee Deloney's chapter in this volume.

> Then I'll commend her volubility,
> And say she uttereth piercing eloquence:
> If she do bid me pack, I'll give her thanks,
> As though she bid me stay by her a week:
> If she deny to wed, I'll crave the day
> When I shall ask the banns and when be married.
> But here she comes; and now, Petruchio, speak. (2.1.169–181)

Jonathan Miller, director of the 1980 BBC video production of this play, argues that Petruchio's goal with Katharine is to free her from her shrewishness by providing her an escape into the kind of "companionate marriage" preached by the Puritans of Shakespeare's day. And indeed, though it seems somewhat combative, their first conversation shows a pair of equally matched wits who genuinely enjoy the give and take of verbal sparring with one another:

Petruchio: Good morrow, Kate; for that's your name, I hear.

Katharina: Well have you heard, but something hard of hearing:
They call me Katharina that do talk of me.

Petruchio: You lie, in faith; for you are call'd plain Kate,
And bonny Kate and sometimes Kate the curst;
But Kate, the prettiest Kate in Christendom
Kate of Kate Hall, my super-dainty Kate,
For dainties are all Kates, and therefore, Kate,
Take this of me, Kate of my consolation;
Hearing thy mildness praised in every town,
Thy virtues spoke of, and thy beauty sounded,
Yet not so deeply as to thee belongs,
Myself am moved to woo thee for my wife.

Katharina: Moved! in good time: let him that moved you hither
Remove you hence: I knew you at the first
You were a moveable.

Petruchio: Why, what's a moveable?

Katharina: A join'd-stool.

Petruchio: Thou hast hit it: come, sit on me.

Katharina: Asses are made to bear, and so are you.

Petruchio: Women are made to bear, and so are you.

Katharina: No such jade as you, if me you mean.

Petruchio: Alas! good Kate, I will not burden thee;
For, knowing thee to be but young and light—

Katharina: Too light for such a swain as you to catch;
And yet as heavy as my weight should be. (2.1.182–205)

Note how in each of their exchanges they each pick up on particular words the other has used and then twist them back on the previous speaker: "hear" becomes "heard" in Petruchio's speech and "hard of hearing" in Kate's response. And though he plays at length upon her name, she picks up his word "moved" and spits it back to him twice before changing it to "remove" and insulting him with "moveable," which she defines for him. He takes the insult and asks her to sit on him, which she turns into a deeper insult, which he turns back upon her with a patriarchal put-down, which she counters again. And so on throughout much of the rest of the play. Yes, the very notion of taming a woman is demeaning, potentially reducing her to the level of an animal (a prized falcon, in fact). And the play does end with Katharine giving a long speech reaffirming the traditional submissive role of the wife to her husband ("Thy husband is thy lord, thy life, thy keeper,/ Thy head, thy sovereign . . ." [5.2.146–7]). This speech is essentially an extended elaboration of the injunction in Ephesians 5:22: "Wives, submit yourselves unto your own husbands, as unto the Lord."

Some critics and directors have seen this as evidence that Shakespeare here succumbed to the misogyny of his age in constructing his plot. Charles Marowitz, for instance, declares, "The modern technique of brainwashing is, almost to the letter, what Petruchio makes Katharine undergo,"[20] and in his notorious 1973 production he had Katharine deliver this lengthy speech like a zombie, battered black and blue and bloody, as though Petruchio had beaten the old patriarchal doctrine into her thick skull.[21]

Marowitz misses the distance Shakespeare has traveled from his source. Katharine at the end is in many ways still the old Katharine, and she gives this speech with all of the feisty spirit she once had. With Petruchio, Katharine has learned how to play the game of love and marriage that society demands of them, and they play it together with gusto.[22] Katharine

20. Marowitz, *Marowitz Shakespeare*, 18.

21. Bate and Jackson, *Shakespeare*, 164.

22. This notion is consistent with "the theatrical theory of the self" that Colin McGinn finds throughout Shakespeare's plays (12), as expressed most notably in Jaques's famous lines from *As You Like It*: "All the world's a stage,/ And all the men and women merely players . . ." In Shakespeare's characters, McGinn argues, "this makes

and Petruchio are an intellectual and verbal match for each other, and they each rejoice in finding someone worthy of their wit. In her spirited final speech, she offers to place her hand beneath her husband's foot, in hyperbolic concession to the prevailing paradigm of marriage. But Petruchio takes her by the hand and raises her to an equal stature with him, as he says, "Why, there's a wench! Come on and kiss me, Kate" (5.2.180).

Yes, Kate has just given a lengthy paraphrase of the traditional view of wifely submission. And yes, Petruchio the patriarchal braggart is the one who raises her from the ground at the end. Yet he does raise her, in appreciation of her spirit and intellectual spark. These two combatants have become friends with a mutual respect for each other. Jack Jorgens argues that the so-called taming in this play has gone both ways: "Their struggle, really a mutual taming, is 'the old game'—they test each other, school each other."[23] Harold Bloom hears in their final scenes in the play the "subtly exquisite music of marriage at its happiest."[24] To accentuate this interpretation, eighteenth-century actor-manager David Garrick added this speech to the end of his adaptation of the play when he performed the part: "Petruchio here shall doff the lordly husband;/ An honest mask, which I throw off with pleasure./ Far hence all rudeness, willfulness, and noise,/ And be our future lives one gentle stream/ Of mutual love, compliance, and regard!"[25] Katharine and Petruchio are companions who enjoy each other's company. They have begun, in fact, a "companionate marriage," clearly superior to the marriage that her sweet, simpering, hypocritical sister Bianca has entered with the wealthiest of her suitors. Compared with his source material, the misogynistic ballad of *A Merry Jest of a Shrewd and Curst Wife*, Shakespeare's play reflects a revolution in the view of marriage.

For Shakespeare, the revolution had just begun. *Shrew* was written in 1593, fairly early in his career. In 1594 he wrote *Romeo and Juliet*. Both plays dramatize in different ways the tension between dynastic marriage, stuck in the traditions of patriarchal privilege and power, and egalitarian marriage, based on compatibility and choice. In *Romeo and Juliet*, he demonstrates how the old hatreds between two powerful dynasties

---

personality not a given but a choice, not determined but free. . . . [P]eople try out one role and then another, until one seems to fit. . . . I am what I make myself, according to my own aesthetic and practical standards. I am always acting a part . . ." (11).

23. Jorgens, *Shakespeare on Film*, 68.

24. Bloom, *Shakespeare*, 33.

25. *Taming of the Shrew*, 159.

destroy the young love between two members of their clans who dare to defy patriarchal authority to forge their own companionate love and marriage. As we saw in *The Taming of the Shrew*, the first conversation between potential lovers can demonstrate their immediate compatibility. The first conversation between Romeo and Juliet at the crowded Capulet masked ball is in fact a shared sonnet, with Romeo taking the first quatrain, Juliet the second, and the two of them sharing the third as well as the concluding couplet. Though indeed they are very young and subject to the throes of erotic love, they share an intellectual and poetic sensibility that makes them kindred spirits in ways that they cannot be with any others in the play. Romantic love is not the same as companionate marriage, but in this play Shakespeare brings the two together in a way that is revolutionary. Despite their impetuosity and emotional immaturity, their shared poetic sensibility and facility with language evidence a potential for a companionate marriage, had not the dynastic hatreds intervened.

Shakespeare returned to this prospect twice with his comedy *A Midsummer Night's Dream*, written in 1595. The play within the play, rehearsed throughout the play and performed as entertainment after the wedding of the three noble couples, farcically enacts the tragic story of Pyramus and Thisbe. Like their counterparts Romeo and Juliet, these two lovers die because of the animosity between their two houses. The farce also demonstrates what might well have happened in the larger plot of the play, which begins with a father, Egeus, demanding that his daughter Hermia marry the man of his choice. Duke Theseus agrees, reminding Hermia that

> To you your father should be as a god;
> One that composed your beauties, yea, and one
> To whom you are but as a form in wax
> By him imprinted and within his power
> To leave the figure or disfigure it. (1.1.47–51)

She is her father's property, and he is free to do with her as he pleases, which includes marrying her to the man of his own choosing, based presumably on financial and political benefit to himself. If she fails to comply with his wishes, Duke Theseus says she will be condemned either to die or to while away her years as a nun, "chanting faint hymns to the cold fruitless moon" (1.1.73).

Hermia, however, rejects all of these options and chooses to run off with her lover, Lysander. After a night of misadventures in the forest, they are discovered by Theseus and Egeus, who asks Theseus to enforce the penalties against his daughter. True to his comic vision, however, and to his desire to call into question the dynastic view of marriage of his time, Shakespeare has Theseus reverse his earlier decree and override Egeus's absolute control over his daughter to allow her own choice based on affection and compatibility. He invites Hermia and Lysander (and Helena and Demetrius) to join him and Hippolyta to celebrate a triple wedding in the palace that very day. It is after their weddings that they watch the performance of the tragedy of Pyramus and Thisbe, which, though hilarious, reminds them of how easily their own joyful ending might have turned tragic because of dynastic power and animosity—as in fact was the case with Romeo and Juliet.

In all three of the plays we have examined thus far, we have seen how Shakespeare has dramatized the tension between the patriarchal dynastic view of marriage and a new egalitarian view of marriage based on choice, affection, and compatibility. In *Taming of the Shrew*, Katharine and Petruchio form a relationship that proves a foil to the traditional relationship of her sister Bianca and Lucentio. In *Romeo and Juliet*, the two lovers defy their fathers to form a relationship that is a foil to the one Juliet's father had chosen for her with the County Paris. In *A Midsummer Night's Dream*, Hermia and Lysander defy her father to form a relationship that is a foil to the one Hermia's father had chosen for her with Demetrius. But in each of these plays, in dramatizing the tension between these opposing views of marriage, Shakespeare leaves open a range of interpretations between them. We have already seen how some critics and directors have chosen to interpret *The Taming of the Shrew* as reinscribing the patriarchal view of marriage. Might not one argue as well that *Romeo and Juliet*, and even *A Midsummer Night's Dream*, with its tragedy of "Pyramus and Thisbe," serve as cautionary tales against the folly of defying the dynastic view of marriage?

Exploring the New Ideal in the Middle Plays

Shakespeare pits these two views of love against each other again in *Much Ado About Nothing*. This play, written in 1598, reflects a more mature effort on Shakespeare's part to critique the dynastic model by means of the egalitarian, without reverting to the traditional view of wifely submission, as Katharine seems to do in her final speeches in *Taming of the Shrew*. In *Much Ado About Nothing*, two relationships prove a foil for each other on this very point. Hero and Claudio fall in love at first sight, are relatively silent about it, and must have their marriage approved and arranged by Hero's father. Beatrice and Benedict, on the other hand, insult each other incessantly, can't stop talking to each other, and—very significantly—she has no father to arrange her marriage. Beatrice and Benedict begin the play with as vicious a repartee as Petruchio and Katharine's first conversation.

> Beatrice: I wonder that you will still be talking, Signior
> Benedick: nobody marks you.
>
> Benedick: What, my dear Lady Disdain! are you yet living?
>
> Beatrice: Is it possible disdain should die while she hath such meet food to feed it as Signior Benedick? Courtesy itself must convert to disdain, if you come in her presence.
>
> Benedick: Then is courtesy a turncoat. But it is certain I am loved of all ladies, only you excepted: and I would I could find in my heart that I had not a hard heart; for, truly, I love none.
>
> Beatrice: A dear happiness to women: they would else have been troubled with a pernicious suitor. I thank God and my cold blood, I am of your humour for that: I had rather hear my dog bark at a crow than a man swear he loves me.
>
> Benedick: God keep your ladyship still in that mind! so some gentleman or other shall 'scape a predestinate scratched face.
>
> Beatrice: Scratching could not make it worse, an 'twere such a face as yours were.
>
> Benedick: Well, you are a rare parrot-teacher.
>
> Beatrice: A bird of my tongue is better than a beast of yours.
>
> Benedick: I would my horse had the speed of your tongue, and so good a continuer. But keep your way, i' God's name; I have done.
>
> Beatrice: You always end with a jade's trick: I know you of old. (1.1.115–145)

On the surface, Benedick and Beatrice despise each other; yet they are unable to stop talking to each other. Their first conversation uses the same device as Petruchio and Katharine's: repeating words the other has used and twisting them back on the other to heighten the insult. They obviously enjoy this game and each other's company, despite their venom, and they keep up their patter throughout the play, even after their friends trick them into confessing their hidden love for each other.

Benedick's friend Claudio, however, woos his love Hero by proxy, through his friend the prince, Don Pedro. So by the time Claudio has won Hero's hand in marriage, he has never even spoken to her, and has had to overcome the suspicion that the prince has wooed Hero for himself. Here is the conversation surrounding their betrothal:

> **Don Pedro:** Here, Claudio, I have wooed in thy name, and fair Hero is won: I have broke with her father, and his good will obtained: name the day of marriage, and God give thee joy!
>
> **Leonato:** Count, take of me my daughter, and with her my fortunes: his grace hath made the match, and all grace say Amen to it.
>
> **Beatrice:** Speak, count, 'tis your cue.
>
> **Claudio:** Silence is the perfectest herald of joy: I were but little happy, if I could say how much. Lady, as you are mine, I am yours: I give away myself for you and dote upon the exchange.
>
> **Beatrice:** Speak, cousin; or, if you cannot, stop his mouth with a kiss, and let not him speak neither.
>
> **Don Pedro:** In faith, lady, you have a merry heart.
>
> **Beatrice:** Yea, my lord; I thank it, poor fool, it keeps on the windy side of care. My cousin tells him in his ear that he is in her heart.
>
> **Claudio:** And so she doth, cousin. (2.1.298–317)

Beatrice has to speak for both Hero and Claudio. Hero is speechless, in stark contrast to her cousin Beatrice. Based on so little communication, Claudio and Hero's relationship is easily broken by a rumor planted by the villain Don John. On their supposed wedding day, Claudio denounces Hero as a whore, breaks off the marriage and runs off, leaving a very distraught Beatrice weeping for her cousin. Benedick, whose heart has warmed to her, comes to comfort her, and in one of the most remarkable scenes in all of Shakespeare we get several layers of emotional complexity occurring at once: Beatrice's grief and anger over the false accusation against her cousin, Benedick's gentleness of repressed love about to be expressed, both of them retreating for a moment into the brittle defensiveness of their old verbal badinage, Beatrice's sweet vulnerability of repressed love finally revealed, then her anger against patriarchal injustice suddenly erupting into full blown rage, ending with Benedick placating the raging Beatrice by agreeing to defend her (and her cousin's) honor by adopting the traditional role of male chivalry.

Benedick: Lady Beatrice, have you wept all this while?

Beatrice: Yea, and I will weep a while longer.

Benedick: I will not desire that.

Beatrice: You have no reason; I do it freely.

Benedick: Surely I do believe your fair cousin is wronged.

Beatrice: Ah, how much might the man deserve of me that would right her!

Benedick: Is there any way to show such friendship?

Beatrice: A very even way, but no such friend.

Benedick: May a man do it?

Beatrice: It is a man's office, but not yours.

Benedick: I do love nothing in the world so well as you: is not that strange?

Beatrice: As strange as the thing I know not. It were as possible for me to say I loved nothing so well as you: but believe me not; and yet I lie not; I confess nothing, nor I deny nothing. I am sorry for my cousin.

Benedick: By my sword, Beatrice, thou lovest me.

Beatrice: Do not swear, and eat it.

Benedick: I will swear by it that you love me; and I will make him eat it that says I love not you.

Beatrice: Will you not eat your word?

Benedick: With no sauce that can be devised to it. I protest I love thee.

Beatrice: Why, then, God forgive me!

Benedick: What offence, sweet Beatrice?

Beatrice: You have stayed me in a happy hour: I was about to protest I loved you.

Benedick: And do it with all thy heart.

Beatrice: I love you with so much of my heart that none is left to protest.

Benedick: Come, bid me do any thing for thee.

Beatrice: Kill Claudio.

Benedick: Ha! not for the wide world.

Beatrice: You kill me to deny it. Farewell.

Benedick: Tarry, sweet Beatrice.

Beatrice: I am gone, though I am here: there is no love in you: nay, I pray you, let me go.

Benedick: Beatrice,—

Beatrice: In faith, I will go.

Benedick: We'll be friends first.

Beatrice: You dare easier be friends with me than fight with mine enemy.

Benedick: Is Claudio thine enemy?

Beatrice: Is he not approved in the height a villain, that hath slandered, scorned, dishonoured my kinswoman? O that I were a man! What, bear her in hand until they
come to take hands; and then, with public accusation, uncovered slander, unmitigated rancour,—O God, that I were a man! I would eat his heart in the market-place.

Benedick: Hear me, Beatrice,—

Beatrice: Talk with a man out at a window! A proper saying!

Benedick: Nay, but, Beatrice,—

Beatrice: Sweet Hero! She is wronged, she is slandered, she is undone.

Benedick: Beat—

Beatrice: Princes and counties! Surely, a princely testimony, a goodly count, Count Comfect; a sweet gallant, surely! O that

I were a man for his sake! or that I had any friend would be
a man for my sake! But manhood is melted into courtesies,
valour into compliment, and men are only turned into tongue,
and trim ones too: he is now as valiant as Hercules that only
tells a lie and swears it. I cannot be a man with wishing, therefore I will die a woman with grieving.

Benedick: Tarry, good Beatrice. By this hand, I love thee.

Beatrice: Use it for my love some other way than swearing by it.

Benedick: Think you in your soul the Count Claudio hath
wronged Hero?

Beatrice: Yea, as sure as I have a thought or a soul.

Benedick: Enough, I am engaged; I will challenge him. I will
kiss your hand, and so I leave you. By this hand, Claudio shall
render me a dear account. As you hear of me, so think of me.
Go, comfort your cousin: I must say she is dead: and so, farewell. (4.1.256–336)

Benedick goes off to challenge his friend Claudio to prove his love for
Beatrice, but before this can happen Don John's villainy is discovered,
and Hero and Claudio's relationship is restored.

All's well that ends well, perhaps, but I have quoted this passage at
length because it brilliantly conveys how Shakespeare is playing with the
tension between different ways of seeing male and female relationships.
Not only is Beatrice much more vocal than Hero in speaking her mind,
she also has no father to proscribe her choices and arrange for her a marriage that suits his convenience and financial and political benefit. Shakespeare intentionally makes Beatrice fatherless so that he can make her
free to shape her own love and marriage. And though in this conversation
with Benedick she defers to the traditional chivalric gender roles ("Oh,
that I were a man!"), she is the one who initiates the traditional male role
of revenge and drives the action forward. The upshot is that, in the end,
the audience may have more confidence in the long-term prospects of the
marriage between Beatrice and Benedick than they do in that between
Claudio and Hero. Not only do Beatrice and Benedick love talking with
each other, they also love matching wits and intelligence with a worthy
contestant—and more than that, they love talking about love, as they
will do through the rest of the play, and they use their intelligence and
verbal powers to share with each other the full range of human emotion.

And because Beatrice is free to keep her feisty spirit, she and Benedick sharpen each other, and each is made better for the continuing exchange. Rather than "mutual submission," a phrase sometimes used to describe egalitarian marriages, Beatrice and Benedick evidence a "mutual empowerment" in their relationship.

Another couple in Shakespeare who demonstrate a deep compatibility of spirit are Brutus and Portia in *Julius Caesar* (1599). Portia has only one scene in the play, but in it she reveals that she and her husband have a history of sharing deeply their thoughts, concerns, and anguish. In this scene she confronts her husband about his secrecy concerning what has been troubling him lately. She has seen several hooded men this very evening who have met with him in the shadows of their orchard, and she pleads with him on her knees to confide in her:

> **Portia:** Within the bond of marriage, tell me, Brutus,
> Is it excepted I should know no secrets
> That appertain to you? Am I yourself
> But, as it were, in sort or limitation,
> To keep with you at meals, comfort your bed,
> And talk to you sometimes? Dwell I but in the suburbs
> Of your good pleasure? If it be no more,
> Portia is Brutus' harlot, not his wife.
>
> **Brutus:** You are my true and honourable wife,
> As dear to me as are the ruddy drops
> That visit my sad heart.
>
> **Portia:** If this were true, then should I know this secret.
> I grant I am a woman; but withal
> A woman that Lord Brutus took to wife:
> I grant I am a woman; but withal
> A woman well-reputed, Cato's daughter.
> Think you I am no stronger than my sex,
> Being so father'd and so husbanded?
> Tell me your counsels, I will not disclose 'em:
> I have made strong proof of my constancy,
> Giving myself a voluntary wound
> Here, in the thigh: can I bear that with patience.
> And not my husband's secrets?
>
> **Brutus:** O ye gods,
> Render me worthy of this noble wife! (2.1.233–309)

"Dwell I but in the suburbs of your affection?" In this exchange Shakespeare explores the perspective that a "true wife" is one who shares equally in everything of significance with her husband; to be anything less is to be merely his harlot. Portia asks pointedly, "Am I your whore, or your wife?" Brutus acknowledges Portia a worthy match in nobility to his own soul, and promises to confide in her the secrets of his heart.

Ambiguity in the Later Plays

One couple in Shakespeare's later plays does not share such compatibility of spirit as Brutus and Portia, and thus does not communicate as well or share as deeply. As a consequence, they suffer deeply, in a tragic sense enacting the wife/whore dichotomy Portia describes above. In *Othello* (1604), the beautiful Desdemona falls in love with the noble moor Othello when she hears him recount his wondrous exploits to her father. She has obviously been entranced by his manly exploits, but even more, she feels that she is enlarged by listening to him. Her imagination has been sparked by his stories, and something in her has been awakened. He, however, is so entranced by her beauty that he treats her with a kind of dangerous idolatry, foisting onto her an image of perfection that no human can bear. Shortly after they are married, Othello's malevolent lieutenant, Iago, triggers in him an unfounded jealousy against Desdemona. Othello never bothers to discuss his suspicions with his new wife; he allows his imagination to run wild with the prospect of her infidelity. When he finally does speak with her, he is too far gone with jealousy to recognize her innocence, and in his imagination she falls from the paragon of virtue to a whore.

Desdemona's lady-in-waiting, Emilia, who is also the wife of Iago, sees the injustice of this imbalance and rails against men who treat women in this belittling and dehumanizing way. In an angry manifesto for poorly treated wives, she declares:

> 'Tis not a year or two shows us a man:
> They are all but stomachs, and we all but food;
> They eat us hungerly, and when they are full,
> They belch us. (3.4.103–106)

And later, when Othello's jealousy escalates, so does Emilia's complaint:

> But I do think it is their husbands' faults
> If wives do fall: say that they slack their duties,
> And pour our treasures into foreign laps,
> Or else break out in peevish jealousies,
> Throwing restraint upon us; or say they strike us,
> Or scant our former having in despite;
> Why, we have galls, and though we have some grace,
> Yet have we some revenge. Let husbands know
> Their wives have sense like them: they see and smell
> And have their palates both for sweet and sour,
> As husbands have. What is it that they do
> When they change us for others? Is it sport?
> I think it is: and doth affection breed it?
> I think it doth: is't frailty that thus errs?
> It is so too: and have not we affections,
> Desires for sport, and frailty, as men have?
> Then let them use us well: else let them know,
> The ills we do, their ills instruct us so. (4.3.86–103)

Emilia here sounds similar to Shylock in *The Merchant of Venice* in his famous "Hath not a Jew eyes" speech (3.1.59–73), wherein he argues that Jews are as fully human as Christians are. In both of these speeches, Shakespeare gives expression to the emerging Christian humanism of the time that affirmed the value of every human being regardless of race, class, nationality, and gender. Emilia argues that wives are as fully human as husbands are, but, as with Shylock, the imbalance that has led to this manifesto is so severe that it cannot be resolved peacefully.

Shakespeare suggests that the power of Othello's unbridled imagination does him in. Othello can imagine all too vividly what isn't true in his wife, and this imagination, coupled with his idolatry and his inability to see women other than in the traditional polarized categories of virgin and whore, drives a wedge between them, leading him finally to murder his wife in the insanity of his jealousy. He had placed her on an impossibly high pedestal, and this unequal status left them unable to communicate with each other or to become genuine companions in marriage. The wife who had been a goddess of purity to him becomes a whore to him in his imagination, and he kills her for it.

The ideal of the companionate marriage suggested that the partners would share in every significant aspect of their lives together, without strict regard to the traditional gender roles of the past. But what if husband and wife become partners in *evil*? This is the basis for what Harold

Bloom calls "the happiest married couple" in Shakespeare—the Macbeths.[26] As soon as Macbeth hears the prophecy of the three witches that he shall become king someday, he sends his wife a letter to include her in his imaginings. He writes, "This have I thought good to deliver thee, my dearest partner of greatness, that thou mightest not lose the dues of rejoicing by being ignorant of what greatness is promis'd thee. Lay it to thy heart, and farewell" (1.5.10–14). She immediately sets out to fulfill their mutual ambition. It is clear that they have discussed such things before and that she knows his hesitations about killing the king. Macbeth, as she says, is "too full of the milk of human kindness" (1.5.17). She will supply whatever ambition he might lack, but to do so she decides that she will have to play the traditional role of the man, and so she prays in a chilling soliloquy:

> Come, you spirits
> That tend on mortal thoughts, unsex me here,
> And fill me from the crown to the toe top-full
> Of direst cruelty! make thick my blood;
> Stop up the access and passage to remorse,
> That no compunctious visitings of nature
> Shake my fell purpose, nor keep peace between
> The effect and it! Come to my woman's breasts,
> And take my milk for gall, you murdering ministers,
> Wherever in your sightless substances
> You wait on nature's mischief! (1.5.40–50)

When Macbeth arrives, she greets him warmly and begins to plot with him the deed that they decide together must be done. But later, when Macbeth hesitates again, she calls his manhood into question and forcefully reminds him of their mutual ambition:

> Was the hope drunk
> Wherein you dress'd yourself? hath it slept since?
> And wakes it now, to look so green and pale
> At what it did so freely? From this time
> Such I account thy love. Art thou afeard
> To be the same in thine own act and valour
> As thou art in desire? Wouldst thou have that
> Which thou esteem'st the ornament of life,
> And live a coward in thine own esteem,

---

26. Bloom, *Shakespeare*, 518.

Letting 'I dare not' wait upon 'I would,'
Like the poor cat i' the adage?

Macbeth: Prithee, peace:
I dare do all that may become a man;
Who dares do more is none.

Lady Macbeth: What beast was't, then,
That made you break this enterprise to me?
When you durst do it, then you were a man;
And, to be more than what you were, you would
Be so much more the man. Nor time nor place
Did then adhere, and yet you would make both:
They have made themselves, and that their fitness now
Does unmake you. I have given suck, and know
How tender 'tis to love the babe that milks me:
I would, while it was smiling in my face,
Have pluck'd my nipple from his boneless gums,
And dash'd the brains out, had I so sworn as you
Have done to this. (1.7.35–59)

Though she takes it to horrifying excess, Lady Macbeth is nonetheless saying, "We are a team, you and I, my dearest partner of greatness. My intelligence matches yours. My courage exceeds yours. My spirit is as tough as yours." This is why "marriages such as that between Macbeth and his 'dearest partner of greatness' have been adduced as evidence . . . for the rise of the affective companionate marriage in which both husband and wife understand themselves as embarked on a joint emotional and social enterprise."[27] As such, the play can also be read as a cautionary tale against such marriages, especially when the wife denies her sexuality and traditional gender role to play the traditional violent and ambitious male role. She taunts him for his lack of "manliness," and taunts him further by bragging that she is more man than he. In the end she, like Beatrice, strong as they both appear to be, must rely on their man to do the work of violence. "Oh, that I were a man!" cries Beatrice before commissioning Benedick to "Kill Claudio." Lady Macbeth, after sending her husband to kill King Duncan, says plaintively, "Had he not resembled my father as he slept, I had done it," revealing at last and too late a touch of the "milk of human kindness" that she berated in Macbeth. Clearly, Shakespeare was not so naïve as to believe that companionate marriage was a panacea for social problems, or he wouldn't have written this play with

27. Dobson and Wells, *Oxford*, 280.

its depiction of a companionate marriage gone horribly wrong. It is clear that Shakespeare enjoyed exploring all the possible consequences, comic and tragic, of lifting the traditional gender boundaries that had defined and restricted women's roles in the past.

One thing is true of all of the great couples in Shakespeare: Petruchio and Katharine, Beatrice and Benedict, Romeo and Juliet, Brutus and Portia, a different Portia and Bassanio in *The Merchant of Venice*, and Rosalind and Orlando in *As You Like It*. Of none of these women can we say, as Hamlet says of his mother Gertrude—and later implies of his love Ophelia—"Frailty, thy name is woman!" (1.2.146). In their relationships with their men, these women fulfill the biblical description of true friendship: "iron sharpens iron, and one person sharpens the wit of another" (Prov 27:17, NRSV). But with Macbeth and Lady Macbeth, surely the tragedy is that such greatness of intelligence and imagination is given over to such evil. Greater is their fall as a consequence, and the fall drives a wedge between them. As his murders escalate, Macbeth leaves his wife out of his deliberations. She is no longer his "dearest partner of greatness." They no longer even communicate, and they are left to encounter their guilt alone—she in madness and he in nihilistic despair. He comes to see that their lives are "full of sound and fury,/ Signifying nothing." This is the tragedy of two noble intelligences, their friendship, and their marriage destroyed by ambition. These are two great souls who fall into damnation even before they die.

Conclusion

Our discussion ends in the tragedies, where we see Shakespeare's explorations of the consequences of the dangers both of unequal and idolatrous love, on the one hand (*Othello*), and of companionate marriage dedicated to evil on the other (*Macbeth*). Yet in the earlier plays we considered, Shakespeare had already explored the positive potential of this new model of companionate marriage. In his comedies, Shakespeare suggests that the couples who argue together stay together—they enjoy their repartees because they sharpen an already lively intelligence and imagination in each other, revealing a strong undercurrent of respect that is essential to love.

Shakespeare frequently delights in complicating the strict polarities in gender relationships that encouraged misogyny to flourish in his culture.[28] His plays, in fact, evidence a culture in transition regarding the nature of marriage and gender. Shakespeare's primary purpose was to dramatize the prevailing conflicts regarding these and other issues, not necessarily to resolve them. He succeeded in this in powerful and compelling ways, which continues to make his dramas intriguing and relevant today, honestly provoking questions we still struggle to answer.

Bibliography

Ackroyd, Peter. *The Life of Sir Thomas More*. New York: Anchor, 1999.

Bate, Jonathan, and Russell Jackson, editors. *Shakespeare: An Illustrated Stage History*. Oxford: Oxford University Press, 1996.

Bevington, David. "The Difficult Ideal of the Companionate Marriage." *The Journal of Religion* 74/3 (July 1994) 372–78.

Bloom, Harold. *Shakespeare: The Invention of the Human*. New York: Riverhead, 1998.

Boose, Lynda E. "The Family in Shakespeare Studies." In *Shakespeare: An Anthology of Criticism and Theory 1945–2000*, edited by Russ McDonald, 606–33. Oxford: Blackwell, 2004.

Dobson, Michael, and Stanley Wells, editors. *Oxford Companion to Shakespeare*. Oxford: Oxford University Press, 2001.

Greaves, Richard L. *Society and Religion in Elizabethan England*. Minneapolis: University of Minnesota Press, 1981.

Greenblatt, Stephen. *Renaissance Self-Fashioning*. Chicago: University of Chicago Press, 1983.

———. *Shakespearean Negotiations: The Circulation of Social Energy in Renaissance England*. New Historicism, Studies in Cultural Poetics, 84. Berkeley: University of California Press, 1989.

———. *Will in the World: How Shakespeare Became Shakespeare*. New York: Norton, 2005.

Grudem, Wayne, and John Piper, editors. *Recovering Biblical Manhood and Womanhood*. Wheaton, IL: Crossway, 1991.

Jardine, Lisa. *Reading Shakespeare Historically*. London: Routledge, 1996.

Jorgens, Jack J.. *Shakespeare on Film*. Bloomington: Indiana University Press, 1977.

Keats, John. "Letter to George and Thomas Keats on December 22, 1817" and "Letter to Richard Woodhouse on October 27, 1818." In *Criticism: Major Statements*, edited by Charles Kaplan and William Davis Anderson, 282–86. 4th ed. Boston: Beford/St. Martin's, 2000.

Kostenberger, Andreas J. *God, Marriage and Family: Rebuilding the Biblical Foundation*. 2nd ed. Wheaton, IL: Crossway, 2006, 2010.

Lewis, C. S. "Donne and Love Poetry in the Seventeenth Century." In *Selected Literary Essays*, edited by Walter Hooper, 106–25. Cambridge: Cambridge University Press, 1979.

Marowitz, Charles. *The Marowitz Shakespeare*. London: Marion Boyars, 1978.

28. Again, see Woodbridge, *Women and the English Renaissance*, for a thoroughly detailed elaboration of the misogyny rampant in the literature of Shakespeare's time.

McGinn, Colin. *Shakespeare's Philosophy: Discovering the Meaning behind the Plays.* New York: Harper, 2007.

Miller, Jonathan. "Interview with Jonathan Miller." With Tim Hallinan. *Shakespeare Quarterly* 32/2 (1981) 134–45.

Novy, Marianne. "Demythologizing Shakespeare." *Women's Studies* 9/1 (1981) 17–27.

Packer, J. I. *A Quest for Godliness: The Puritan Vision of the Christian Life.* Wheaton, IL: Crossway, 1994.

Piper, John. "A Vision of Biblical Complementarity: Manhood and Womanhood Defined According to the Bible." In *Recovering Biblical Manhood and Womanhood*, edited by John Piper and Wayne Grudem, 31–59. Wheaton, IL: Crossway, 1991.

Richardson, Herbert W. *Nun, Witch, Playmate: The Americanization of Sex.* New York: Harper and Row, 1971.

Ryken, Leland. *Worldly Saints: The Puritans as They Really Were.* Grand Rapids: Zondervan, 1986.

Shakespeare, William. *The Riverside Shakespeare.* Edited by G. Blakemore Evans and J. J. M. Tobin. 2nd ed. Boston: Houghton Mifflin, 1997.

———. *The Taming of the Shrew: Texts and Contexts.* Edited by Frances E. Dolan. Boston, New York: Bedford, 1996.

Tilney, Edmund. *The Flower of Friendship: A Renaissance Dialogue Contesting Marriage.* Edited by Valerie Wayne. Ithaca, NY: Cornell University Press, 1992.

Vickers, Brian. *Appropriating Shakespeare: Contemporary Critical Quarrels.* New Haven, CT: Yale University Press, 1993.

Wayne, Valerie. "Introduction." In *The Flower of Friendship: A Renaissance Dialogue Contesting Marriage*, by Edmund Tilney, 1–94. Ithaca, NY: Cornell University Press, 1992.

Woodbridge, Linda. *Women and the English Renaissance: Literature and the Nature of Womankind, 1540–1620.* Urbana and Chicago: University of Illinois Press, 1984.

11

Beloved Sex

Healing Shame and Restoring the Sacred in Sexuality

Tina Schermer Sellers

'Kiss me there where pride is glittering
Kiss me where I am ripened and round fruit
Kiss me wherever, however I am supple, bare and flare
(Let the bell be rung as long as I am young:
Let ring and fly like a great bronze wing!)
Until I am shaken from blossom to root.'

'I'll kiss you wherever you think you are poor,
Wherever you shudder, feeling striped or barred,
Because you think you are bloodless, skinny or marred:
Until, until
your gaze has been stilled—
Until you are shamed again no more!
I'll kiss you until your body and soul
the mind in the body being fulfilled—
Suspend their dread and civil war!'

—Aria in *Kilroy's Carnival* by Delmore Schwartz

From my personal experience, the message was hardcore. Along with "sexual purity" was "emotional purity" and living within certain boundaries so you didn't give pieces of yourself away by going "too far" physically or even having serious emotional connections, conversations with the opposite sex. You were told to have clear relationship boundaries—but this was never clearly defined and was hard to understand. A lot of the pressure came from my parents, and certain church groups and para-church organizations. This story kind of describes the overall idea and concept that was constantly driven home:

> *Imagine for a moment one of those huge lollipops, the kind that you buy at an amusement park candy store. Take off the wrapper, and pass it around to ten people. Allow them to lick as much as they want. The leftover is saved for the husband or wife, the rightful owner of the lollipop.*

Yuck! Who would want that?! Imagine being told this—so now you feel dirty, unwanted, yucky and worthless. If I have given anything away even just emotionally, this is how I feel about myself. Here is a quote from a book I was given as a teen, "When we give away pieces of ourselves emotionally and spiritually . . . what is left over for the rightful owner? . . . Keeping yourself emotionally pure is a gift that should be left and given to the rightful owner—your spouse." (twenty-four-year-old female graduate student)[1]

For many like this woman, the "no sex before marriage" discourse expanded in the early 1990s to include the idea that they must remain "sexually pure" before marriage, which meant no expression of sexual desire was to be entertained (masturbation, kissing, longing, touching, fantasizing, etc.). This notion was punctuated by the purity movement that gained popularity in 1993 with the Love Waits purity pledge, sponsored by LifeWay Christian Resources. Here is the pledge, which, according to this organization, over two million adolescents signed:

> Believing that true love waits, I make a commitment to God, myself, my family, my friends, my future mate, and my future children to a lifetime of purity including sexual abstinence from this day until the day I enter a biblical marriage relationship.[2]

1. Paulson, *Emotional Purity*, 52. Approximately thirty books with this ascetic purity message were published between 1995 and 2005, along with t-shirts, calling cards, bracelets, and purity rings. *I Kissed Dating Goodbye*, published in 1997, was frequently mentioned as another book promoting condemnation and shame in interviews with graduate students who were adolescents during this movement.

2. Lifeway, "True Love Waits."

Vague and undefined mandates in this pledge and throughout this literature leave a young person lost in self-condemnation. Desperately wanting to "be a good Christian," earnest adolescents feel damned for developmentally appropriate thoughts and desires.

Phrases such as the following, in particular, leave no room for normal desires for intimacy or intimate touch:

> "*understand that purity begins with **what is in your heart and your mind**"*

> "*A lifetime of purity is contingent upon **setting boundaries** and living within them*"

> "*If you have already given in to **physical desire**, pledge today that from this day forward you will remain physically pure.*"[3]

These phrases disregard that God hard wires each of us for intimacy, connection, and pleasure. We see this everyday in the lives of children, who, in normal play, love, hug, touch, and engage in many acts of pure joy-filled pleasure. What is stunning to me is how this "purity message" resembles the most extreme ascetic movements of the early church, where to serve God required renouncing all sexual thoughts and actions. I have heard twenty-somethings say they were told that even when they desired someone (real or fantasy) they were impurely "lusting" after them and thus "sinning against themselves, the other, their future mate, and God." Since desire is as natural as breath, this has left millions of Christian youth isolated, feeling deep shame and condemnation. Inside this dark vault, they persecute themselves with the belief that these wants and desires are evidence of their depravity. The tragedy for many of these earnest young Christians is learning that this assault on desire does not lift when they get married. Many, both men and women, develop significant sexual dysfunction and chronic low desire issues persisting well into their marriages.

What is shocking to those who supported the purity movement is the lack of protection this movement provided. Research on the effect of the purity pledge indicated only a slight delay of the onset of sexual activity (by twelve to eighteen months), a *reduced* use of contraception in intercourse, an *increase* in unwanted pregnancy, and a significant increase in shame, condemnation, and self-loathing.[4] In other words, if you are told

---

3. Ibid.

4. Charles, "Almost Everyone's Doing It," 65. The National Campaign to Prevent

that something core about yourself—in this case your emotional, physical, and spiritual desire for intimate and sexual touch—is wrong and bad, then it stands that you—your very being—is wrong and bad. Donna Freitas interviewed students at public, Catholic, and evangelical colleges around the United States about their sexual beliefs, attitudes, and behaviors. She writes the following about students at evangelical colleges: "Of all the students I interviewed at all four types of institutions, the only students who spoke of pregnancy scares and having unprotected sex came from the evangelical colleges. [A student], who also had a pregnancy scare, confirms this tendency, which is supported by statistics about Christian students, who are more likely to delay sex, yes, but when they do engage in sex, they are more likely to have unprotected sex."[5]

The effect of the purity movement on these students severely hinders healthy young adult development. As Freitas comments, "The idealization of sexual purity is powerful at evangelical colleges and it exacts demands on students that can be severe, debilitating and often unrealistic. The pressures to marry are extreme for women, and college success is often determined by a ring, not a diploma. Because of the strong hold of purity culture, many students learn to practice sexual secrecy, professing chastity in public while keeping their honest feelings and often their actual experiences hidden. Students are aware that officials at evangelical colleges see it as their duty to monitor male-female romantic relationships and to strictly enforce campus rules about visitation in the residence halls."[6]

> *Self-rejection is the greatest enemy of the spiritual life because it contradicts the sacred voice that calls us the "Beloved." Being the Beloved expresses the core truth of our existence.*[7]

Shame is the core belief that something is bad or unworthy about me. Shame attributes to the whole self—not to a behavior. When a child or adolescent is condemned for something core to their being, they feel deep and abiding shame. When a person believes they are bad, they learn

---

Teen and Unplanned Pregnancy reveals that, of Christians eighteen to twenty-nine who are sexually active, 30 percent have experienced a pregnancy. This is actually 1 percent higher than among those who do not claim an evangelical Christian faith. According to the Guttmacher Institute, nearly half of all pregnancies in the U.S. are unintended, with 40 percent ending in abortion. Of those, 65 percent self-identify as Christian (28 percent Catholic, 37 percent Protestant).

5. Freitas, *Sex and the Soul*, 281.

6. Ibid., 219.

7. Nouwen, *Life of the Beloved*, 68.

to hide their core self. Their own self-rejection causes them to discount any love received because they believe that if that person *really* knew them, they would reject them. No love in. Not God's, not others'. When a person filled with shame gives love from this false self, they doubt their sincerity, which leads to more shame. When we as Christians participate in causing and sustaining shame, we assault the ability to receive the love that would heal or give the love that sustains. Rather than loving like Christ loved the woman at the well, we heap more shame and condemnation on her.

Our created nature—God's Beloved. No shame. God calls us to love. No doubt.

The Effect of These Messages on Sexual, Spiritual, and Esteem Development

Beliefs versus Actions

From findings collected through the National Survey of Family Growth, conducted every few years with approximately five thousand male and female subjects from all over the United States (eight large cities and twenty-five smaller and rural cities) by the Center for Disease Control and Prevention, we know that traditional religious teaching about sexuality changes attitudes, not behaviors; in other words, religious beliefs about sexuality affect the talk more than the walk.[8] Here are some pertinent statistics: When participants were asked if they think it is okay for an eighteen-year-old to have sex with someone they love, 74 percent of those who claimed no religious affiliation said yes, 54 percent of those who claimed Catholic affiliations said yes, and 29 percent of those who claimed a fundamentalist Protestant affiliation said yes. But when asked questions about their age at first intercourse, those who claimed no religion on average lost their virginity at 16.4 years old, while those with a Catholic affiliation were 17.7 years old and those with a fundamentalist Protestant affiliation were 16.9 years old. Similar statistics echo in beliefs versus actions pertaining to virginity at marriage. While the vast majority of conservative Christians might believe that sex before marriage is wrong, of those that actually were virgins at marriage, 12 pecent had no religion, 15 percent were Catholic, and 17 percent were fundamentalist

8. Center for Disease Control, "National Survey for Family Growth."

Protestant. As Freitas explains, "A series of studies have shown that young Christians find it difficult to keep the covenant these ['covenant rings'] symbolize. In many cases, abstinence pledges do little more than post-pone sexual intercourse for a few months or turn those who try to keep them in the direction of other sexual activity."[9] Further, young adults who believe that sex before marriage is wrong yet still become secretly sexual-ly active outwardly condemn others and inwardly condemn themselves. This situation creates both a hypercritical and isolating tendency in their social life and a shame-filled inner life. As one tearful eighteen-year-old recently said to me, "Adults have no idea how lonely and isolating it is to deal with all the pressures around sex while also trying to figure out what is right for you. It is horrible!"

Nowhere to Turn

In this underground world of sexual activity clothed in pretense and si-lence, students suffer under their ignorance, isolation, misinformation, and sexual mythology. While abstinence-only education does not lower the incidence or onset of sexual intercourse, it actually *increases* the inci-dence of unwanted pregnancy.[10] Certainly the aftershocks of an unwanted pregnancy can ripple through a family and community for years—if not generations. As Christine Gudorf, a theological ethicist, says, "Children of sexually ignorant or silent parents, in school systems with poor or nonexistent sex education programs, without adequate health resources, will grow up to have sexually ignorant children like themselves. . . . All human activity which causes unnecessary suffering without producing any greater good should be understood as sinful."[11]

Through Freitas's interviews, she learned that evangelical colleges

> often combine monitoring with legislation about sexual activity on campus (including, in some instances, requiring students to sign agreements that, under penalty of expulsion, they will not have sex during their college years). Such monitoring can create an unfortunate communications breakdown—a campus atmo-sphere akin to a high school environment that fails to recognize and trust that students are already powerfully bound by the

9. Freitas, *Sex and the Soul*, 77.
10 Strayhorn and Strayhorn. "Religiosity and Teen Birth Rate."
11. Gudorf, *Body, Sex, and Pleasure*, 23.

> sexual tenets of their faith traditions, particularly in the area of restrictions on premarital sex. As a result of this oversight, many students feel compelled to hide their sexual practices not only from friends but also from all adults with whom they come into contact, including clergy. This stops them from seeking adult advice about sex and helps to create a culture of fear regarding sexual activity and identity on campus.[12]

A chief complaint of students on evangelical campuses is the deafening silence and condemnation leaves them no safe place to turn.[13] In contrast to this situation, evangelical students need an environment that is informed, grace-filled, encouraging, and compassionate when sharing their stories, their desires, and their histories. They need wise guidance to integrate faith values while navigating the sexual pressures of youth culture, and conversations about God's purpose in sexual desire. These changes to the current culture on evangelical college campuses must happen in order for students to be able to deal with sexuality in a healthy way and affirm their sexual desire as a God-given life force.

Premature Marriage Decisions

Another effect of the purity message is the social and religious pressure to get married prematurely. Not surprisingly, the age of marriage is lower in this population, which then increases the risk of coupling before an adequate understanding of self or other has been obtained. This trend persists in spite of research showing that divorce rates for those who marry prior to age twenty-four are significantly higher than those who marry after age twenty-five.[14] Another related byproduct of the purity message is halting the developmental teacher that dating or courting has been historically. Freitas finds that students at evangelical colleges exist in a culture that nearly obliterates dating, while at the same time putting extreme pressure to find one's mate before graduation.[15] In my office, I hear students talking about what is referred to as "ring by spring" pressure. One young woman at an evangelical college, while interviewing me

12. Freitas, *Sex and the Soul*, 219.
13. Ibid., 10, 222–23.
14. Bramlett and Mosher, "First Marriage Dissolution," 5.
15. Freitas, *Sex and the Soul*, 210.

for a newspaper article, shared that within a month of dating a person, people begin to ask if they plan to get married.

Patiently dating someone provides the time to gather many experiences with a person you are romantically interested in. Through dating, you learn about yourself, what kind of person fits well with you, what is important to you in romantic partnership, and what are the habits, beliefs, values, and behaviors of another. When dating, the jury stays out. You have *not* decided to marry this person. Dating is a time of discovery, with options open to learn and stay or learn and leave. *This all changes* the minute a person decides formally or informally they will marry the person they are dating. As soon as that happens, even if it is only two months into a relationship, the dynamics of learning and observing change. Now whatever creates serious doubt is either ignored or placed in the category of "things that will change." When young Christian adults with little to no dating experience prematurely make the decision to marry, they often tend toward an overly romantic and unrealistic choice. Such a decision is made with logic such as, "This is my *only* chance to find a suitable spouse," "A wedding would be fun," "He/she seems perfect," and "We want sex!"

Marriage Decisions Driven by a Fear of Sexual Expression Outside of Marriage

Many young Christian men and women learn this formula from religious culture: sex equals intercourse, intercourse is what God cares about, and sex should only happen after you are married. This formula prompts unmarried Christians to separate romance, which is an accepted feeling in their religious culture, from sexual feelings and expression, which is unacceptable. Yet love separated from sex creates a focus on behaviors, instead of on the quality of the relationship.

Prior to a romantic interest, young Christians often think idealistically of being in love, being married, and enjoying a great sex life. They often believe if they "remain pure" in thoughts and actions prior to marriage, this dynamic and loving sexual life is a reward for their faithfulness. However as soon as a youth or young adult becomes romantically involved, desires to express those feelings through verbal and physical action become driving desires. Sexual desire and romantic expression are natural drives of attraction, romance, and love. It is at this point that adolescents or young adults begin to feel ashamed of their thoughts and desires. They begin to separate their feelings of love and attraction from their desire to physically and verbally express this love. Since the church has been primarily silent, withholding guidance and open conversations of learning, youth are alone and isolated as they experience this shame. While the feelings may be acceptable, the desires to touch and express are not. If a Christian begins to experience mutual romantic attraction at fifteen, but does not marry until twenty-six, they will have eleven years of condemning themselves for sexual desire, all the while separating the role a loving relationship can play in cultivating desire.

This pattern of separating sexual desire from the quality of the relationship carries forth into many Christian marriages. For example, a spouse might judge their sex life only on the basis of how often sex, aka intercourse, occurs. "We are not having enough sex" or "You never want sex" or "When did we last have sex?" These comments focus on a behavior, *not* on the quality of the relationship, whether there is trust or connection in the relationship in which sexual expression is taking place. When sexual expression becomes primarily a behavior-centered routine that ends in intercourse, many couples become bored, sexually dissatisfied, or sexually disinterested. There remains a focus on intercourse while ignoring how or if a couple is cultivating a loving relationship. Sexual desire does not exist in a vacuum. Just as in the beginning of a romance, a loving relationship cultivates sexual desire.

With an emphasis on intercourse as the only sex act that matters, young Christian men and women fail to learn that sacred, sexual experiences begin first with a loving bond and can include much more than intercourse. They do not understand the reason God gave men and women desires for sexual intimacy, what being a good lover really means, or how sexual intimacy can help to express and participate in God's love. They have not been directed to consider how the discipline and desire of loving, sexual touch in a committed relationship can become one of the most profound ways to practice and experience ourselves as Beloved. And they do not know the ingredients necessary for lovemaking to be sacred, sustainable, and satisfying.

Men and Women at Sexual Odds

In evangelical Christian circles, young brides often receive the message to abdicate their sexuality, sexual desire, and sexual power to men. The woman then is placed at odds from the man because she doesn't know what kinds of touch she likes, or even that she has the right to want and ask for multiple forms of intimate touch or no touch at all. She likely brings emotional baggage from years of silencing herself and being treated as an object by media and other men. She might find that she judges herself by how pretty she thinks she is and how much she thinks her partner desires her. If sex has been dominated by his sexual desires and the absence of hers, eventually she will likely wonder why her sexual desire has dropped, and he will wonder why she doesn't seem present at intimate moments.

Men are also at a disadvantage because they have been taught that intercourse is the real deal, thus they can feel entitled to intercourse in marriage. They have grown up in a social culture that views sex through a male lens and portrays women as objects for men's pleasure. If men are also taught that their emotional and relational desires are not masculine, they sublimate these desires through sex while failing to learn the nuances of loving expression. This leaves many Christian men feeling isolated and ashamed of their sexual thoughts and actions prior to marriage. In turn, this shame causes men to feel insecure about their abilities as a lover and even more awkward at sexual conversation and romance with their partner. Neither the church nor culture has taught men the art of loving a woman and the difference between women and men in sexual expression and desire. Further, they have not been given sacred teaching, like the Vow of 'Onah, which I discuss below, to ensure that their wife receives pleasure (which doesn't always mean intercourse), and that pleasurable intimate sex is about more than how often intercourse happens and whether they both have an orgasm.

A Sensual God Who Gives Sexual Desire with Intention and Purpose

> *Body and spirit marry in the chapel of the soul. They marry every minute of every day, in all activities and in all inactivity, in all thoughts and in all actions, or they marry not at all. If they don't marry, we do not know sexuality with soul, and therefore our sexuality remains incomplete and insufficiently human. We do not find the soul of sex by spiritualizing the body **but** by coming to appreciate its mysteries and by daring to enter into its sensuousness.*[16]

16. Moore, *Soul of Sex*, 24.

I believe that God wants us to experience a kind of sexuality that reflects God's own love—extravagant and abundant in pleasure and blessing. To that end, I set out to explore writings on sexuality from the Judeo-Christian tradition that are unknown to the Christian men and women I encounter in my private counseling practice or in my classroom. In particular, I studied Jewish writings on sexuality. While not a Hebrew scholar, after reading books and talking with Hebrew scholars, I found magnificent stories of sexuality that show the depth of God's love and devotion. Here are a few examples from my discoveries.

The Lion of Desire

The Lion of Desire is an ancient mystic Jewish tale that offers a glimpse into the ways in which early Jewish mystics understood the power and purpose of sexual desire and managed their fear of the force inside.[17]

> The masters of the day were distressed. Adultery was spreading rampant as plague among the people. The authorities were at a loss as to how to curb this powerful drive. Finally, driven to desperation, they began to pray. For three days they fasted, weeping and pleading with God, "Let us slay the sexual drive before it slays us."
>
> Finally God acquiesced. The masters then witnessed a lion of fire leap out from within the Temple's Holy of Holies. A prophet among them identified the lion as the personification of the primal sexual drive.
>
> They sought to slay the lion of fire. But the result was that for three days thereafter the entire society ground to a standstill. Hens did not lay eggs, artists ceased creating, businesses faltered, and all spiritual activity came to a halt. Realizing that the sexual drive was about more than sex that it somehow echoed with the Divine, the masters relented.
>
> They prayed that only its destructive shadow be removed while retaining its creative force. Their request was denied on high with the insightful response: "You cannot have only half a drive." The greater the sacred power of a quality, the greater its shadow; the two are inseparable. So they prayed that the lion at least be weakened, and their prayer was granted. The lion, less potent but no less present, reentered the Holy of Holies.[18]

17. Gafni, *Mystery of Love*, 7.
18. Ibid., 8.

In this lovely Jewish story, we encounter the power, paradox, and dilemma in sexual desire. While the core drive in sexual desire was forceful and needed management, it remained at the heart of all creative endeavors. From this it is possible to extrapolate that when we let our core desires find expression in loving and just ways, we participate in the creative process that reflects the image of God within us. We are the only created creature with drives to create complex relationships with deep intimate bonds—this is the face of the image of God within us. Is it powerful? Yes, desires can be very powerful. Do we need God's guidance and wisdom to discern and decipher how to manifest desire? Yes, we do. After all, we look in a mirror dimly (1 Cor 13:12). But are our core desires and drives a gift from God? Most certainly yes. Another subtle but important point in this story is how the lion of sexual desire came out of the temple's Holy of Holies.[19] This is where the presence of God, the *Shekinah*, was said to reside. This is one of many affirmations in Jewish writings where we see the eros of desire emanating from God to God's people and between God's people.[20]

Entering the Holy Tabernacle and Entering Sacred Union

Jewish author and psychologist Rick Blum notes that when a couple joins together in a carefully prepared time of union, in essence they are partners in creating a tabernacle of love.[21] A dwelling place for God.[22] This tabernacle, some texts of Kabbalah (a branch of Jewish mysticism) teach, expresses God's desire to make a home for the Divine in the material world, just as the Holy of Holies was a home for the presence of God in the temple. So sanctified and physical is this image that the same Jewish preparation practices for priests to ready themselves to enter the Holy of Holies is also applied to a husband and wife in preparation for entering their tabernacle of love. Each is expected to know they are entering into a place where no one is allowed or could ever go without God's invitation.[23] When sexual touch is entered into with sanctified purpose and loving intention, the fire of passion can brightly burn at the heart of the union

19. Ibid.
20. Idel, *Kabbalah and Eros*, 34.
21. Blum, "Most Sacred of Places."
22. Idel, *Kabbalah and Eros*, 33.
23. Blum, "Most Sacred of Places."

and a couple's sexual life can remain vibrant and deeply satisfying across their lifespan.

However, when entered into lightly, the blaze will burn you to dust. If we think about it, we see this Hebrew lesson in our current culture every day. When handled incorrectly, as we see in various forms of sexual addiction and sexual compulsivity, sex can become an insatiable drive threatening to extinguish all other creative life a person may have. Or as we often see in marriages where sex is routine and thoughtless, sexual desire burns itself out leaving the couple withdrawn and alone—unable to emotionally connect even in sex. Making sex (versus making love), in or out of marriage, will either burn itself out or burn out those involved. Sex, outside its purpose in love and connection, is unsustainable and unsatisfying over time. It falls to the law of diminishing returns. Making love requires preparation of the space, heart and body. It requires a sincere intention to enter into love, with full attention and mindfulness. And it requires awareness that you are entering a holy communion as the Beloved with each other and with God.

The Cherubs in the Holy of Holies of the Jerusalem Temple

A conceptualization of the divine-human relationship in Jewish literature was the divine presence that resided between the two cherubs over the ark of the covenant in the Holy of Holies within the temple. The cherubim were thought to have an amount of life in them and were said to turn toward each other when Israel followed God's commandments, and turn away from each other when Israel sinned.[24] While there were gold cherubim in each rebuilding of the temple, the dimensions, depictions, and positions of the cherubim varied. Sometimes they were presented as open-winged in mutual protection of the ark. Sometimes they were thought to be seated in sexual embrace over the ark.[25]

> As late as the 3rd and 4th centuries C.E., the memory of the original function and the significance of the Cherubim in the Sanctuary survived among the Babylonian Talmudic masters. According to one of them, a certain Rabh Qetina, who flourished in the late 3rd and early 4th century, "When Israel used to make the pilgrimage, [the priests] would roll up for [the people] the parokhet [or the curtains separating the Holy of Holies],

24. Patai, *Hebrew Goddess*, 84.
25. Idel, *Kabbalah and Eros*, 31; Patai, *Hebrew Goddess*, 67–68.

and show them the cherubim which were intertwined with one another, and say to them: 'Behold! Your love before God is like the love of male and female.'"[26]

The famed eleventh-century commentator Rashi explains the passage in this way: "The Cherubim were joined together, and were clinging to and embracing each other like a male who embraces a female."[27] According to Moshe Idel, the nature of the intertwining cherubim functions as a metaphor of the divine eros that God has for God's people. When the last temple was destroyed toward the end of the first century CE, Idel conjectures, the role of the cherubim as a dwelling place for the presence of God was believed to be preserved through the sexual union of a husband and wife, when the couple prepared to enter their sacred space with the same kind of intention and preparation as a priest entering the Holy of Holies.[28]

Song of Songs

> My beloved called out to me and he said, "Rise up, my dear mate, my beautiful one and come to me. Behold, the chill has fled and the rain has ceased and gone on its way. The blossoms have appeared throughout the land. The time for pruning has arrived and the voice of the turtledoves can be heard around our land. The figs have livened up their hue and the vines are bursting with their bouquet. Arise, my dear mate, my beautiful one, come to me. My dove who is nestled is hidden in the crevice of the rock, in the hollow of the steps' ascent, reveal your form unto me and let me hear your voice, for oh, how sweet is your voice, My love is mine and I am his, who grazes me amongst the roses.[29]

The famous rabbi Akiva (ca. 50–135 CE) is reputed to have said, "All of Scripture and its texts are holy, but the Song of Songs is the Holy of Holies."[30] Here an early Jewish teacher reminds us that this cherished Jewish text, which would be included in the Jewish canon, involved the highly evolved and deeply sensual love of God for God's people, God's

26. Patai, *Hebrew Goddess*, 84.
27. Ibid.
28. Idel, *Kabbalah and Eros*, 33.
29. Song of Songs 2:10–17.
30. Schiffman, "Mishnah Yadayim 3:5," 119–20.

Beloved. This text can be interpreted to refer to experiencing God's presence and essence through a passionate, awe-inspiring, and boundless love. It is an erotic message of union of love, God's love and human love, merged into an experience of the God of love. When a couple makes love with the embodied awareness of God's gift of love within the space of sacred commitment, the lines between giving and receiving, pleasure and love, are no longer distinct. God dwells in this holy place. So sanctified and holy is this physical union in Jewish practice that the same elaborate rules of ritual purity apply. This involved intentional and mindful practices of readiness to enter God's presence. Repeatedly in rabbinic Judaism we read, "If a man and a woman are [religiously] worthwhile, the divine presence dwells between them."[31] There is an enticing parallel process between the priest's entry into the Holy of Holies and a couple's entry into sexual communion.

The Vow of 'Onah

The last old Jewish wisdom I will share comes from the Vow of 'Onah, taken by a young Jewish man at the time of marriage. The Vow of 'Onah reminds us of a few important elements for sexual fulfillment. In fulfilling the 'Onah, men are taught that sexual pleasure is the right of the woman—not the man.[32] Moshe Idel says it this way: "The term 'onah as a religious obligation is commonly connected not to the sexual satisfaction of the husband but to the special sexual needs of his wife."[33] The responsibility is given to a husband to become the lover of a woman—his wife. He is to study her, how to bring pleasure to her and how to love her.[34] This is a wise and elegant request that invites a young man to expand his relational and sexual skills—inviting his love for his beloved to guide his sexual touch instead of his sexual desire alone being the primary drive of his touch.

This vow leads, if we engage it creatively, to a critical component of intimacy. Careful attending by her husband invites a young woman to not only feel desired but to engage a more active voice and involvement in sexual touch. Here she is encouraged to express her sexual desires while

31. Idel, *Kabbalah and Eros*, 32.

32. Ibid., 18.

33. Ibid.

34. Magonet, *Jewish Explorations of Sexuality*, 222.

in the safety of his love. Both the skill of a man to open a woman's heart and the skill of a woman to own and express her sexual preferences are lovemaking skills often not seen until midlife, if at all. These are areas a couple needs to develop in order to create a vibrant, intimate, and meaningful sex life that can stand the test of time. Men who learn how to connect to a woman's heart will open her, allowing her to feel safe enough to share her sexual desires and vulnerabilities. This pathway allows desire to linger and grow, providing more satisfying sexual encounters—emotionally, spiritually, and physically.

A young man's growing edge in marriage is to see, hear, learn, and study his partner in order to meet his lover's needs. Loving well relies less on competition, conquests, or goals and more on learning the nuances of his beloved. In loving well, husbands are not competing with other men, they are learning to grow their relationship and lovemaking skills. This practice of truly learning their wives helps men to connect their sexual and accomplishment drives to their heart. The sooner men learn the value of their relationships to ground their life purposes, the less mistakes they make, the less pain they inadvertently cause, and the less meaningful time they lose with children and spouses.

American culture often fails to introduce skills to men or women that help them grow into good lovers. Men are often taught through secular and religious channels that sex is about intercourse (the penis), to which they are entitled after marriage. How much and how often are based on *their* wants. They are the sexual creatures. This belief *reinforces* the tendency of men to lead from their core drives and ignores their need to learn the skills of the heart and the skills of how to love a woman, how to be her great lover.

In turn, women in American religious and secular culture often learn that sex is about intercourse and about the man's sexual drive. They learn that sex is not about them, but what they can do for a man. They learn to be sexually passive. This idea eclipses their need to claim their sexual wants, power, and voice—and may have communicated that their sexual power was shameful. The focus on intercourse and a man's pleasure inadvertently teaches women to ignore their sexual pleasure while focusing on the rest of the relationship. A woman can fail to learn how boldly and clearly to own her sexual power with her husband. This Jewish vow, however, reminds women and men that sexual *intimacy* is not an option, an act, but a relationship quality needed for a satisfying marriage. Sex is not just *for him*. Sex is not just *about him*. Sex is not *his job*, and the relationship *her job*. *Intimacy* is their job. When women try to drive the relationship alone and men try to drive the couple's sexual life alone, the sex *and* the relationship will become void of emotional connection and passion. It will become routine and monotonous. And eventually desire will burn out . . . for her, for him, or for both. At best this leads to a lifeless and loveless sex life.

Conclusion

As believers and educators, we must begin to develop a New Covenant sexual ethic and concomitant sexual curriculum that can open grace-filled dialogue with our children and youth, while sharing the vision and capacities in God's gift of sexual desire and sexual intimacy. At the heart of the study of romance, sexuality, and spirituality is the understanding that our created nature is to know that God calls us his Beloved. And our created call from God is to love—to live love, be love, and stand up for love. When I listen deeply to the sexual pain of our Christian youth and see the opportunity we have to impart a much-needed integration of sexual health with our belovedness, I think the time is well overdue.

Bibliography

Blum, Rick. "The Most Sacred Places." *Parabola* (2007) 14–17.

Bramlett, Matthew, and William Mosher. "First Marriage Dissolution, Divorce, and Remarriage: United States." Division of Vital Statistics. *Advance Data*, May 31, 2001, 1–19.

Center for Disease Control. "National Survey for Family Growth." Online: http://www.cdc.gov/nchs/nsfg.htm.

Charles, Tyler. "Almost Everyone's Doing It." *Relevant* (2011) 64–69.

Freitas, Donna. *Sex and the Soul: Juggling Sexuality, Spirituality, Romance, and Religion on America's College Campuses.* New York: Oxford University Press, 2008.

Gafni, Marc. *The Mystery of Love.* New York. Atria, 2003.

Gudorf, Christine. *Body, Sex, and Pleasure: Reconstructing Christian Sexual Ethics.* Cleveland: Pilgrim, 1994.

Idel, Moshe. *Kabbalah and Eros.* New Haven, CT: Yale University Press, 2005.

LifeWay Christian Resources. "True Love Waits." http://www.lifeway.com/Article/true-love-waits.

Magonet, Jonathan. *Jewish Explorations of Sexuality.* Providence, RI: Berghahn, 1995.

Moore, Thomas. *The Soul of Sex: Cultivating Life as an Act of Love.* New York: Harper, 1998.

Nouwen, Henri J. M. *Life of the Beloved: Spiritual Living in a Secular World.* New York: Crossroad, 1992.

Patai, Raphael. *The Hebrew Goddess*. 3rd ed. Detroit: Wayne State University, 1990.

Paulsen, Heather Arnel. *Emotional Purity: An Affair of the Heart*. Wheaton, IL: Crossway, 2007.

Schiffman, Lawrence. "Mishnah Yadayim 3:5: The Debate over the Biblical Cannon." In *Texts and Traditions: A Source Reader for the Study of Second Temple and Rabbinic Judaism*, edited by Lawrence Schiffman, 119–20. Hoboken, NJ: KTAV, 1998.

Strayhorn, Joseph, and Strayhorn, Jillian. "Religiosity and the Birth Rate in the United States." *Reproductive Health Journal*, September 2009, n.p. Online: http://www.reproductive-health-journal.com/content/pdf/1742-4755-6-14.pdf.

12

Impossible Promises and Broken Hearts[1]
Sexuality and Spirituality in Campus Culture

Antonios Finitsis

A Startling Realization

By the time the first week of our Lilly Fellows Summer Seminar on Gender and Christianity ended, I came to a startling conclusion. I realized that I was almost oblivious to the challenges gender and sexuality posed in the everyday lives of students on campus. This was an unsettling realization, to say the least, since I had been teaching classes on gender and sexuality for four years and had engaged my students in conversation both inside the class and outside. I teach the Hebrew Bible, so most of our conversations were based upon biblical texts. When students shifted to the contemporary world, we discussed the implications of these texts for our lives, and we talked about what we might learn about the influence of the Hebrew Bible on the contemporary world. Our conclusions often highlighted the relationship between biblical literature and life. However, after I read Donna Freitas's *Sex and the Soul* and discussed campus culture with other seminar participants, I realized that my work as a college

---

1. This presentation can be found online at:
   https://sites.google.com/site/impossiblepromisespresentation/.

teacher was one-sided.[2] It is one thing to have an academic conversation on gender and sexuality and quite another to discuss the day-to-day impact of gender and sexuality in the lives of students. I found this realization unsettling since, as a teacher, I work hard to empower students by equipping them to find sustained meaning in their lives.

Because I wanted to be more successful at empowering students, I explored models of intellectual development that are based upon the observation of students during their college years.[3] These models show that college students make changes in their thought processes that allow for increasingly complex ways of understanding. College teachers can play a key role in this development if—and this is a big "if"—they participate in ways that make sense to college students. For instance, Sharon Daloz Parks, in her book *Big Questions, Worthy Dreams: Mentoring Emerging Adults in the Search for Meaning, Purpose, and Faith*, discusses the importance of teachers as mentors.[4] She remarks that a mentor "becomes significant only if he or she 'makes sense' in terms of the young adult's own experience."[5] As a college professor, I understand her comment to mean that mentors have a meaningful impact upon protégés when they are able to address the day-to-day lives of students. She also adds that a mentor "recognizes in practical terms *the promise and the vulnerability* of the young adult life."[6]

During the course of the summer seminar on gender and Christianity, I wanted to develop practical strategies for nurturing the promise of my students' lives while respecting their vulnerability. In particular, I wanted to discover a hands-on way to empower them to meet the challenges posed by the intersection of gender, sexuality, and faith. This goal I tried to achieve with the presentation that you may find in the following url:

https://sites.google.com/site/impossiblepromisespresentation/

Prompting an Honest Conversation

Starting an honest conversation about gender and sexuality can be a daunting task, particularly when the conversation addresses others whom

2. Donna Freitas, *Sex and the Soul.*

3. See for example, a useful summary of the generative model of William Perry and the alternative model of Baxter Magolda in McKeown, *First Time Effect*, 31–38.

4. Parks, *Big Questions, Worthy Dreams*, 127–57.

5. Ibid., 131.

6. Ibid., 129.

one barely knows—a situation in which many administrators, faculty, and staff (e.g., student life staff who work in dorms) find themselves on a college campus. Notwithstanding this challenge, my teammates in our seminar small group, Dr. Mikee Delony, (Abilene Christian University), Dr. Katrina Karnehm (Indiana Wesleyan University), and Dr. Carrie Pierce (Azusa Pacific University), and I wanted to find a way to prompt conversations on our own campuses. Therefore, we created a video that features fictional students on a university campus. While our characters are fictional, their problems are *real*. We wrote their thoughts based on the results of recent published research on these topics. In this way, you will be able to ease into a discussion that addresses the concerns college students have on gender and sexuality without making them, and their professors, uncomfortable. The current generation of students is used to responding to visual stimuli. The video presentation works with this facility to elicit a reaction on a relatively taboo topic.

Before the Presentation

I have used this video in my university to address the growing need for positive conversations about gender, sexuality, and religion. While there are myriad ways of making the best use of this video, let me explain what I have done. My experience is not normative but illustrative.

When I showed this video, I demonstrated the need for a conversation before I played the video. For starters, I asked participants to close their eyes, to take a few deep breaths, and to relax. I then informed them that I was going to take a poll through a show of hands, and I assured them that I was the only person in the room who could see the result. I also assured them that I would respect their privacy. I continued by asking the participants to raise their hands if they thought that one of their friends had been dishonest with them in discussions around gender and sexuality. Subsequently, I asked them to raise their hands if they thought they had been dishonest with a friend, at least once, on discussions about gender and sexuality. The results, both times I used this technique, were surprising. The vast majority of the participants (almost 90 percent) raised their hands to both questions. When they opened their eyes again, I reported back to them the results of my informal poll.

My next question was, "Why do people feel the need to lie about this topic even to their friends?" The purpose of this question was to help the students to articulate what generates a culture of duplicity among peers on a college campus. Their answers revealed a series of problems that inhibit communication and productive conversation on these challenges. I continued by asking students to imagine ways in which they might address these problems and facilitate conversation that would break the "silence" and engender honest discourse.

Only after I had set the scene in this way and established the need for this video did we view it. I used it in a particular way because of my campus setting. You will use it, of course, in a way that best fits the needs of your campus and the group you are asking to participate (e.g., a dorm floor, a classroom). Let me illustrate a few ways to maximize the benefit of this video after you have shown it.

After the Presentation

The video is designed to launch conversations, but you will achieve the best results if you provide structure to the ensuing conversation. For example, you can provide the participants with prompts before playing the video and ask the participants to write down their thoughts on these prompts after viewing the video. For example, based on the statistics on college rape found in the first case of the booklet, you might want to ask, "How many female college-aged students, do you think, have been the victims of an attempted rape? How many, do you imagine, reported it?" On the basis of the second case you may want to consider asking, "How important is it for you to meet your future spouse in college?" You may develop similar prompts for all twelve cases, tailor-made to address the particular interests of your audience.

There are many ways to analyze afterwards the cases presented on the video. For instance, if you want to focus the conversation on the content of the video, a handout with either the thought balloons of the actors or the statistics could be effective. Or perhaps participants could be asked to imagine hypothetical consequences that these statements have for the characters in the video.

If you want to use the video to generate a more personal conversation, a handout with questions that address the participants directly will be useful. For example, ask the participants to select a test case that stood out in their opinion and why this test case is the most important. The video is created with a menu that allows one to play each test case separately after the initial viewing. You might want to show that particular test case again to refresh the participants' memories and to jog further dialogue. Further, you may ask the participants to evaluate statements made in the video on the basis of their own experience and invite them to propose ways to face these challenges. (Remember, once again, that you can show whatever cases are mentioned by using the menu.)

There are a few rules of thumb for every conversation that uses this video. First, remember what Sharon Daloz Parks said: students engage when the discussion makes sense in light of their experience. (Given the experience of sexuality by so many on college campuses, this rule may not be especially difficult to keep.) Second, use the video prompts to review the cases. You may want to have a summary list of the cases available; this would be a useful tool. Third, provide the sort of structure for the conversation that will achieve the ends you have in mind.

Other Venues and Audiences

Although my intention during the summer seminar was to create an instrument that would catalyze conversation and empower college-age students to deal with issues around gender and sexuality, young adults in several phases of life, including those who do not attend a college or university, can benefit from such a conversation. Members of institutions other than college and university campuses will find this presentation beneficial for facilitating discussions about gender, sexuality, and faith. It can be used in venues as different as theological schools and seminaries, youth group meetings, and retreats for adults of all ages.

Bibliography

Freitas, Donna. *Sex and the Soul: Juggling Sexuality, Spirituality, Romance, and Religion on America's College Campuses.* Oxford: Oxford University Press, 2008.

McKeown, Joshua S. *The First Time Effect: The Impact of Study Abroad on College Student Intellectual Development.* Albany: SUNY Press, 2009.

Parks, Sharon Daloz. *Big Questions, Worthy Dreams: Mentoring Young Adults in Their Search for Meaning, Purpose, and Faith.* San Francisco: Jossey-Bass, 2000.

Index